AF904658

Century of Shanghai Trade

Wang Shengqiao

Century of Shanghai Trade

Rethinking of Chinese Cultural Identity

復旦大學出版社
Fudan University Press

Springer

Wang Shengqiao
College of Business Administration
Shanghai Business School
Shanghai, China

ISBN 978-981-96-8700-8 ISBN 978-981-96-8701-5 (eBook)
https://doi.org/10.1007/978-981-96-8701-5

Jointly published with Fudan University Press.
The printed edition is not for sale in Mainland China. Customers from Mainland China please order the print book from Fudan University Press.

© Fudan University Press Co., Ltd. 2025

This work is subject to copyright. All rights are solely and exclusively licensed by the Publisher, whether the whole or part of the material is concerned, specifically the rights of translation, reprinting, reuse of illustrations, recitation, broadcasting, reproduction on microfilms or in any other physical way, and transmission or information storage and retrieval, electronic adaptation, computer software, or by similar or dissimilar methodology now known or hereafter developed.
The use of general descriptive names, registered names, trademarks, service marks, etc. in this publication does not imply, even in the absence of a specific statement, that such names are exempt from the relevant protective laws and regulations and therefore free for general use.
The publishers, the authors, and the editors are safe to assume that the advice and information in this book are believed to be true and accurate at the date of publication. Neither the publishers nor the authors or the editors give a warranty, express or implied, with respect to the material contained herein or for any errors or omissions that may have been made. The publishers remain neutral with regard to jurisdictional claims in published maps and institutional affiliations.

This Springer imprint is published by the registered company Springer Nature Singapore Pte Ltd.
The registered company address is: 152 Beach Road, #21-01/04 Gateway East, Singapore 189721, Singapore

If disposing of this product, please recycle the paper.

Preface

Shanghai, a city made great by the sea, thrived on commerce and flourished through trade. Spanning over a century, what was once a small fishing village has become a world-renowned jewel. Shanghai gave birth to China's first modern shopping mall, the first modern bank, the first church university, the first newspaper and magazine, the first commercial street, the first telephone booth, the first stock, and so on. Today, Shanghai boasts the world's largest container port, the first commercial magnetic levitation train, the first quantum secure communication line, China's first large passenger aircraft C919, and the first China International Import Expo.

From "Westernization of the East" to an international shopping paradise, from "metropolis infested with foreign adventurers" to an international consumption center city, from "Southeast Metropolis" to a global international trade center, from ancient water towns to the old city, and then to the Bund and Nanjing Road, Shanghai has been continuously unfolding its inexhaustible commercial legends for over the past century. Luxury, modernity, classicism, and elegance are the impressions of Shanghai in the eyes of the world; innovation, fairness, service, and efficiency are becoming the world projection of Shanghai.

The development of Shanghai's retail industry is a microcosm of the city's commercial evolution. The prosperity of traditional department stores, represented by the "Four Major Department Stores" on Nanjing Road-Xianshi, Yong'an, Xinxin, and Daxin-marks the 1.0 era of Shanghai's retail. In the 1990s, with the advent of the "supermarket" format to China, various formats such as department stores, supermarkets, convenience stores, and specialized shops coexisted, featuring competitors like Carrefour, Walmart, RT-Mart, Lianhua Supermarket, and Bailian Group. This marks the 2.0 era of Shanghai's retail. Entering the 21st century, with the development of information technology, new technologies such as big data, cloud computing, artificial intelligence, and virtual reality have been widely applied in the commercial sector, especially with the emergence of electronic commerce and mobile intelligence, leading Shanghai's retail into the new 3.0 era.

As early as the Qianlong and Jiaqing eras of the Qing dynasty, Shanghai was known as "a thoroughfare of rivers and seas, a metropolitan city of the southeast." In 1833, the German missionary Karl Friedrich August Gützlaff depicted the bustling scene in Shanghai in his book: "This place has a huge advantage for foreign trade, and what is even rarer is that it has not yet been discovered." This marked the first time Shanghai entered the international stage as a center for commerce and trade. After its opening in 1843, Shanghai rapidly rose to become the international trade hub of the Far East and a world-renowned metropolis. Since the reform and opening-up, especially with the current "14th Five-Year Plan" and new development pattern of "dual circulation", Shanghai is striving to build a global trade hub, create an Asia-Pacific investment gateway, develop an international consumption center city, establish an international exhibition capital, and construct an Asia-Pacific supply chain management center, thereby form a highland of innovative trade and investment systems.

Over a century, the spirit of openness, contractuality, innovation, and craftsmanship has always accompanied and promoted the growth of Shanghai's commerce and trade, which in turn has fostered the development of Shanghai. Shanghai is also the birthplace of the Chinese Communist Party, from where it originated and led the Chinese people in constructing the New China, reaching out to the world, and progressively realizing the dreams of the Chinese people to stand up, become prosperous, and grow strong. The significance of reviewing the century-long history of Shanghai's commerce, extracting the characteristics of Shanghai's business, and promoting the spirit of the city holds immense practical value in commemorating the centenary of the Party's founding. The purpose of compiling and publishing the Shanghai Centennial Series is precisely for this reason.

The Shanghai Centennial Series is divided into three volumes, titled "Century of Shanghai Business," "Century of Shanghai Trade," and "Century of Shanghai Retail." Each volume stands as a complete book with its distinct features; yet, they also could be integrated as a whole, complementing each other.

"Century of Shanghai Business", edited by Liu Hong as the chief editor and Yin Yanhai as the deputy editor, is divided into four chapters. The authors' contributions are as follows: Chap. 1 "Beachhead Landing" by Liu Xin, Chap. 2 "Building Dreams of Prosperity" by Di Rong, Chap. 3 "Moving Forward with Burdens" by Cheng Zhengrong, Chap. 4 "Rebuilding Brilliance" by Fu Dongliang, Yin Yanhai, and Liu Hong.

"Century of Shanghai Trade", edited by Wang Shengqiao as the chief editor and Liu Hong as the deputy editor, is divided into four chapters. The authors' contributions are as follows: Chap. 1 "Live Towards the Sea (1843–1919)" by Liu Xin and Jiang Jiang, Chap. 2 "The Convergence of East and West (1919–1949)" by Di Rong and Yuan Junxia, Chap. 3 "Forging Ahead (1949–1990)" by Cheng Zhengrong and Shao Wei, Chap. 4 "Standing on the Tide (1991–2024)" by Zhao Lili, Kang Xiuqiu, and Fu Dongliang.

"Century of Shanghai Retail", edited by Jiao Yue as the chief editor and Feng Rui as the deputy editor, is divided into five chapters. The authors' contributions are as follows: Chap. 1 "The Light of Opening" by Liu Xin, Chap. 2 "Metropolis Infested with Foreign Adventurers" by Di Rong, Chap. 3 "Breaking Old to Establish New" by Feng Rui, Chap. 4 "Gathering Strength to Soar" by Kang Xiuqiu, Chap. 5 "Ever-Changing" by Fu Dongliang and Jiao Yue.

The Shanghai Century Series was authored by a team of experts composed of professors, associate professors, and doctors from Shanghai Business School, based on years of research and practice in Shanghai's commerce. It has also referenced a large number of previously published textbooks, theses, audiovisual materials, and research resources. The publication of the series was funded by the Shanghai Municipal Higher Education Project for Plateau Disciplines in Business Administration and the Project for the Construction of First-Class Undergraduate Programs, and it also received strong support from the Haipai Commercial Culture Research Institute, for which we express our gratitude. The conception, initiation, and completion of the Shanghai Century Series took over two years, with each volume undergoing multiple revisions. Due to time and capacity limitations, some errors may inevitably appear in the book, and some articles or materials may be difficult to trace due to their age, resulting in the inability to fully cite the original authors, for which we sincerely ask for your understanding and correction where necessary.The pubicatian of "Shanghai Trade Century" (English Version) has received funding from "China Classic International" and we would like to express our gratitude.

Shanghai, China
September 2025

Professor Wang Shengqiao
Dean of the College of Business Administration

Competing Interests The author has no competing interests to declare that are relevant to the content of this manuscript.

Contents

Chapter 1
Live Towards the Sea (1843–1919)

1 Introduction

Shanghai's trade success is rooted in its unique geographical advantage of being nestled between the river and the sea. From Qinglong Town and Shiliupu to the iconic Bund, these places have been witnesses to Shanghai's trade evolution from its humble beginnings to becoming a thriving trade hub. Over the past century, Shanghai has been a competitive ground for merchants from all directions, attracting talents from the south of the Yangtze River. The city has also seen the active participation of Westernization enterprises, comprador businesses, and national capital in its trade expansion. Shanghai has been the starting point for Chinese people to broaden their global perspective, humbly embracing various modern systems. Moving from reluctantly opening its doors to proactively engaging with the world, Shanghai is bound to foster limitless trade opportunities.

2 The Transformation of Trade Ports

2.1 *The Famous Qinglong Town*

The Qinglong Town Ruins stand at the ancient mouth of the Wusong River, a pivotal point where the north and south sea routes converge. The Wusong River and the Yangtze River communicate inland, so its geographical location is exceptional. The archaeological excavation of the Qinglong Town Ruins officially began in 2010, unearthing a significant number of trade ceramics and architectural remnants over the nine-year period. This gradual unveiling paints a picture hidden for centuries. The archaeological discoveries at Qinglong Town Ruins act as a bridge between the past and present, affirming that Shanghai was a major coastal port city in southeastern China even before the opening of the port.

© Fudan University Press Co., Ltd. 2025

W. Shengqiao, *Century of Shanghai Trade*,
https://doi.org/10.1007/978-981-96-8701-5_1

If you were to ask about the location of ancient Shanghai's first commercial port, most would point to Qinglong Town, which is now Baihe Town in Qingpu District and was formerly Qingpu Town. In the year 746 AD (fifth year of the Tang Tianbao era), Qinglong Town was established (old Qingpu in the northeast of today's Qingpu County). Having a town magistrate and deputy magistrate, it marked the birth of Shanghai's second trade port, Qinglong Town Port, after Huating Town. Qinglong Town Port, situated near Wusong River, provided access upstream to Suzhou (a prosperous economic center in the Tang Dynasty), serving as Suzhou's gateway to the sea. Connected through the nearby Grand Canal, Qinglong Town Port had convenient transportation links to cities like Jiaxing, Huzhou, and Changzhou. Qinglong Town was the earliest foreign trade port in the Shanghai region and a crucial stop on the maritime Silk Road during the Tang and Song dynasties. Shanghai, now globally renowned as a trade, shipping, economic, and financial center, can trace its roots back to Qinglong Town, located in Qingpu during the Tang and Song periods, acting as the "ancestor" of the world-class Yangshan Port (Fig. 1).

With a long and storied history, Qinglong Town stands as a trailblazer and representative among towns in Jiangnan. In the era of Eastern Wu during the Three Kingdoms period, Qinglong Town served as a military stronghold where Sun Quan strategically defended river crossings with a formidable navy, It was named after the Qinglong battleship was built here. The town, named after these warships, became a natural and sheltered harbor, evolving into a key training ground for the Eastern Wu navy. As the coastline advanced, the mouth of the Wusong River gradually shaped into a well-defined trumpet-shaped bay, commonly referred to as the "Triangle Port."

Fig. 1 Old images of Qinglong Harbor

with vast waters and an ocean-like shape. Historical records document that Qinglong Town once housed three pavilions, seven pagodas, and thirteen temples, including a shrine dedicated to Mazu. Archaeological findings indicate that during the Song Dynasty, the settlement area of Qinglong Town expanded to 25 km^2, four times its size during the Tang Dynasty, accompanied by ongoing bridge construction.

Qinglong Town marks the genesis of Shanghai's expansion towards the sea and its transformation into a thriving harbor city. In the Tang and Song Dynasties, Qinglong Town, strategically positioned at the mouth of the Hudu River (now the downstream Huangpu River), Benefiting from the developed regions of Suzhou and Xiuzhou (now Jiaxing, Zhejiang Province), Qinglong Town flourished. Transitioning from a military stronghold, Qinglong Town emerged as a pivotal port for foreign trade during this period, standing on par with prominent trade ports such as Guangzhou, Quanzhou, and Yangzhou. The Tang Dynasty poet Pi Rixiu, in his poem "Hudu," vividly describes the abundant marine life and bustling fishing activities in Qinglong Town. Starting as a fishing settlement, it evolved into a market town and expanded further to become a significant port. With the development of the upstream Wusong River area (Taihu Lake region) and the growth of foreign trade, Qinglong Town became the earliest center for internal and external trade distribution in the Shanghai region, solidifying its position as the earliest maritime port in Shanghai.

Qinglong Town underwent a temporary name change to Tonghui Town, embodying the concept of "mutual trade and reciprocity" both domestically and internationally. This era witnessed a flourishing trade in goods and services, laying the foundation for the early stages of modern free trade. Benefiting from the impetus of foreign trade, Qinglong Town experienced accelerated development, taking the lead among other towns in the Jiangnan region. Additionally, Qinglong Town manifested the early signs of an emerging urban center, fostering advanced economic and cultural achievements.

Qinglong Town, as a vital market town port in the Yangtze River Delta and a pivotal economic hub in Jiangnan, Shipping routes originating from Qinglong Town reach as far as the waters of Northeast Asia and Southeast Asia. Traders from Nanyang, Japan, Silla (an ancient Korean kingdom), and other regions gathered here annually for commerce. Qinglong Town played a central role in the distribution of both domestic and international trade from places like Suzhou and Xiuzhou. Tribute goods from the Suzhou area were also transported here through the Wusong River and redirected north via the Hudu River. Every month, merchant ships from Suzhou, Hangzhou, Huzhou, Changzhou, and other areas frequented Qinglong Town. Ships from Fujian's Zhangzhou and Quanzhou, as well as those from Zhejiang's Ming, Yue, Wen, and various states in Taiwan, visited two to three times a year, bringing vitality to the land and leaving no space unoccupied.

Particularly during the Song Dynasty, Qinglong Town entered its most illustrious era. The Song Dynasty had a highly developed foreign trade system, establishing market supervisors in three key port cities: Guangzhou, Hangzhou, and Mingzhou (modern-day Ningbo). These market supervisors, collectively referred to as the "Three Offices," were responsible for overseeing overseas trade and served as the primary foreign trade ports during the Song Dynasty. In the first year of the

Shaoxing era (1131 AD) of the Song Dynasty, a dedicated market supervision office for managing maritime trade was established in Qinglong Town. This office, exclusively handling overseas trade, became a symbol of Qinglong Town's flourishing maritime trade during this period.

Qinglong Town stood as the earliest trade distribution center in Huating County during that period. Not only did the local economy flourish, but tax revenues also steadily increased. Qinglong Town exhibited a prominent trend towards urban development, accompanied by the early emergence of urban cultural forms. The ancient economic and cultural exchanges in the Shanghai region can be segmented into two phases, marked by the decline of Qinglong Town's port and the rise of Shanghai's port. In the earlier phase, the Shanghai region's involvement in maritime Silk Road exchange activities revolved around town ports. In the later phase, the focus shifted to the port city, with Shanghai County and its port taking a central role.

Qinglong Town represents the earliest fusion and development of Songze culture and maritime civilization in Shanghai. Rooted in maritime trade, it thrived during the culturally active Tang and Song Dynasties. Before the emergence of Shanghai Town, Qinglong Town paved the way for the maritime Silk Road, evolving into a vital port and trade distribution center for external exchanges in Shanghai and the broader Yangtze River basin since the late Tang Dynasty. During this era, the bustling Qinglong Town was home to foreign expatriate merchants.

Qinglong Town held a prominent position in maritime trade for 500 years, especially during the late Tang Dynasty to the end of the Southern Song Dynasty. The most splendid period spanned over a century from the Northern Song to the late Southern Song. During this time, Qinglong Town pioneered routes for the maritime Silk Road. Qinglong Town stands as a vital symbol of Shanghai's involvement in the maritime Silk Road, catalyzing the entire Huating County's development and further propelling external economic and cultural exchanges in Shanghai and the Jiangnan region. Its contribution to trade promotion, benefiting various parties, and leading Silk Road trade activities for centuries laid a robust foundation for Shanghai to become a major hub for river and sea transport in modern times and an international center for economy, finance, trade, and shipping (Fig. 2).

2.2 *Port Trade Is on the Rise*

After the Northern Song Dynasty, the waterways and coastal features of Qinglong Port faced severe constraints, resulting in the gradual deterioration of the water network. Those reclaiming land prioritized their own needs over navigational convenience, arbitrarily converting water areas into farmland. Merchants, with little regard for agricultural water management, extensively destroyed farmland and dismantled floodgates to facilitate ship passage. This led to the siltation of rivers, coastline expansion, and the narrowing of waterways, resulting in challenging navigation. By the end of the Song Dynasty and the beginning of the Yuan Dynasty, the once-broad

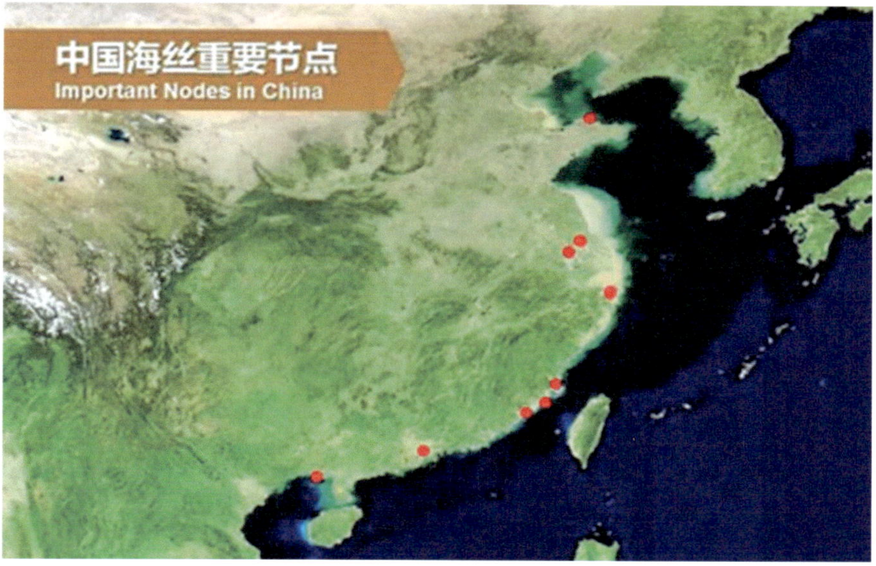

Fig. 2 Diagram of maritime Silk Road Nodes

Wusong River had become extremely narrow. The upstream Wusong River progressively shoaled, and the downstream area constricted, making it impossible for sea vessels to anchor. Incoming and outgoing ships could no longer navigate the Qinglong Port through the Hudu River, leading to the port's relocation to Liujiagang in Taicang, Jiangsu (now known as Liuhe River). This shift caused a significant decline in Qinglong Town's prominence.

In the late Yuan Dynasty and early Ming Dynasty, Qinglong Town faced plundering by both officials and bandits, leading to a gradual decline in its prosperity. By the Jiajing period of the Ming Dynasty, Japanese pirates repeatedly invaded, resulting in the burning and looting of Qinglong Town. Most houses and temples were destroyed. After the late Ming Dynasty, many of the town's famous historical sites ceased to exist. When the Ming Wanli era reinstated the county in the first year, the county seat was moved to Tangxing Town. Qinglong Town experienced further decline, was renamed Old Qingpu Town, and eventually became a rural market town before the establishment of the People's Republic of China. Over the centuries, Qinglong Town gradually faded into the historical mist. However, along the Huangpu River, a new harbor began to emerge.

Wang Hui (Director of the Qingpu District Museum): The Taihu region is inherently economically developed, acting as a significant export production hub for products such as silk and porcelain. To fulfill export responsibilities, the port of Qinglong Town played a crucial role in redirecting goods to Japan, Korea, and other Southeast Asian countries.

The primary ports in the Shanghai region moved eastward to Shanghai Town, now in the Sixteen Pu area. As the saying goes, "First Sixteen Pu, then Shanghai

Fig. 3 Old images of Shiliupu

Bund." During the Ming and Qing periods, this area evolved into a central hub for the distribution of goods, with boats and ships densely populating the river, shops proliferated and a dense population. Shanghai was consequently known as the "hub of river and sea, the metropolis of the southeast." During this period, Shanghai played a crucial role not only in domestic trade but also as a vital port for trade with Japan. In the year 1684, the establishment of the Jianghai Customs led to a significant increase in the traffic of ships entering and leaving Shanghai Port. According to "Famous Streets of Shanghai" compiled by the Shanghai Archives, after the maritime bans were lifted in the Qing Dynasty during the reign of Emperor Qianlong, the Shanghai port, due to its superior geographic location, became a connection point for maritime trade between the northern and southern seas of China (Fig. 3).

Historical records indicate, "All trade, whether near or far, entered the Wusong mouth and anchored in Huangpu." During this era, the Sixteen Pu region had already emerged as China's largest port, giving rise to five major maritime routes: (1) Northern Coastal Route (commonly known as the Northern Ocean Route), connecting to Tianjin, Niuzhuang (Yingkou), and Yantai. Primary transportation vessels were sand boats, carrying goods like cotton, cotton fabric, soybean cakes, soybeans, and soybean oil. (2) Southern Coastal Route (referred to as the Southern Ocean Route), linking to Ningbo, Dinghai, Taizhou, Wenzhou, Fuzhou, Quanzhou, Xiamen, Taiwan, Chaozhou (Shantou), and Guangzhou. Types of vessels included bird boats, egg boats, and estimated boats, handling the import and export of commodities such as sugar, fuel, cotton, and tea. (3) Yangtze River Route, reaching Zhenjiang, Jiangning (Nanjing), Wuhu, Datong (Tongling), Jiujiang, and Hankou. Cargo transported included rice, miscellaneous grains, and timber. (4) Inland River Route, connecting to Suzhou, Wuxi, Changzhou, Hangzhou, Jiaxing, Huzhou, and various

Fig. 4 The prosperous business scene of Shiliupu

major towns along the Grand Canal. (5) Oceanic Route, extending to Japan, Korea, and the archipelago of Southeast Asia (Fig. 4).

In the late Ming Dynasty, the coarse cloth produced in Songjiang, Shanghai, had already gained widespread recognition. Departing from Shanghai, this fabric found its way to Nagasaki, Japan, where it became a highly popular Chinese product. Concurrently, Shanghai ships, upon reaching Nagasaki, brought back Japanese goods, predominantly silver, along with coal and other mineral resources, cultural items, and folding fans.

In 1832, the British East India Company sent the HMS Amherst to explore trade prospects with Britain and the Qing Dynasty along the Chinese coast. Navigating from Fuzhou and Xiamen, the HMS Amherst noted Shanghai as a pivotal hub for North–South trade. Weekly, around 400 ships entered and departed from the Shanghai port, half from the north and the other half from the southern regions, including Fujian, Taiwan, Guangdong, and Siam (Fig. 5).

The "Report on the Voyage of the HMS Amherst to China in 1833" states: "This is the initial exposure of Shanghai, a commercial hub, to European eyes, dispelling any prior limited assessments. Shanghai boasts tremendous advantages in foreign trade, and notably, it has remained unnoticed." Starting from Shanghai, the Yangtze River provides access to the inland regions, connecting to Jiangnan's water networks, extending to Suzhou. The canal system enables the expansion of inland trade, a key factor behind Western nations strongly urging the opening of Shanghai for commerce (Fig. 6).

Fig. 5 Native cloth from Songjiang

Fig. 6 Amherst cargo ship of the British East India Company

> Professor Dai Angang from the History Department at Fudan University explains that the underwater environment on the north and south sides of the Yangtze River estuary differs, to the south, there are reefs, while to the north, there are mudflats. This leads to distinct vessel requirements. For example, vessels with pointed bottoms are not suitable for northern routes, and those with flat bottoms are impractical for southern routes. Consequently, a port facilitating the exchange of vessel types is crucial, and Shanghai is positioned ideally at this boundary point.

Located at the mouth of the Yangtze River, the maritime gateway to the Yangtze River Delta, and the central hub of north–south shipping routes, Shanghai's strategic position, coupled with the prosperous hinterland of the Yangtze River basin, makes it an indispensable port on the East China Sea for conducting both domestic and foreign trade. Despite the development of Sixteen Pu Port following Shanghai's opening, it was eventually surpassed by the modernized Shanghai Port. While coastlines and waterways undergo transformations, Shanghai's role as a major trading port has remained constant.

Wu Songdi (Professor at Fudan University's Institute of Historical Geography): The development of foreign trade inevitably requires a vast hinterland, which must be relatively advanced and economically and culturally developed. If the hinterland is too small, trade cannot expand; if it is impoverished without a well-developed market economy, foreign trade cannot prosper. Fortunately, the Yangtze River Delta, where Shanghai is located, can be considered the most developed region in China since the turmoil of the An Lushan Rebellion during the Tang Dynasty.

At this moment, adventurers are flocking to claim the Shanghai Bund, and a myriad of people from across the nation are converging at the waterfront, assimilating into the vibrant Shanghai. Merchants, sailors, missionaries, diplomats, and even criminals and opportunists traverse this lively space.

2.3 *The Establishment of Major Trade Port Status*

In the turbulent waters of history, Shanghai faced a bloody and ruthless onslaught on June 16, 1842. China, at this juncture, was amidst an unprecedented transformation labeled as the "Great Changes of Three Thousand Years." The signing of the Nanjing Treaty and the Humen Treaty led to the addition of Xiamen, Fuzhou, Ningbo, and Shanghai to the existing Guangzhou, forming the "Five Treaty Ports" for trade. While these new ports redirected Guangzhou's foreign trade, they also brought forth fresh opportunities for growth. However, early customs reports revealed limited foreign trade development in the ports of Xiamen, Ningbo, and Fuzhou. Despite Shanghai's substantial growth, it still maintained a considerable distance from Guangzhou.

Shanghai emerged as a dominant trading port, surpassing Guangzhou in total import and export trade from the year 1853 onwards. The city's proximity to silk and tea-producing areas, coupled with the disruption caused by the Taiping Rebellion breaking down artificial barriers imposed by the Qing government and damaging tea transportation routes to Guangzhou, played a pivotal role. The stimulations of the First Opium War, the Taiping Rebellion, and the Second Opium War gradually unveiled Shanghai's potential in foreign trade, firmly establishing its position as a significant trading hub (Figs. 7 and 8).

Shanghai distinguishes itself among the four new ports. Beyond being one of the original five trade ports, known as "Tianshi," and benefiting from the geographical advantage of the prosperous Yangtze River Delta as its "Dili," Shanghai adds the factor of "Renhe." Unlike Guangzhou, entrenched in exclusionary traditions, Shanghai, as a newly opened port, avoided such practices. Historically, Guangzhou upheld its tradition, confining foreigners to trade outside the city. To enter, Harry Smith Parkes repeatedly negotiated with Qiying, who was then the Viceroy of

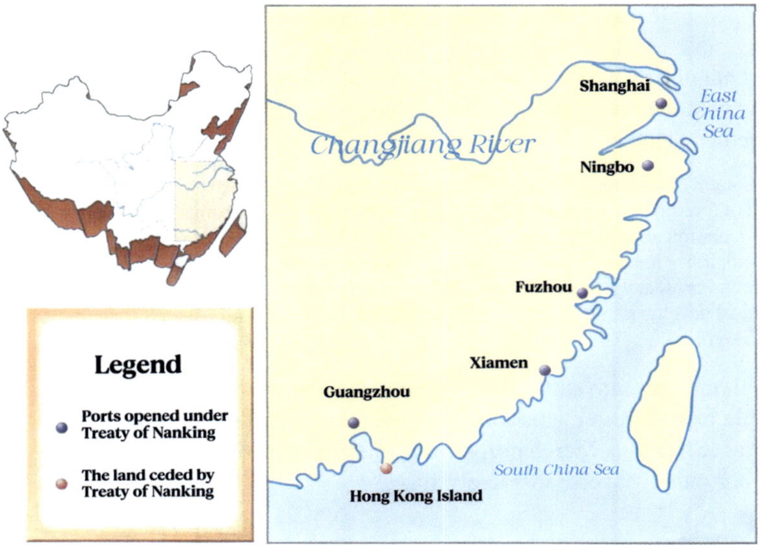

Fig. 7 Diagram of ports opened and territories ceded by the Treaty of Nanjing

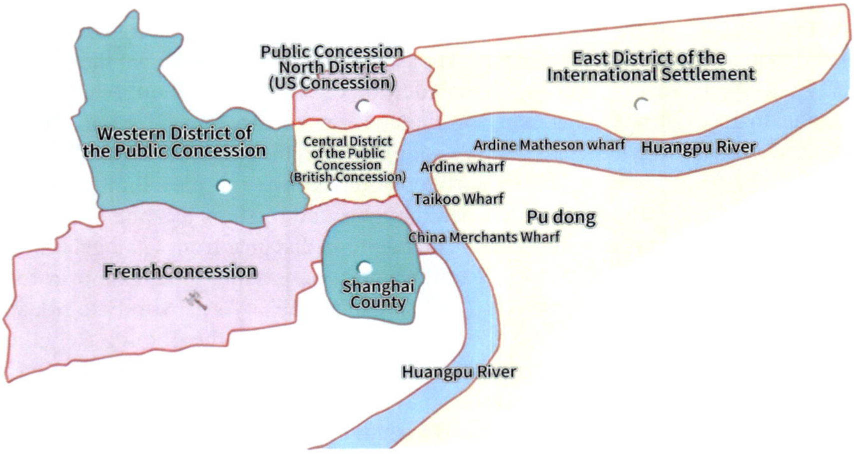

Fig. 8 Distribution map of Shanghai concessions

Liangguang, and his successors Xu Guangjin and Ye Mingchen, while faced strong resistance of local gentry and people and prolonged conflicts. In contrast, Shanghai enjoyed a pleasant climate and friendly locals. Foreigners were respected, freely exploring within a day's journey to take walks and ride horses around. As a residence, Shanghai surpassed Guangzhou in advantages. Its inclusive local customs

Fig. 9 Captain ward of the ever-victorious army

facilitated smoother interactions between foreign powers and local authorities. While Guangzhou resisted foreign entry, Shanghai had established concessions, forming a foreign community (Fig. 9).

In the year 1853, the Taiping Army launched an attack on Shanghai, leading to an uprising by the grassroots anti-Qing organization, the Small Sword Society, which escalated the unrest. Despite its small size, Shanghai served as the main base for British and French concessions, commonly known as the "The International Settlemen". Foreign powers proposed an expansion of their administrative control in the concessions and restructured customs, fully integrating Shanghai's foreign trade into the treaty system. Confronted with an almost uncontrollable situation, the Qing government had no choice but to acquiesce. Additionally, foreign armed forces were aiding the Qing government in suppressing the Taiping Army during that period.

Amidst the spreading turmoil of the Taiping Rebellion, refugees sought refuge in the relatively secure foreign concessions. In 1854, concession authorities initiated taxation on immigrants, and the increased revenue from property and land taxes led to concessions encouraging local populations to enter. Many high-ranking officials of the Qing Dynasty, including governors of the Liang Jiang provinces, fled to Shanghai, prompting attention from the Qing government. The Taiping Heavenly Kingdom showed no hostility to their "foreign brothers" who sharing one belief in

"God". They actively supported trade in the Yangtze River region, even establishing the Tianhai Customs near Nanjing Xiaoguan to boost revenue. Shanghai witnessed an unprecedented opportunity for development. Before the Taiping Heavenly Kingdom approached Shanghai, there were around 500 Chinese residents in the concessions. However, as the threat neared, the Chinese population surged to 20,000 in the concessions. For the people of that era, foreigners were perceived as safer than the Taiping Army.

Until 1860, the Taiping Army had made three unsuccessful attempts to conquer Shanghai, as they were consistently rebuffed by the British and French forces. This situation accelerated the migration of economic and human resources from the Jiangnan region to Shanghai. Consequently, Shanghai accumulated substantial energy, propelling it into a phase of extraordinary development. Each military conflict Shanghai experienced seemed to enhance its prosperity. By the year 1862, Shanghai's population had surpassed 700,000, and its GDP had surged to 6.5 million silver taels (Fig. 10).

In 1860, Shanghai's total import and export value reached 80,544,710 taels, marking an almost 16-fold increase from the early days of its opening. The United Kingdom and the United States dominated as Shanghai's primary trading partners, with the UK holding a significant advantage. Analyzing the tonnage distribution of ships entering and leaving Shanghai Harbor, in 1849, the UK accounted for 70%, while the United States represented 24%. By 1852, the UK's proportion decreased to 49%, and the United States increased to 47%.

Analyzing trade volumes, the export of tea to the United Kingdom constitutes 54.1% of Shanghai's total tea exports, while exports to the United States make up 31.2%. In the case of raw silk, the trade volume exported to the United Kingdom

Fig. 10 Former Shanghai concessions

makes up 98.6% of Shanghai's total raw silk exports, with only 1.4% exported to the United States. The United Kingdom displays substantial demand for both raw silk and tea, influenced by its domestic needs and the simultaneous re-exportation of raw silk and tea from China to Europe.

During that period, the United States primarily imported tea, and its demand for raw silk was comparatively smaller. Tea made up 60%-80% of China's exports to the United States, and tea remained the largest commodity exported to the U.S. by 1860, followed by raw silk and silk products. The growth in Sino-American trade from 1845 to 1860 can be attributed to the strengthened maritime capabilities of the United States, often with ship owners also engaging in trade. Furthermore, the U.S. Congress passed the "New Tariff Act" in 1846 to promote free trade, granting tariff exemptions on many goods, including duty-free import of tea, while the average tariff on various other goods was set at 30%.

The enactment of the "New Tariff Act" by the U.S. Congress contributed to the swift growth of Sino-American trade routed through Shanghai. However, the United States still couldn't disrupt the absolute dominance of the United Kingdom in foreign trade in Shanghai. Two main factors contributed to this situation. On the diplomatic front, internal divisions emerged within the U.S. State Department and Navy Department regarding the diplomatic stance towards China. The State Department aimed to strengthen diplomatic ties with China for enhanced penetration, while the Navy Department focused on Japan, prioritizing the opening of Japan's doors. This divergence resulted in insufficient military support for the State Department, limiting the depth of U.S.-China diplomacy, including trade. Additionally, in 1860s, the United States is in the midst of the Civil War, experiencing rapid domestic development. The commercial returns in China were relatively lower compared to the U.S., attracting a significant capital inflow back to the U.S. Consequently, there were fewer interactions in Sino-American trade during this period.

Examining the composition of exported goods, raw silk and tea emerged as the principal categories. In 1850, raw silk represented 52% of Shanghai's total export value, while tea constituted 46%, and miscellaneous goods accounted for 2%. By 1860, the proportion of raw silk further escalated to 66%, while tea decreased to 28%, and miscellaneous goods increased to 6%. In 1846, raw silk exports through Shanghai comprised 81% of the national total, soaring to 92.7% by 1853. The export volume of raw silk witnessed a substantial rise from 56,211 bales in 1855 to 85,970 bales in 1858. As for tea exports through Shanghai, it constituted 61% of the national total in 1852, with the absolute export volume surging from 1,149,000 pounds in 1844 to a peak of 80,221,000 pounds in 1855. In the subsequent years, tea export volumes experienced a modest decline, reaching 53,463,800 pounds in 1860.

Analyzing the composition of imported goods, cotton textiles and opium emerged as the principal categories. From 1843 to 1845, an overestimation of the demand for cotton textiles by foreign merchants led to a surplus in imports, causing sales stagnation. This resulted in a continuous decline in import trade values until recovery in 1853, while export trade maintained steady growth. To counter the trade deficit, foreign merchants engaged in significant opium smuggling into China, with Shanghai serving as a major entry port. In 1847, the estimated opium imported through

Shanghai reached 16,500 chests, comprising 49.6% of the national import volume. From 1856 to 1857, opium entering through Shanghai constituted around 50% of the national opium import volume. Until 1857, opium import value surpassed that of all other goods. This dynamic gradually shifted from 1857 to 1860, with the import value of other goods surpassing opium. By 1860, the import value of other goods and opium constituted 64% and 36% of the total import value, respectively, reflecting an improved trade structure.

3 The Competitive Development of Maritime Trade

3.1 The Establishment of the Customs Management System

Established in 1685, China introduced its initial customs system, featuring four distinct offices: Yuehai Customs in Guangzhou, Minhai Customs in Xiamen, Zhehai Customs in Ningbo, and Jianghai Customs in Shanghai (Fig. 11).

With the opening of Shanghai, trade flourished, and the trade volume at Shanghai Port saw a rapid surge. Jianghai Customs emerged as the primary source of customs revenue for the Qing government, yielding an annual income surpassing 1.3 million taels of silver. Since 1853, the value of imports and exports and the number of ships entering and leaving supervised by Jianghai Customs have ranked first nationwide, making Shanghai's position as a pivotal national trading port.

The grand clock adorning the Customs House on the Bund in Hankou Road was once acclaimed as the "largest clock in Asia" and stands as a symbol of Shanghai to this day. However, this building underwent four phases of evolution. The earliest Jianghai Customs was situated within Shanghai's old county town (Fig. 12).

In 1853, during the Small Sword Society's occupation of Shanghai County, Wu Jianzhang, the Shanghai Circuit Intendant and Jianghai Customs Supervisor, sought refuge in the concession. To facilitate customs duty collection, he temporarily established customs offices in Pudong Lujiazui, the north bank of Suzhou River, Minhang Town, and Baihezhu. Faced with resistance and challenges from foreign officials and merchants, these customs offices became virtually ineffective, resulting in a suspension of customs operations. Driven into a corner by foreign aggressors, Wu Jianzhang devised a plan to "entrust foreigners with customs duties."

In 1854, consuls from the United Kingdom, France, and the United States, in collaboration with Wu Jianzhang, signed the "Jianghai Customs Organization Agreement." This agreement designated the British individual William Medhurst, the American Jardine Matheson, and the Frenchman Siaas as tax commissioners, establishing the Customs Management Committee. As a result, the administrative control of Jianghai Customs shifted to foreign invaders, with foreigners overseeing Chinese customs for more than half a century (Fig. 13).

Fig. 11 Old images of Jianghai Customs

Fig. 12 Wu Jianzhang, Shanghai Daotai and Supervisor of Jianghai Customs

In 1859, the Minister of Foreign Trade of Nanyang, He Guiqing, appointed Li Taiguo as the first Commissioner of Customs for China, establishing the Commissioner's Office headquartered in Shanghai. In July of that year, Li Taiguo appointed the British individual Dodd as the Customs Commissioner of Jianghai. Consequently, the trilateral Customs Management Committee ceased to exist, granting sole dominance over customs to Britain. The system of foreign Commissioners of Customs was officially established in Shanghai, and subsequently, this system gradually extended to customs at various ports nationwide.

Feng Jinniu, Deputy Director of the Historical Documents Center at the Shanghai Library, states that the first ispector of Customs was the British figure Li Taiguo. He had a notable drawback of arrogance, and offending many people due to his self-righteous attitude. The Chinese government, dissatisfied with him, worked to find a way to replace him, resulting in the relocation of Hurd to Shanghai.

On September 12, 1863, Hurd, a British national, was appointed as the Inspector of Customs for Jianghai, with additional responsibility for the customs in Hankou, Jiujiang, Zhenjiang, and Ningbo, as per the appointment by the Prime Minister's Yamen. On November 15 of the same year, due to Li Taiguo's unauthorized signing of the "Li-Ashburne Contract" with Ashburne, British Navy, the Qing government's Prime Minister's Yamen relieved Li of his duties as Inspector General of Customs,

Fig. 13 Li Taiguo (Horatio Nelson Lay), Customs Inspector General

and Hurd took over. Hurd continued to lead Chinese customs until 1908 when he went back to his home country on leave, marking an impressive 47-year tenure as the head of Chinese customs and becoming the longest-serving Commissioner of Customs in China.

Shi Liangping (Consultant to the People's Government of Shanghai): After Hurd took charge of Chinese customs, one negative aspect is that he gained control over the entire customs import and export duties, along with access to data on China's overall trade. On the positive side, Hurd introduced a system that significantly modernized the statistics, inspection, taxation, and billing of the entire customs operation. This brought about a substantial difference from the previous Qing government era.

Throughout the half-century under Hurd's leadership of Chinese customs, he implemented the United Kingdom's financial system and rotation avoidance system. Furthermore, he systematically organized administrative structures, personnel management, and taxation standards under a rigorous and unified framework. Hurd introduced a modern management system for Chinese customs, encompassing aspects such as the recruitment, promotion, and assessment of customs officers. The customs management system established by Hurd had a profound and far-reaching influence on the development of trade in Shanghai (Fig. 14).

Fig. 14 Robert Hart, Inspector General of Customs

3.1.1 Defining the Powers and Responsibilities of the Commissioner of Customs

The Commissioner of Customs centralized the administrative and personnel appointment authority of customs offices across various regions, enforcing a vertically unified leadership structure for individual customs offices. This management style simplified the organizational structure, promoted unified directives, facilitated quick decision-making, defined responsibilities, and allowed for flexible centralized command, making it more easier to uphold discipline and order. In contrast to the prior customs supervision, which was merely labeled as having "the name of supervision without actual inspection duties," this restructuring indeed played a positive role in organizing the chaotic state of both domestic and foreign trade at that time.

3.1.2 Establishment of a New Personnel System

Hard insisted that every new recruit to the customs office had to pass an examination, without exception, regardless of any recommendations, even those from Hard himself. Recruitment was based on exam performance and the potential for development. Hard adhered to a strict principle of "rejecting anyone not meeting the standards, even if they were the son of the Commissioner of Customs." He conducted rigorous performance assessments for his subordinates, directly linked to their ranks and benefits. Regular assessments were conducted to determine promotions or dismissals. The Commissioner of Customs introduced Western personnel management systems to maximize the efficiency of customs officers, representing a relatively advanced approach in China at that time.

In Hard's perspective, the income of customs officers was composed of three components: basic salary, incentive salary, and welfare allowances. Salaries were aligned with the significance of the position and the difficulty of the work, providing a comprehensive reflection of officers' job performance. Considering the living standards of that era, the salary package for customs officers was quite generous, far exceeding those of equivalent government officials in other departments of the Qing government. Additionally, there were substantial prospects for salary growth, allowing customs personnel to dedicate themselves diligently to their responsibilities.

3.1.3 Establishment of a New Accounting System

Before 1865, the customs accounting records were a general ledger resembling the traditional Chinese four-column inventory. Starting in 1865, under the supervision of James Duncan Campbell, who had undergone rigorous accounting training, customs accounting underwent a series of reforms. This accounting system was recognized as a novel treasury system at that time. Through the rigorous enforcement by Hard and Campbell, the previous issues of unclear accounts and customs funds being embezzled by various tax commissioners were eliminated. This not only improved and clarified the customs figures but also cracked down on the practice of embezzlement by corrupt officials.

3.1.4 Establishment of a New Statistical System

Before Hard took over as the head of the General Customs Administration, China had not established a systematic trade reporting and statistics system. In 1864, various customs produced trade statistics with inconsistent specifications. From 1866 onward, this work was centralized in Shanghai. In 1873, the Trade Registration Office was established, responsible for printing quarterly and annual trade statistics reports for all customs and compiling a comprehensive trade report. The statistics covered various aspects of China's finances, economy, currency, and finance, especially focusing on major imports and exports like opium, tea, silk, hemp, and soybeans. These meticulous statistics serve as precious historical documents.

3.1.5 Establishment of an Inspection System

To enhance financial scrutiny within the Customs Administration, a specialized Audit and Taxation Department, responsible for accounting, was established under the General Customs Administration. This department had authority over customs accounting and conducted audits of customs accounting across various regions. Inspections were carried out at least once a year in each location, with Deputy Tax Commissioners stationed in Beijing overseeing the examination of customs reports. The Audit and Taxation Department wielded significant power, allowing them to inspect financial conditions at any time. In the event of significant issues, they had the authority to take over the customs operations, awaiting instructions from the General Customs Administration. Throughout Hard's nearly fifty years in office, instances of such takeovers could be counted on one hand. Hard also devised the "Regulations for the Examination of Goods Entering Customs" to curb widespread smuggling. This not only served as an "effective warning" for wrong-doers but also contributed to fostering a stable and sound atmosphere. It prevented numerous cases from progressing to the point where an examination was necessary, effectively addressing them before they escalated.

During Hart's tenure, he rescued the Chinese Customs from its previous state of chaos and rampant corruption, establishing a rational and effective management system. Under his leadership, the Chinese Customs underwent a revolutionary transformation, and the revenue functions of the customs were fully utilized. As a result, the tariff revenue for the Qing government witnessed a steady increase year after year.

Dai Angang (Professor in the Department of History at Fudan University): Back then, China didn't have officials with the necessary expertise in customs management. Consequently, they had to turn to foreigners for assistance. Hard was essentially a conscientious customs leader. Before his time, China's customs operated on a personal basis rather than following a legal framework. The collection of customs duties was often arbitrary, posing significant challenges to customs trade and the expansion of overseas imports and exports. The modern customs system in China was introduced thanks to Hard.

It's disheartening to note that the Chinese customs under Hard's administration was surprisingly the most honest institution within the Qing government. By 1899, one-third of the Qing government's financial revenue came from customs duties. Under Hard's guidance, the customs applied a remarkably low tariff rate of "five percent ad valorem" on imported Western goods. This was the world's lowest tariff at the time, attracting numerous merchant ships loaded with Western goods to venture into China. These ships brought more than just trade; they brought a plethora of goods and opportunities previously unseen by many Chinese.

Foreign tax officials introduced the disciplined, scientific, and rational civil service system from Western countries into the management structure of Chinese customs. This guided Shanghai's trade to a leading position in the nation's standardization and rule of law processes. In terms of supervising inbound and outbound goods and items, Shanghai Customs established a relatively comprehensive declaration system and assessment system. Concerning tariff collection, they developed a system for classifying and valuating tariffs. In the realm of statistics, a considerable amount of valuable trade data was accumulated. In customs enforcement, procedures for handling cases were established, and these systems indeed played a positive role in organizing the chaotic domestic and international trade order of that time.

3.2 Shipping, Competition, and Commercial Warfare: A Tripartite Standoff

Ship merchants not only held a central position in Shanghai's shipping industry but also played a leading role in various sectors. Initially, Shanghai's shipping relied on manually operated sand boats, with Shanghai Port having over 5000 sand boats at its peak. However, after the opening of the port, under the pressure from foreign steamships, the number of Shanghai's sand boats sharply declined. Following the signing of the "Treaty of Tianjin" in 1858 and the "Beijing Treaty" in 1860, several more commercial ports were opened in addition to the five designated ports. This allowed foreign cargo ships direct access to the Yangtze River. Foreign merchant ships were faster, could carry more cargo, and offered cheaper freight rates, leading to the rapid decline of China's shipping industry.

> Xiong Yuezhi (Researcher at the Shanghai Academy of Social Sciences and Visiting Professor at Fudan University): Western steamships, powered by machinery, had a large cargo capacity, high transit speed, and could adapt to various locations. Consequently, they could generate substantial profits, impacting our traditional wooden ships. Many profits from transportation were plundered by foreign entities.

Transporting grain through the Grand Canal was a crucial guarantee for the national finances during the feudal era, with a substantial amount of grain transported annually from the south to the north. If the transportation of grain was also seized by Western fleets, China's entire trade would be completely controlled by Western merchants. Therefore, many insightful individuals raised a question at that time: we need our own fleet and cannot allow Western fleets to freely navigate along our coastline.

Led by Li Hongzhang, the Westernization Movement ministers vigorously advocated the establishment of the China Merchants Steam Navigation Company, aiming to secure a share in China's shipping industry. This initiative aimed to prevent all shipping interests from falling into the hands of foreigners. Simultaneously, it involved transporting official grains, providing the capability to transport troops and military supplies in case of war. Although there was agreement on collectively financing the purchase of steamships and organizing shipping, serious differences arose between

Fig. 15 China Merchants Steam Navigation Company

the government and business sectors regarding operational policies. The "Westernization Faction," represented by Li Hongzhang, insisted on prioritizing the transportation of grains for the imperial court, with canal transportation taking precedence. In contrast, the business sector insisted on prioritizing seeking freight, actively participating in business competition, and competing for profits with foreign steamships (Fig. 15).

After rejecting the business sector's "Business Capital and Commercial Management" proposal, on December 26, 1872, the Qing government approved the establishment of the China Merchants Steam Navigation Company. This marked the first "wealth-seeking" enterprise of the Westernization Movement. Li Hongzhang enlisted the services of Zhu Qiang, a wealthy sand boat operator with both official and commercial ties, to oversee the establishment of the company. Zhu Qiang proposed a strategy of combining merchant shares with official operations, known as "merchant shares, official management." However, this policy failed to garner support from merchants. Without merchant investments, the China Merchants Steam Navigation Company struggled to meet its initial plan of raising 500,000 taels of silver in the first year. Additionally, Zhu Qiang lacked management experience in dealing with foreign entities, as well as proficiency in operating modern shipping. Consequently, the company quickly found itself in a predicament with no available shares and funds. In the more than a year that Zhu Qiang served, the development of the China Merchants Steam Navigation Company progressed very slowly. Hence, Li Hongzhang began exploring the strategy of "official supervision of business operations," a response that originated from his aide, Sheng Xuanhuai.

Li Hongzhang appointed Tang Tingshu as the general manager of the China Merchants Steam Navigation Company, with the equivalent position of a CEO. He also designated Xu Run and Sheng Xuanhuai as as associates, equivalent to deputy general managers. Tang Tingshu, a comprador of Jardine Matheson in Shanghai, and Xu Run, a comprador of Dent & Co., not only excelled in foreign languages but also had significant influence in the business community. Tang Tingshu, especially, was hailed as the "first comprador in China."

Originally from Xiangshan, Guangdong, Tang Tingshu received a comprehensive education in Hong Kong from an early age. Consequently, he spoke fluent English, facilitating seamless interactions with foreigners. Some even considered him an authentic Englishman. Coupled with his comprador background, experience as a Chinese director for the Beiyang Union Steam Navigation Co., and involvement in launching steamship companies, Tang Tingshu brought valuable expertise to his role (Fig. 16).

> This kind of initiative, if entrusted to the people, would be beyond their capability; if entrusted to businessmen, they lack the authority; if entrusted to the government, it cannot persist without issues over time. Only by having businesses contribute their capital, people contribute their labor, and the government oversee the overall process can the benefits be shared among the government, businesses, and the people.
>
> —Sheng Xuanhuai
>
> Eight Articles on the Trial Operation of Hubei Coal Mines

In Tang Tingshu's first strategic move upon his arrival in Shanghai, he relocated the original China Merchants Steam Navigation Company from Yong'an Road to within the British concession. He submitted a request to Li Hongzhang to rename the "China Merchants Steam Navigation Company" to the "China Merchants Steam Navigation General Bureau." Changing "Bureau" to "General Bureau" was a subtle yet impactful shift, altering the operational policy from "official management" to "official supervision of business operations." This change significantly allayed concerns and suspicions within the business community. Tang Tingshu personally invested a substantial capital of 80,000 taels and mobilized relatives and friends to join as shareholders. Tang Tingshu's four ships and the steamship company he ran between Hong Kong and Shanghai were also discounted and contributed as capital to the China Merchants Steam Navigation General Bureau. This boosted the confidence of Shanghai's businessmen, and the recruitment of commercial shares progressed smoothly. According to the articles of association, for every hundred shares, a business director would be elected, and among these business directors, one business general would be nominated. Both the General Bureau and its various branches would be presided over by the business general and business directors, providing investors with a certain degree

Fig. 16 Sheng Xuanhuai

of say in the affairs. Major shareholders enjoyed management rights. The prospectus also clearly outlined the use of funds, profits, and returns. As a result, businessmen flocked in, and in no time, 500,000 taels in commercial shares were raised. The assets of the China Merchants Steam Navigation General Bureau quickly expanded, and its transportation capacity increased (Fig. 17).

In July 1873, the thoroughly transformed China Merchants Steam Navigation General Bureau embarked on a new journey, involving not only the transportation of official grains for the government but also participating in civilian shipping business. With abundant funds from the business sector and robust support from the government, it became a mutually beneficial collaboration. As the China Merchants Steam Navigation General Bureau set sail on its inaugural river journey, the route extended from Shanghai through Zhenjiang and Jiujiang to Hankou, marking a significant shift from the previous dominance of British and American steamship companies over China's "Golden Waterway." The China Merchants Steam Navigation General Bureau pioneered China's first coastal route from Shanghai to Shantou, the first Yangtze River route from Shanghai to Hankou, and the first oceanic commercial route from Shanghai to Kobe, Japan. With Shanghai as its hub, the company's routes interconnected various Chinese ports, forging closer connections between China and the world (Fig. 18).

Fig. 17 Tang Tingshu

Fig. 18 Swire Group

Fig. 19 Jardine shipping

However, the success of China Merchants Steam Navigation Company has touched upon the vested interests of other merchant ships, provoking resentment from foreign shipping companies. The American Flag Line, Jardine Matheson of UK and Swire, jointly waged a trade war against China Merchants Steam Navigation Company, employing the most straightforward tactic - price pressure. Among them, the oldest company in the competition, American Flag Line, dramatically reduced freight rates by 70%, reaching as low as one-tenth of the original. This aggressive strategy was aimed at pushing China Merchants Steam Navigation Company out at any cost (Fig. 19).

In response to the challenge, the newly launched China Merchants Steam Navigation Company had no choice but to lower prices. The company's own secret weapon boiled down to two words—grain transport. Early in its establishment, Sheng Xuanhuai secured an annual transportation order for 400,000 piculs of grain from the government. Sheng Xuanhuai effectively pulled the national business into his shipping enterprise. Grain transport involved the transportation of grains collected by local governments for the central government. The authority to operate and transport these grains rested with the ship fleet chosen by local governments. At this point, Sheng Xuanhuai visited households, leveraging Li Hongzhang's influence and emphasizing national interest, combined with economic strategies. With the grain transport business in hand, China Merchants Steam Navigation Company could break even. Sheng Xuanhuai then issued the directive: "Negotiate from a position of strength, never show weakness." He knew well that continual weakness would allow foreign interests to prevail, and Chinese enterprises would have no chance to rise.

Relying on the coordination between government and merchants and supported by the annual transportation of 400,000 piculs of grain, China Merchants Steam Navigation Company engaged in a three-year business war against foreign merchants. Sheng Xuanhuai noticed that despite the collaboration between the Jardine Matheson of UK and Swire, there were conflicting interests. Proactively, he alternately pressured Swire against the Jardine Matheson and vice versa. By the end of the third year, the once-thriving China Merchants Steam Navigation Company barely made a profit of over ten thousand taels of silver, and the atmosphere within the company was filled with sighs. Despite Sheng Xuanhuai's deep concerns, he was confident that his opponents were also facing difficult times. The ultimate victory depended on endurance. As expected, shortly after, the Jardine Matheson of UK and Swire sought a truce with Sheng Xuanhuai. By the end of 1876, the competitors found themselves in an unprofitable situation. The initiator, Flag Line, suffered substantial losses, leading to a sharp decline in its stock value. Faced with severe losses, Flag Line had to liquidate its entire fleet, reducing its maritime operations in China. Tang Tingshu, seizing the opportunity, astutely acquired Flag Line Steamship Company, inadvertently eliminating a competitor.

With an initial profit margin of only 7%, how did China Merchants Steam Navigation Company secure two million taels of silver to acquire Flag Line Steamship Company? Sheng Xuanhuai turned to Li Hongzhang, writing a letter seeking aid. He emphasized the urgency of raising a down payment of one million taels within two months for the Flag Line acquisition and hoped for assistance from the central government. Li Hongzhang's reply approved the purchase of Flag Line but advised Sheng Xuanhuai to explore fundraising options with local governments.

During the Self-Strengthening Movement, Sheng Xuanhuai gained the moniker "using authority to oppress merchants and using merchants to deceive authorities." While somewhat critical, this description reflected his adept maneuvering between the government, the public, and the business world. Wielding the influence of Li Zhongtang and backed by Southern Minister Shen Baozhen, Sheng Xuanhuai remarkably raised the needed one million taels down payment within two months. In a significant move, the four-year-old China Merchants Steam Navigation Company acquired all the ships and docks of the financially robust American-owned Flag Line Steamship Company. This historic acquisition, marking the first time a Chinese enterprise competitively absorbed a sizable foreign company, caused a stir in the shipping industry and saw the retrieval of some of China's maritime rights from foreign hands. On March 1, 1877, both companies issued a joint statement in "Shen Bao," announcing that all former Flag Line customers would be transferred to China Merchants Steam Navigation Company and receive equivalent services.

Flag Line Steamship Company, with its 7 ocean liners, 9 river vessels, numerous chartered and towed boats, totaling 27 ships, along with docks, warehouses, shipyards, and an ironworks, all switched allegiance from the Stars and Stripes to the vibrant Yellow Dragon Flag under the banner of China Merchants Steam Navigation Company. China Merchants Steam Navigation Company became the largest shipping company in China. Almost overnight, the company's fleet expanded by 20 ships, more than doubling the total tonnage, surpassing any foreign shipping company operating in China. The strength and reputation of China Merchants Steam Navigation Company soared. Sheng Xuanhuai's strategic acquisition of Flag Line Steamship Company for two million taels yielded a full return on investment within just four years. Besides major cities, new docks and warehouses emerged along the entire Yangtze River, signifying substantial growth. At its zenith, centered around Shanghai, China Merchants Steam Navigation Company's routes extended eastward to Japan and the United States, westward through the South Seas, passing through the Suez Canal directly to London, covering more than half the globe.

After acquiring Flag Line's wharf and four additional wharves owned by the Jin family, China Merchants Steam Navigation Company unified them under the name "Jinliyuan Wharf," also known as "Nanzhan Wharf." Along the Pujiang River, they constructed 13 floating docks, laying the foundation for what would become the Sixteen Pu Wharf. Subsequently, due to the company's business expansion, China Merchants Steam Navigation Company carried out extensive renovations on the Sixteen Pu Wharf, transforming it into Shanghai's largest commercial center and transportation hub. By 1880, the Bund had taken shape, attracting prospectors from across the globe. During that period, the Bund served as a major dock, connected to the Sixteen Pu Wharf. Almost 300 foreign ships anchored on the Huangpu River daily, with these international shipping companies handling routes along the Chinese coast, the Yangtze River, and even across the open seas (Fig. 20).

In 1883, Shanghai experienced a financial crisis, plunging numerous fledgling enterprises into hardship. The Shanghai Steam Navigation Company was no exception. Under economic and political pressures, Li Hongzhang reorganized the Shanghai Steam Navigation Company in 1885. He appointed Sheng Xuanhuai as the supervisor. Sheng, having a background as a government official, maintained his official position during his tenure as supervisor. In comparison to businessmen,

Fig. 20 The Bund in 1880

Fig. 21 Steamships of the China Merchants Steam Navigation Company

he displayed a strong official demeanor, accustomed to the ways of the bureaucratic field. Compared to government officials, however, he resembled a businessman, often taking actions to protect the interests of merchants.

The acquisition of Flag Line marked a significant leap forward for China Merchants Steam Navigation Company, solidifying a triumvirate with British Jardine Matheson and Swire. The burgeoning China Merchants Steam Navigation Company provoked increased animosity from Jardine Matheson and Swire, leading them to join forces against China Merchants Steam Navigation Company. In January 1890, a price war unfolded among the three shipping companies (Fig. 21).

In April 1893, after years of intense rivalry, the three longstanding competitors finally sat down for negotiations, once again signing a comprehensive contract. In this contract, it is evident that Shen Xuanhuai's China Merchants Steam Navigation Company emerged as the ultimate winner. The news of China Merchants Steam Navigation Company' triumph spread, prompting cheers among the Chinese business community. Whistles echoed on the Huangpu River as Chinese ships celebrated. In this moment, China Merchants Steam Navigation Company' merchant vessels navigated through the Yangtze River and coastal cities, heralding their golden age.

3.3 Sustained Growth in Shanghai's Foreign Trade

With the rapid development of inland navigation on the Yangtze River and the opening of new ports such as Nanjing, Hankou, Niuzhuang, Dengzhou, and Tianjin after the Second Opium War, Shanghai's position in national trade, especially foreign trade, became more prominent. Shanghai witnessed a period of rapid growth in its foreign trade, with the total trade volume increasing from an average of 70.04 million customs taels in the 1860s to an average of 131.96 million customs taels in the 1890s, indicating a substantial growth rate. From 1864 to 1894, the cumulative value of Shanghai's imports, calculated at the landed price, reached 2,334,510,000 customs taels, and the cumulative value of Shanghai's exports, calculated at the departure price, reached 2,686,440,000 customs taels.

This can be attributed to four main factors: Firstly, the pacification of domestic wars and the initiation of the Self-Strengthening Movement, aiming for prosperity and strength. Secondly, the continual increase in the number and reach of Yangtze River ports led to Chinese and foreign merchants in Shanghai establishing numerous branch offices and making substantial investments in Yangtze River shipping. Thirdly, the preliminary formation and gradual improvement of Shanghai's modern foreign trade system. Fourthly, the significant progress in transportation and communication brought about by global technological changes. Since 1871, direct telegraphic communication between China and Europe ensured the swift and accurate delivery of information, profoundly impacting foreign trade. In 1874, a commercial report in Shanghai stated, "Due to the convenience of banks and telegraphs, European silk merchants can directly procure most of the raw silk they need from China, eliminating the need to go through the London market. Last year, approximately half of the raw silk directly shipped to the European continent accounted for the total exports."

An illustrative instance is the swift sale of raw silk purchased in the Shanghai market in the London. The opening of the Suez Canal brought about a fundamental shift in Shanghai's approach to foreign trade. Preceding this canal's opening, trade between China and Britain necessitated circumventing the Cape of Good Hope, involving a journey of about 120 days. Since the inauguration of the Suez Canal on November 17, 1869, the journey was shortened to just 55–60 days, ensuring optimal freshness of goods and reducing shipping costs to a considerable extent.

From the perspective of major trading nations, the United Kingdom and its colonies were the primary focus of Shanghai's foreign trade during this period. The European continent witnessed a significant rise in its export trade with Shanghai, while the United States experienced a resurgence in its position in Shanghai's foreign trade.

Before the 1870s, Shanghai primarily conducted its foreign trade with the European continent through the United Kingdom as an intermediary. The most significant imported commodity during that period, opium, largely originated from British India. In 1864, Shanghai's imports from the United Kingdom amounted to 11,311,964 customs taels, making up 33% of the total imports. Imports from Hong Kong stood at 1,922,092 customs taels, comprising 6%, while imports from India accounted for 16,134,995 customs taels, representing 48%. Shanghai's exports to the United Kingdom totaled 25,484,654 customs taels, constituting 84% of the city's overall exports.

Post the 1870s, the widespread use of telegrams and the opening of the Suez Canal led to a significant increase in direct foreign trade between Shanghai and the European continent, resulting in a diminished trade position for Britain. By

1894, Shanghai's imports from the United Kingdom were 29,138,061 customs taels, constituting 30% of Shanghai's total imports. Imports from Hong Kong accounted for 21,837,233 customs taels, making up 23%, and imports from India were 19,929,092 customs taels, representing 21%. Shanghai's exports to the United Kingdom reached 8,575,575 customs taels, comprising 15% of Shanghai's total exports. Exports to Hong Kong were 7,252,078 customs taels, accounting for 12%, and exports to India amounted to 2,542,592 customs taels, making up 4%. Despite a decline in Britain's trade position in both imports and exports, it is evident that Britain remained a key trading partner for Shanghai's import trade (Fig. 22).

As the United States heightened its focus on East Asia in the late nineteenth century, its foreign trade with Shanghai experienced a resurgence. Shanghai's import trade with the European continent showed a slight upward trend, while export trade to the European continent notably increased. The European continent's share of Shanghai's total imports rose from 0.3% in 1864 to 6% in 1894. In terms of total exports, its share surged from 4% in 1864 to 32% in 1894, surpassing Britain and becoming the primary destination for Shanghai's export trade.

The United States' role in Shanghai's foreign trade has seen an upward trajectory, with its proportion of Shanghai's total imports increasing from 1% in 1864 to 9% in 1894. Similarly, its share of Shanghai's total exports rose from 8% in 1864 to 19% in 1894. With the heightened interest of the United States in East Asia during the late nineteenth century, its foreign trade with Shanghai experienced a revival.

Fig. 22 Great Northern Telegraph Company in 1871

While Shanghai's import trade with the European continent exhibited modest growth, export trade to the European continent showed a significant increase. The European continent's share of Shanghai's total imports increased from 0.3% in 1864 to 6% in 1894. In terms of total exports, its share skyrocketed from 4% in 1864 to 32% in 1894, surpassing Britain and emerging as the primary recipient of Shanghai's export trade.

During this period, the composition of Shanghai's exported goods continued to be dominated by raw silk and tea, while the significance of miscellaneous goods in Shanghai's export trade witnessed an uptick. Despite facing competition in categories such as raw silk and tea from countries like India and Japan, the proportion of Shanghai's total export trade represented by raw silk and tea decreased from an initial 90%. However, by 1894, these categories still comprised over 50% of the total export trade. Raw silk and tea remained the principal product categories in Shanghai's export trade, with raw silk consistently holding its position as the most crucial export. Shanghai's unique geographical advantage, being close to renowned raw silk production areas like Huzhou and Nanxun, solidified its role as the primary export port for raw silk.

Shanghai's portion of the national raw silk export trade had reached 70% in the 1860s and 1870s. Despite the continual increase in port openings during the 1880s and 1890s, Shanghai maintained a share of over 60%, reaching 68.7% by 1894, showcasing its notable advantage in raw silk exports. Apart from raw silk and tea, the late 1880s witnessed an uptick in the export trade of miscellaneous goods such as straw hats, beans, fur, seeds, vegetable oil, and raw cotton. By 1893, miscellaneous goods like pig bristles from Sichuan, and hides and leather from Hunan and Henan, comprised 37% of Shanghai's total export trade. During the maritime conflicts, the opening and expansion of ports along the Yangtze River and its routes allowed Shanghai to expand its hinterland from the Jiangnan region to the upstream Yangtze as a source of raw materials. This change facilitated the export of previously less weighty miscellaneous goods via steamships, contributing to the growing significance of miscellaneous goods in Shanghai's export trade.

Regarding the structure of imported goods, cotton textiles overtook opium as the primary category, and there was a significant increase in the import volume of sugar, rice, kerosene, and hardware. In the 1860s and 1870s, opium remained the most crucial imported commodity in China, making up over 40% of the total imports. By the 1880s, opium's import share dropped to around 30%. In 1893, opium's share further decreased to 20%, while the import share of cotton textiles reached approximately 30%, surpassing opium. Shanghai continued to be the primary port for opium imports, with 70% of the opium imported to China passing through Shanghai in the 1870s and 1880s. However, there was a gradual decline, and by 1894, opium imported through Shanghai accounted for 57% of the national total.

In terms of absolute numbers, Shanghai's opium imports decreased from 41,984 piculs in 1871 to 35,804 piculs in 1894. Analyzing the proportion of opium imports to the total import volume, in 1860, opium represented 48% of Shanghai's total imports, while cotton textiles made up 44%. By 1894, opium's proportion had declined to 19.8%, whereas cotton textiles maintained a substantial share at 43.7%. The declining share of opium in import trade persisted through the 1890s, with cotton textiles surpassing opium to become the predominant imported commodity in Shanghai.

During this period, the significant growth in the import trade of sugar, rice, kerosene, and hardware is a noteworthy change. By 1894, the import volume of these four categories constituted over 20% of Shanghai's total import trade, with sugar alone accounting for over 30% of the total import volume for these goods. Additionally, starting from the 1880s, the increase in domestic cotton and woolen mills led to a rising demand for machinery. By 1894, the import of machinery through Shanghai accounted for 6.4% of the city's total import volume, marking a stage of progress in Shanghai's modernization process.

The flourishing trade has shaped this city and influenced its inhabitants. Adventurers from all corners of the country have flocked to this feng shui treasure land, tirelessly pioneering new territories, engaging in gold rushes, contributing back to society. Their successes have vividly marked the pages of Shanghai's trading history.

4 The Rapid Development of Foreign Trade After the First Sino-Japanese War

4.1 The Continuous Improvement of Foreign Trade Fundamentals

The enhancement of trade fundamentals owes much to the sustained growth in shipping, the ongoing refinement of railway networks, and the rapid expansion of telecommunications. These improvements in the exchange of information and goods have rendered Shanghai's trade environment exceptionally appealing.

4.1.1 The Continuous Improvement of Shipping Promoted Trade Growth

During the first ten years of the twentieth century, Shanghai witnessed rapid growth in its shipping sector. In 1902, the total import and export tonnage at Shanghai Port amounted to 11,812,535 tons, with Britain accounting for 48%, China for 15%, and Japan and Germany both at 14%. In 1911, the total tonnage had surged to 18,179,472 tons, with Britain's share dropping to 40%, Japan's rising to 22%, China's remaining at 17%, and Germany's at 9%. Throughout this decade, Shanghai's shipping industry experienced an overall growth of 53.9%, particularly with Japan's significant increase in both shipping and trade activities in Shanghai. This rapid advancement in maritime transportation greatly bolstered the swift expansion of domestic and international trade in and out of Shanghai.

4.1.2 The Continuous Improvement of Railway Network Promoted Trade Growth

Between 1895 and 1911, China saw the construction of 9,253.83 km of railway, including key lines like Zhongdong, Jingfeng, Huning, Jinpu, Jiaoji, Pinghan, and Guangzhou-Guiping. These developments significantly eased trade expansion. In 1897, after nearly two decades of disuse, the Songhu Railway was restored, reopening on September 1, 1898, spanning 16.09 km and sparking vital opportunities for the development of towns along its route. Subsequently, in 1907, the Rizhao Port branch line of the Shanghai-Hangzhou railway was completed, followed by the opening of the Shanghai-Nanjing and Shanghai-Hangzhou lines in 1908 and 1909, respectively. The continuous expansion and enhancement of the railway network not only expanded Shanghai's urban landscape but also transformed its traditional reliance on waterways for internal and external transportation. Shanghai gradually solidified its central role in the Yangtze River Delta, facilitating the distribution of imported goods to the hinterland while also propelling exponential growth in its export commodities (Fig. 23).

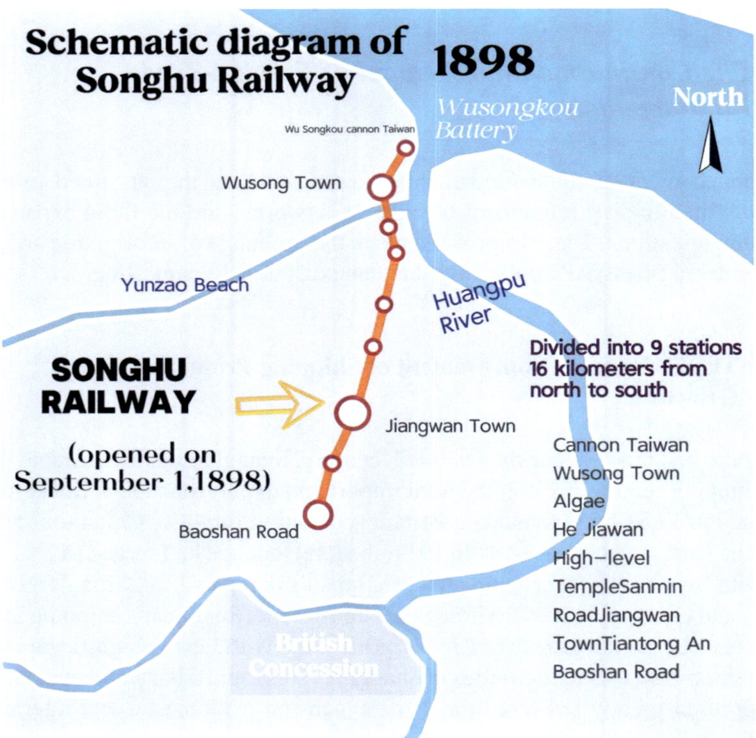

Fig. 23 Songhu Railway schematic diagram

4.1.3 The Establishment of Telecommunications Further Highlighted the Attractiveness of the Business Environment

After the First Sino-Japanese War, telegraphs sent from Shanghai could reach as far as Beijing to the north, Guangzhou to the south, Hankou to the west, and Shanhaiguan to the northeast, solidifying Shanghai's pivotal role as a domestic telecommunication hub. By the end of 1897, Shanghai had established direct telegraphic links with Southeast Asia, Japan, Europe, and beyond, facilitated not only by submarine cables but also telegraph lines stretching from Shanghai to Beijing, reaching Kyakhta and Siberia. Furthermore, Shanghai led the way in embracing wireless telegraphy. In 1908, telegraph stations were established in Chongming and Wusong, along with a wireless telegraph bureau. The first commercial wireless telegraphy station in modern China was erected at the Palace Hotel. The continuous refinement of the telecommunications network gradually elevated Shanghai to become the nation's foremost communication hub. The burgeoning telecommunication industry completely overturned the previous predicament of obstructed business communications due to inadequate postal routes, creating highly favorable conditions for the dissemination and exchange of domestic and international business information, thereby further enhancing Shanghai's business environment.

4.2 The Degree of Internationalization of the Foreign Trade System Has Deepened

The internationalization of the foreign trade system is mainly reflected in a series of activities and reforms within various foreign trade sectors, including customs, foreign firms, compradors, and Chinese merchants.

4.2.1 Customs Reforms Improved Clearance Efficiency, Further Promoting Trade Development

The reform of customs primarily involved the continual expansion of customs functions, encompassing a variety of modern business operations. In 1888, the Jianghai Customs initiated the trial operation of customs warehouses, allowing imported and exported goods to be temporarily stored pre-clearance, enjoying deferred tax treatment, thus reducing storage costs and winning favor from numerous businesses. Furthermore, leveraging its authority and efficiency, the customs secured cooperation from the Qing government and extended its jurisdiction to encompass regular tariffs within 25 li of treaty ports. Beginning in 1896, the customs undertook postal services, with the Tax Commissioner L.S. Rocher concurrently serving as the Postal Commissioner. By 1907, its branches had proliferated to 2800 locations, spanning a broad area. On March 1, 1898, the Qing government borrowed funds through likin, entrusting the Jianghai Customs with likin collection on April 21, utilizing the proceeds for debt repayment. On June 6 of the same year, the Qing government approved British steamships' passage through the inner harbor, assigning management and licensing authority to the Jianghai Customs. In April 1899, the Jianghai Customs dissolved the riverboat associations, assuming responsibility for dock dues formerly collected by the Shanghai Municipal Council and the Public Board, subsequently establishing a dedicated dock dues office. In 1904, the Qing government further empowered the Jianghai Customs to oversee trademark registration, a duty retained by the customs until the establishment of the Nanjing National Government.

To cope with the burgeoning trade and the expanding functions of the customs, the customs workforce saw continual growth. Between 1891 and 1901, the total staff in the Tax Collection Department surged from 448 to 659, marking a 25% increase, with foreign staff in the Internal and External Divisions rising from 97 to 127, and in the Maritime Division from 8 to 24. Concurrently, the staff count in the Ship's Bills Department swelled from 133 to 200, including a rise in foreign staff from 29 to 51. The establishment of the postal bureau saw an additional 168 staff, including 23 foreign staff. By July 1902, the total number of staff in the Tax Collection Department, Ship's Bills Department, and Postal Department in Shanghai had doubled to 1027 compared to 1892. Analyzing the proportion of foreign staff among Jianghai Customs personnel, in 1875, out of a total of 353 staff, 86 were foreign, accounting for 24.4%. By 1914, this proportion had climbed to 30.6%, with most foreign staff occupying pivotal roles, while positions held by Chinese staff tended to be of lower status.

The continual expansion of customs functions and the rising proportion of foreign personnel within the customs workforce underscored the predominantly foreign control over modern customs, exhibiting traits of deepening internationalization or semi-colonialism. Through the modern enterprises facilitated by customs operations, foreigners bolstered their penetration and influence over the Qing government, securing their interests. However, it's worth noting that most foreign-operated customs were relatively incorruptible and introduced more systematic Western management systems. The Qing government tangibly perceived the benefits of increased tax revenue brought about by the introduction of foreign customs systems. While the deepening foreign control over customs compromised Chinese sovereignty, a series of reform measures notably enhanced customs efficiency, ensuring the continuity of foreign trade in Shanghai amidst periods of turmoil and driving trade development.

4.2.2 The Transformation of Foreign Business Practices Has Highlighted the Increasingly Important Role of Chinese Merchants in Foreign Trade

From the early days of the opening of Shanghai until the 1890s, most foreign firms operated as distributors, agents, and shipping merchants. For instance, companies like Jardine Matheson & Co., American Flag Line, and Dent & Co. were comprehensive foreign firms integrating shipping, trade, insurance, and finance, conducting trade through packaged shipping. Others like Gibb, Livingston & Co., Robert S. Walker & Co., and Holliday Wise & Co. acted as agents, trading Chinese silver and gold, silk, tea, and miscellaneous goods for Western-manufactured cotton textiles and other products. Following the First Sino-Japanese War, foreign powers gained privileges to invest in and establish factories in China, leading foreign firms to shift towards investment and conglomerates. This resulted in the formation of major conglomerates such as Swire Group, Anderson Meyer&Co.Ltd., Carlowitz & Co., Mitsubishi, Jardine Matheson, Brunner Mond & Co., Ld, E·D·Sassoon Co., Olivier & Cie, and Mitsui Group. Additionally, specialized import firms were dealing in products ranging from oil, automobiles, and airplanes to films, tobacco, chemicals, Western medicines, paper, soap, and machinery, as well as specialized exporters dealing in products like eggs, silk, tea, leather, casings, lace embroidery, pig bristles, and feathers.

From the twentieth century onward, larger capitalist monopolistic multinational corporations began forging commercial ties with Shanghai's foreign firms through exclusive branding and agency agreements. For instance, the Roberts. Walker&Co. exclusively distributed medicines from the Germany Berlin Pharmaceutical Group Co., limited, while the H.S. Honigsberg & Co. handled exclusive sales of Cadillac cars from the United States, and Anderson Meyer&Co.Ltd. acted as the agent for various machinery and electrical products from American factories. Moreover, some multinational corporations established their own specialized trading companies or sales branches in Shanghai. For example, the DuPont Chemical Group set up Hengxin Trading Company in Shanghai to exclusively market their products like pigments, glazed leather, rubber cloth, paint, and gunpowder. Meanwhile, the British company Imperial Chemical Industries PLC established Brunner Mond (UK) Limited in Shanghai to oversee the import of their chemicals and the export of Chinese goods. Additionally, the British Maucher Trading Company established a Shanghai branch to distribute their heavy machinery such as oil presses, dredgers, and cranes. In Shanghai, the German automotive industry set up Siemens Trading Company and the pigment industry established Defag Trading Company. Seven Belgian steel companies formed the Belgian Steel Union in Shanghai, all dedicated to marketing their products. These foreign merchants leveraged the extensive sales networks of compradors to distribute their products across Shanghai. During this period, the most notable shift in foreign merchant operations was the injection of capital through direct investment in China, followed by the use of comprador networks for importing goods and cultural influence. Compradors played an indispensable role in Shanghai's foreign trade, and their contribution to the city's trade development was continually highlighted.

4.3 National Capital Compradors Emerged

4.3.1 Ningbo Merchants and the Ningbo Chamber of Commerce

In the tide of modern immigration marked by perseverance and ambition, a significant number of people from Ningbo stood out. Generations of Ningbo natives embarked on journeys to Shanghai in search of fortune, fueling an enduring migration between the two cities. The migration wave between Ningbo and Shanghai has remained robust over time. The folk saying "Little Bok Choy, tender mugwort, the husband goes to Shanghai; Returns with Shanghai goods, neighbors envy; Little Bok Choy, tender mugwort, the husband goes to Shanghai; Brings back ten or twenty yuan, what a good husband!" This folk, known as "Little Bok Choy," circulated widely in modern Ningbo society, vividly portraying the impression Ningbo people held of Shanghai in the modern era and the relationship between the two cities: Shanghai represented wealth, the place for entrepreneurial endeavors, while Ningbo was home, Shanghai's backyard, where life flourished (Fig. 24).

According to statistics, by the end of the Qing Dynasty, the number of Ningbo natives in Shanghai had reached 400,000, positioning them as the leading immigrant group in this diverse and cosmopolitan city. With such a large Ningbo immigrant community, Shanghai earned the moniker of the second hometown for Ningbo people, while Ningbo became known as the ancestral home of Shanghainese, with nearly every Ningbo family having relatives in Shanghai. Even today, individuals of Ningbo descent still constitute a significant portion of Shanghai's population. The role and contributions of the Ningbo people to the rise of modern Shanghai were substantial, while Shanghai provided the grand stage for the remarkable achievements of the modern Ningbo people, underscoring the close and interdependent relationship between the two.

Fig. 24 The Ningbo Chamber of Commerce

In the early period of opening, Shanghai implemented a "barter trade" system, where British merchants "could sell goods for cash at a higher nominal price." The ascent of Shanghai deprived Ningbo, once a thriving trading hub, of its economic opportunities. Consequently, Ningbo people surged into Shanghai like a tide. Amidst the rapid development of modern Shanghai, which provided ample space for immigration, the Ningbo people were quick to seize this land teeming with opportunities and potential. Shanghai represented opportunities and hope. Shanghai became the base for Ningbo people's entrepreneurial pursuits, and Ningbo merchants made remarkable contributions across various sectors such as finance, trade, industry, shipping, culture, and philanthropy in modern Shanghai. With the prestigious reputation of "No market without Ningbo," bolstered by the formidable financial resources of the "Suzhe Financial Consortium," the Ningbo clique held a paramount position in Shanghai's socioeconomic sphere.

Ningbo merchants not only pioneered countless "firsts" in China but also held significant sway in Shanghai's most crucial economic entities, such as the Shanghai General Chamber of Commerce and the Bankers' Association. In 1897, China's inaugural modern bank, the Imperial Bank of China, was officially established. Yan Xinhou, regarded as the foremost figure of the Ningbo merchant clique, assumed the roles of its inaugural general manager, chairman of the board, and chairman of the Shanghai branch. In 1908, he went on to establish the Ningpo Commercial Bank, Ltd. Additionally, Yan Xinhou co-founded the Ningbo Tongjiuyuan Textile Mill with Zhou Jinbiao, commencing operations in 1896 with over 17,000 spinning spindles and 216 looms. By 1905, Yan Xinhou had also founded the Tongli Sack Factory in Shanghai and invested in industries such as flour mills, oil mills, and inland shipping. The Shanghai Chamber of Commerce, renowned as one of China's earliest modern business associations, was initiated and founded by Ningbo merchant Yan Xinhou. Subsequently, the majority of its chairpersons were Ningbo merchants, and at its zenith, over half of its board members hailed from Ningbo. Madame Bergere, a notable French historian of modern Chinese history, humorously remarked that the Shanghai Chamber of Commerce could be considered merely a branch of the Si-Ming Gongsuo (Ningbo hometown association) (Figs. 25 and 26).

Ningbo merchants were pivotal in propelling the modernization and advancement of Shanghai, and by extension, the Chinese economy, significantly contributing to Shanghai's establishment as the economic epicenter of China. The eminent Shanghai native businessman, Mu Ouchu, once remarked, "Shanghai is the economic nucleus of our nation, and this remarkable success is largely owed to Ningbo people. Hence, Shanghai is truly the Shanghai of Ningbo people."

Ningbo people in modern times but also facilitated their outreach to both China and the wider world. Throughout modern history, many Ningbo elites have thrived with the influence of "Shanghai elements" in their growth and success, extending beyond merely the realm of commerce. As integral members of the Ningbo clique, Ningbo merchants who journeyed to Shanghai made significant contributions to establishing Shanghai as the epicenter of commerce and trade in China while also actively contributing to the development of their hometowns, fostering a mutually beneficial relationship between Shanghai and Ningbo's economies. Many of these

Fig. 25 Ningbo businessman Yan Xinhou

successful Ningbo merchants in Shanghai harbored deep ties to their hometowns, actively participating in their development by bringing in capital, technology, and talent, as well as introducing new ideas and perspectives, thus serving as a driving force behind Ningbo's modernization. For instance, Li Zhifang, the uncle of the contemporary renowned Ningbo entrepreneur and philanthropist Li Dasan, served as a comprador for a Japanese shipping company in Shanghai for an extended period. Influenced by the Japanese, he placed particular emphasis on education and healthcare. He established schools and hospitals in his hometown of Dongqian Lake, Mozhi, and spearheaded a "toilet revolution," centralizing scattered pit latrines in villages and implementing improved sanitation measures. He also worked tirelessly to enhance drinking water quality, bringing a breath of fresh air to remote mountain villages.

Ningbo merchants not only left a mark in the bustling environment of modern Shanghai but continue to soar on the global stage today. During the early days of Shanghai's opening, Ningbo merchants diversified into new commercial ventures, including foreign cloth and wool. In 1853, Ningbo pharmaceutical merchant Cai Tongde raised 2000 taels and established the Hengxing Foreign Cloth Store at Nanjing Road's Baqi Field. Similarly, in the same year, Sun Zenglai from Cixi opened the Zengtai Foreign Cloth Store at the intersection of Nanjing Road and Henan Road. In 1854, a prominent Ningbo family established the Dafeng Foreign Cloth Store at the

Fig. 26 Si-Ming Gongsuo

same intersection, marking an early transition from traditional to modern merchant practices. By 1858, among the 15 foreign cloth stores in Shanghai, five were operated by Ningbo merchants, constituting one-third of the total. In the 1860s and 1870s, they expanded into sectors such as hardware, foreign oil, and Western medicine, and leveraged money shops and banks to import capital into Shanghai on a large scale, facilitating industrial loans and capital flow. The "Posting system" was one of the financial innovations introduced by Ningbo merchants, characterized by bill exchange for inter-company transactions rather than direct silver payments, which resembled modern banking practices. By the late nineteenth century, spurred on by foreign banks, the modern banking sector of Chinese national capital was burgeoning. Ningbo merchants played pivotal roles in establishing or participating in over 30 modern banks, including the Imperial Bank of China, the Bank of Communication, the Si-Ming Bank, and the China CITIC Bank, with figures such as Yan Xinhou, Ye Chengzhong, Zhu Baosan, Sun Hengfu, Xie Guangfu, and Fu Xiaohan assuming crucial roles. Following the First Sino-Japanese War, with the rise and development of national capitalism, the Ningbo people also heavily invested in modern enterprises.

Xiong Yuezhi (Research Fellow at the Shanghai Academy of Social Sciences and Distinguished Professor at Fudan University): Many Ningbo merchants who migrated to Shanghai hailed from humble backgrounds, known for their perseverance, resilience, and aptitude for learning. In 1893, Shanghai celebrated its fiftieth anniversary since its opening. During this commemoration, two groups emerged as the most active and influential: the Guangdong clique, representing the merchants from Guangdong, and the Ningbo clique. Despite Guangdong being a province and Ningbo being a prefecture, Ningbo merchants were able to compete on equal footing with their counterparts from Guangdong.

Upon their initial arrival in Shanghai, many Ningbo individuals sought various means of livelihood, including apprenticeships in various shops, running errands, working as sailors, laboring in factories, tailoring, or serving as domestic helpers. A notable characteristic of Ningbo people seeking opportunities in Shanghai was their tendency to secure employment through introductions and recommendations from fellow townsmen, which differed from the influx of migrants from northern Jiangsu and northern Anhui who fled to Shanghai due to disasters and famines. The Ningbo clique stood as the largest merchant clique in modern China and one of the "Ten Great Merchant Cliques" in traditional China. It made significant contributions to the development of China's national industry and commerce, spearheading the modernization of China's industrial and commercial sectors. The establishment of the first modern Chinese-owned bank, the first Chinese-owned shipping company, and the first Chinese-owned machinery factory were all attributed to the endeavors of Ningbo merchants.

Although the financial resources of the Ningbo clique were not as abundant as those of the Shanxi clique, their cautious, meticulous, and thrifty approach, devoid of any stubbornness, made them a progressive force. While they may not have possessed the same bold decisiveness as the Guangdong clique, which was active both domestically and internationally, the Ningbo clique was characterized by stability, and pragmatism, and stood on equal footing with the Guangdong clique. According to "The Modern Economic History of Shanghai," Ningbo individuals, in their pursuit of new markets, managed to penetrate various sectors of Shanghai's import and export trade. They infiltrated the comprador circle and industries such as the foreign grocery trade, silk industry, and foreign cloth industry, previously dominated by the Guangdong clique. Gradually expanding their influence, they eventually gained a leading position in these sectors.

4.3.2 The Pioneering Comprador in Ningbo Clique—Mu Bingyuan

The early influential compradors in Shanghai mostly hailed from Guangzhou. However, Mu Bingyuan stood out as the pioneering comprador associated with the Ningbo clique in Shanghai's modern history. Born in Dinghai County, Ningbo Prefecture, Zhejiang Province (now part of Dinghai District, Zhoushan City), Mu started his career as a sailor in the Qing army, having received a basic education. Following his capture in the Battle of Dinghai, the British spared his life and assigned him tasks aboard their ship. Recognizing his youthfulness and industriousness, they even taught him English for daily interactions. Alongside, Mu, with his sharp intellect, absorbed the British strategies and techniques of conducting business.

On June 19, 1842, after the Battle of Wusong, British warships sailed unopposed into the Huangpu River, leading to the swift capture of Shanghai by the British forces. Among the troops entering Shanghai was Mu Bingyuan. Recognizing Mu's command of English and his adept interpersonal skills, British commanders frequently kept him by their side, employing him as a translator and entrusting him with various responsibilities. Seizing this opportunity, Mu commenced his career as a comprador, becoming the pioneer of a new breed of compradors after the opening of Shanghai, earning him the title of "The Founding Father of Shanghai Compradors."

During Shanghai's initial phase of opening up to foreign trade, the prolonged isolation between China and the West presented numerous challenges for foreign merchants conducting business with the locals. Consequently, Mu Bingyuan, possessing a thorough understanding of local customs, English proficiency, adeptness in managing trivial affairs, and earning the trust of foreign traders, naturally assumed a pivotal role. He monopolized all Sino-British foreign trade in Shanghai, frequently serving as an intermediary in major transactions. Mu Bingyuan also facilitated the shipment of foreign goods to Ningbo and other regions in eastern Zhejiang, while also engaging in commercial activities in places such as Hankou, Jiujiang, Niuzhuang, and Yantai. As documented in Yao Gonghe's "Shanghai Gossip," it was a common practice: "Anyone engaging in large-scale transactions inevitably sought Mu's mediation." Evolving into a seasoned professional comprador, Mu Bingyuan astutely amassed wealth through Sino-foreign trade, swiftly ascending to prominence in Shanghai.

Within the first year of Shanghai's opening, 11 British and American trading firms set up permanent bases in the city. Faced with an overwhelming workload, Mu Bingyuan not only served as a comprador himself but also actively recruited young apprentices. He then introduced these apprentices to foreign traders, reducing his workload while earning commissions from their transactions, thus boosting his income. Since most of his apprentices were from Ningbo residing in Shanghai, Mu Bingyuan taught them English and trade secrets, empowering many Ningbo natives to become capable compradors. This initiative not only facilitated the establishment of extensive economic and trade ties between Ningbo natives and foreign merchants but also provided them with opportunities to expand their overseas business ventures.

Following the establishment of the Shanghai Concession, foreign trading firms previously located in Hong Kong, Macau, Guangzhou, and Southeast Asia quickly established branch offices in Shanghai. Additionally, some Guangdong natives employed as compradors and staff migrated to the concession. Utilizing their basic English skills, they served as intermediaries in trade, giving rise to a distinct form of English with non-standard grammar and Chinese accents in the vicinity of the Yangjingbang area, known as "Yang King Pang English." Initially, this language predominantly reflected the pronunciation of the Guangdong region. However, with the increasing presence of Ningbo merchants, it gradually incorporated elements of Ningbo dialect pronunciation.

Mu Bingyuan was the creator of the Ningbo dialect version of "Yang King Pang English". The institution he established likely stands as one of the earliest comprador training centers after the opening of Shanghai, nurturing a cadre of translators desperately needed in Shanghai. In his classes, Mu Bingyuan crafted English phrases into Ningbo dialect rhymes. This approach facilitated rapid comprehension of "Yang King Pang English" by the students. The proficiency in "Yang King Pang English" taught at Mu Bingyuan's comprador training institution undoubtedly played a crucial role in enabling Ningbo clique compradors to seize a dominant position in the market.

The perceptive Ningbo natives, deeply attuned to commercial opportunities, were among the first to recognize the market demand. Leveraging Mu Bingyuan's "Yang King Pang English" as a foundation, they swiftly printed a practical guidebook written in English with annotations based on Chinese (Ningbo dialect) pronunciation and marketed it successfully. In 1860, "An Interpretation of English Speech," compiled by six Ningbo natives including Feng Zefu, emerged as Shanghai's first publication of a "Yang King Pang English" primer. This comprehensive guide included approximately 700 "Yang King Pang English" words, categorized into 40 sections covering areas such as currency, foreign exchange, hardware, exports, imports, astronomy, geography, and seasonal terms. Each category featured several commonly used words annotated with Chinese characters (Ningbo dialect pronunciation). In essence, the publication of "An Interpretation of English Speech" standardized colloquial expressions into a rudimentary "dictionary," marking the formal inception of "Yang King Pang English". "Yang King Pang English" played a pivotal role in modern foreign trade, diplomacy, and cultural exchange, leaving a profound and lasting impact.

4.3.3 The Hardware King—Ye Chengzhong

Ye Chengzhong, known as the Hardware King, was among the most prominent Ningbo merchants. Hailing from Zhuangshi, Zhenhai County, Ningbo Prefecture, Zhejiang Province, he was a renowned pioneer and leader of the Ningbo business community. Gifted in business, he possessed a clear mind, remained optimistic in adversity, conducted himself with integrity, and treated others generously, earning him the title of "a person of utmost virtue" (Fig. 27).

Ye Chengzhong's move to Shanghai was solely driven by economic necessity. His family's poverty, exacerbated by his father's early death and their meager land holdings, made survival challenging. At nine, he briefly attended a local private school before apprenticing at an oil mill. At fourteen, guided by relatives, he ventured to Shanghai, where he apprenticed at a hardware store in the French Concession's Hongkou area by the Huangpu River. In his free time, Ye peddled food and cigarettes to sailors on foreign merchant ships, gathering hardware parts tossed to him and purchasing others at discounted rates from foreign firm managers. With these resources, Ye embarked on establishing a hardware stall by the docks.

Ye Chengzhong's rise to success began at the age of seventeen. A British trading firm manager hired Ye Chengzhong's small boat to cross the river to Shiliupu. Upon docking, the foreigner accidentally left a briefcase onboard, containing a substantial fortune in several thousand US dollars, diamond rings, watches, and checkbooks—a windfall for the young Ye Chengzhong. Despite the temptation, Ye Chengzhong's integrity prevailed, as he chose to wait patiently for the owner's return. When the foreigner finally appeared, late into the night, Ye Chengzhong's steadfastness deeply moved him. In a gesture of gratitude, the foreigner offered Ye Chengzhong a stack of US dollars, but Ye Chengzhong gracefully declined. This foreigner happened to be the

Fig. 27 Photo of Ye Chengzhong

manager of the China branch of a British oil company. Impressed by Ye Chengzhong's honesty, he offered him a position managing the oil warehouse, along with providing Chinese and English tutors to enrich his education. At the age of twenty-two, with the foreigner's support, Ye Chengzhong established "Shunji Hardware Store" in Shanghai, pioneering the importation and sale of hardware—a first in Shanghai and China. Guided by his noble character and unwavering determination, Ye Chengzhong embarked on a successful journey in the business world.

With the increasing bustling foreign trade via steamships, an area near the Hongkou Dock on the Huangpu River gradually transformed into a bustling "Marchet Street" where businesses primarily focused on ship repairs for steamships and supplying provisions and freshwater. Ye Chengzhong realized that proficiency in English and direct communication with foreigners would significantly enhance his business prospects. Carrying a book titled "An Interpretation of English Speech," with phonetic annotations in Ningbo dialect, he seized every opportunity to practice. The foreign sailors, whom he interacted with daily, became invaluable conversation partners for Ye Chengzhong's language acquisition. After achieving success, Ye Chengzhong established short-term English training classes in Shanghai, Hankou, Tianjin, Hangzhou, and other cities, targeting students with a basic understanding of Chinese. These classes were fully funded by Ye's enterprises. Upon completing the

Fig. 28 Ye Chengzhong's "Shunji Hardware Store"

one-year program, students were initially placed in internships within Ye's enterprises before being deployed to various enterprises and foreign trading firms nationwide, where they served as coordinators, assistants, or purchasing agents, thus contributing to the cultivation of a talented workforce for the enterprises (Fig. 28).

The hardware industry boasts a diverse range of products with intricate specifications, and each store specializes in different items, making it impossible to maintain a comprehensive inventory. Confronted with customers' diverse demands, Ye Chengzhong, relying on his honesty and influence, instituted the practice of "inter-store lending." Under this arrangement, stores would borrow items from one another to meet customer needs. The lending store would apply a 5% markup on the purchase price, with this profit evenly split between the two stores involved. Consequently, customers could obtain items at market prices, ensuring utmost convenience. Through this collaborative approach within the hardware industry, modest capital was leveraged to facilitate substantial business ventures.

In the ever-evolving commercial landscape of the "Ten-Mile Foreign Concession," Shanghai's port faced the first waves of impact from new energy brought by the industrial revolutions of the world's great powers. With his keen commercial instincts, Ye Chengzhong always seemed to be one step ahead of others. In 1870, when John D. Rockefeller established Standard Oil Company in the United States, a decade later, Standard Oil ventured into Shanghai, seeking to tap into the Chinese market. However, before they could establish a foothold, they faced fierce competition from British and Russian oil companies. Grappling with the complexities of local dynamics and inconsistent measurement standards in China, Standard Oil found itself at a loss and turned to Ye Chengzhong for help. Leveraging the established channels of Shunji Hardware, Ye Chengzhong continuously supplied Standard Oil products from the Hongkou Dock in Shanghai to the Chinese mainland. The smooth sales channels also facilitated rapid capital turnover for Ye Chengzhong's short-term investments. During the exclusive agency period of ten years, the exact amount of money Ye Chengzhong earned remained a mystery.

Ye Chengzhong was one of China's early industrialists. He founded China's first bank, Imperial Bank of China, and also delved into insurance, money exchange, and supplying steel and coal to the Jiangnan Manufacturing Bureau and several shipyards. Shunji Hardware also established dozens of hardware stores, along with Hualun Silk Mill and Xiechang Match Factory. Over the next decade, Ye Chengzhong gradually expanded his empire with new branches such as Xinshunnanji, Shunji, and Beishunji, eventually ascending to the throne of the " Hardware King."

Despite his accomplishments, Ye Chengzhong remained a diligent, thrifty, and morally upright individual. He preferred walking to traveling by carriage or horseback and politely declined when offered imported cars by foreign merchants. Similarly, he refused to wear the five sets of Western suits gifted to him. His granddaughter, Ye Jimou, recalled, "My grandfather always wore old cloth garments. He believed that wearing them was a way of honoring our ancestors." Ye Chengzhong was a Confucian businessman with a strong sense of social responsibility. Even after achieving success, he remained deeply connected to his roots, prioritizing education, national development, charitable initiatives, and the establishment of schools, thereby making significant contributions to society. In 1871, Ye Chengzhong established the Ye Family Charity, providing underprivileged children with free education, including modern subjects like English. Many distinguished individuals from the Ningbo clique, such as Bao Yugang, Shao Yifu, and Zhao Anzhong, received their early education here and went on to achieve great renown both domestically and internationally (Fig. 29).

In his later years, Ye Chengzhong established the Chengzhong Private School, which became the earliest and most renowned private school in Shanghai (now known as Chengzhong Middle School in Shanghai). Renowned scholar Hu Shi once studied there. Following Ye Chengzhong's passing, his descendants contributed to the establishment of a pulmonary hospital, which is now the Shanghai Pulmonary Hospital located near Wujiaochang. Its precursor was the Ye Family Garden (Fig. 30).

In the article "The Rise and Fall of Ye Chengzhong," Ye Chengzhong was appraised as follows: "Since the opening of Shanghai to foreign trade, among Chinese merchants capable of competing with foreigners, Ningbo has stood out, with Hu Xueyan and Ye Chengzhong as its leaders. Both gentlemen rose to prominence from humble beginnings." Leveraging their unique advantageous conditions, Ningbo merchants swiftly entered the emerging field of foreign trade, forming a new group of businessmen represented by compradors and import–export merchants. This facilitated the development of national capital and industry. Compradors were among the earliest to engage with Western capitalist production methods. Drawing on Western experience in managing joint-stock companies and synthesizing their own experiences in business management, they acquired knowledge of capitalist enterprise management, providing the initial intellectual inspiration for the establishment and development of modern joint-stock companies in China. Compradors directed their investments in new enterprises in two main directions: actively investing in enterprises such as the China Merchants' Steam Navigation Company, as exemplified by Tang Yanshu and Xu Run; and independently establishing new enterprises. Comprador investments across various industries yielded considerable profits,

Fig. 29 China's first modern bank-Imperial Bank of China

serving as a positive demonstration and propelling Shanghai and even China's early modernization process, facilitating trade exchanges between China and the West (Fig. 31).

Although comprador merchants have contributed positively to Shanghai's economic and trade development, it's essential to recognize their historical limitations. Their reactionary and backward nature cannot be ignored, characterized by innate capitalist greed and exploitation, serving as instruments for imperialist economic aggression in China. Collaborating with feudal bureaucrats, they directly obstructed China's economic progress. Despite investing in modern enterprises, they often engage in activities representing outdated production relations. For instance, middlemen in the tea trade reject foreign machinery for processing tea, clinging to traditional methods solely concerned with quick market delivery. Notably, enterprise investment is not a significant part of compradors' economic activities. For instance, Xu Run, active in industrial and transportation investments, allocates only 24% of his wealth to such ventures, while 76% is tied to real estate and pawnshops. Real estate speculation, usury, and various speculative activities form the true essence of comprador existence.

After the 1880s, Shanghai's Ningbo clique compradors surpassed the Guangdong clique and took the first place in the comprador group. Until the comprador system was abolished, Ningbo Bang merchants, mainly new businessmen, invested their business profits in shipping, finance, and industry. In emerging fields, with their strong

Fig. 30 Photo of "Chengzhong Private School"

awareness of the commodity economy and the collective strength and group effect formed by their family ties, they worked hard and arduously started their business, quickly becoming an emerging economic force and making great contributions to revitalizing the modern national economy and promoting foreign trade activities. During this period, the Ningbo clique was based in Shanghai, the bridgehead of China's foreign trade, and created more than 100 national firsts, and a number of "kings" emerged, writing a century of glory in the history of China's industry and commerce.

In addition, during this period, a large number of Chinese merchants directly engaged in foreign trade in Shanghai, including Xiyangzhuang (operating foreign trade with major Western countries and West Asia, India, Ceylon, etc.), Dongyangzhuang (operating foreign trade with Japan, North Korea, etc.), and Nanyangzhuang (operating foreign trade with Southeast Asia). These Chinese businessmen who had originally been mainly responsible for helping foreign businessmen sell imported foreign goods domestically and collecting local products for export, changed to directly ordering imports from abroad or directly operating exports. They played a great role in the rapid development of Shanghai's foreign trade.

Fig. 31 The exterior view of "Chengzhong Private School"

4.4 The New Pattern of Foreign Trade Development Is Beginning to Take Shape

After the First Sino-Japanese War, according to the Treaty of Shimonoseki, China opened additional commercial ports, including Shashi, Chongqing, Suzhou, and Hangzhou, allowing foreign merchants to extend their tentacles to the entire Yangtze River Delta and along the Yangtze River, from Shanghai to Hankou, and then up to Upstream, Chongqing. The most prosperous area in China was included in the business scope of foreign merchants. In addition, the Treaty of Shimonoseki stipulated that the Japanese could invest and set up factories in treaty ports, and the great powers invoked the most-favored-nation treatment clause to enjoy Japan's privileges of opening commercial ports and investing in and setting up factories, thus creating an upsurge for the great powers to export capital to China. The failure of the war further weakened China's sovereignty, significantly weakened its trade autonomy and self-protection capabilities, and made the imbalance in foreign trade even more serious. On the other hand, due to the wide opening of the ports and the widespread use of modern transportation and communication means such as shipping, railways, and telegraphs, Shanghai's foreign trade volume also began to grow rapidly. In the early days, the scale of foreign trade freight forwarding in Shanghai was very small, with only a few customs brokers undertaking short-distance transportation and customs declaration services. After the First Sino-Japanese War of 1895, Shanghai's total and net trade volume far exceeded any previous year. In 1903, the Shanghai-Nanjing and Shanghai-Hangzhou railways were opened to traffic, export customs transit business increased, and the number of customs brokers increased to 140. From 1894 to 1913, the growth of Shanghai's total import and export value was also considerable, from 155 million customs taels to 421 million customs taels, an increase of nearly 1.7 times.

From the perspective of major trading countries or regions, from 1895 to 1910, Hong Kong's status in Shanghai's foreign trade declined significantly, while Japan's position increased significantly. In 1894, the countries or regions that accounted for a large proportion of Shanghai's total import and export volume were the United Kingdom (24.3%), Germany (15.6%), India (14.5%), the United States (13%), Hong Kong (11.3%) and Japan (9.7%); By 1913, Britain, Japan, the United States, India, France, Germany and Hong Kong were the main trading partners, and the trade volume accounted for 21.8%, 13.8%, 13.5%, 10.9%, 9.3%, 6%, and 5.4% of Shanghai's total import and export volume, respectively (Fig. 32).

During this period, significant changes in Shanghai's foreign trade were mainly reflected in the decline of Hong Kong's trade status with Shanghai and the improvement of Japan's trade status with Shanghai. The decline in the trade status of Hong Kong was mainly due to the increase in direct foreign trade between Shanghai and Western countries, which reduced the re-export trade through Hong Kong. Therefore, the total import and export trade volume between Shanghai and Hong Kong showed an obvious downward trend from 1895 to 1910 (Fig. 33).

The improvement of Japan's trade status with Shanghai was mainly due to the fact that during this period, Japan's industry began to show a certain degree of competitiveness after 20 to 30 years of development, while China's industrial development progressed slowly, and the commercial trade status of both parties reversed. In addition, after the First Sino-Japanese War, Japanese capital gradually penetrated the Yangtze River Basin and invested and set up factories in various trading ports, which directly boosted Japan's trade exports to Shanghai. In 1894, Shanghai's total trade with Japan was 15 million customs taels, and by 1913, it increased to 58 million customs taels per year, an increase of nearly 2.9 times. As mentioned above, the ratio of total trade with Japan to Shanghai's total import and export trade increased

Fig. 32 Photo of the Tea King of Modern China-Xu Run

from 9.7% to 13.8%. After the outbreak of World War I, Japan replaced Germany's position in China's shipping industry, and Shanghai's foreign trade transportation once formed a pattern of British and Japanese hegemony (Fig. 34).

After the First Sino-Japanese War, the movement to revitalize industry for national salvation emerged. Western equipment and technology were not only introduced but foreign investment in factories was also recognized. Imports of machinery and production materials increased, while imports of daily necessities decreased. Since 1899, American wheat milling machines, generators, boilers, and various types of machinery and equipment have also been imported. In 1910, Shanghai's machine imports were 1.4285 million taels, accounting for 0.75% of Shanghai's total import value and 20.7% of the country's total imported machine value.

Most of the imported machines in Shanghai are equipped with foreign-owned enterprises, but modern enterprises with national capital in Shanghai have also achieved initial development. The scale of development of textile mills is the largest. In 1910, there were 7 national capital yarn mills in Shanghai, with 172,000 spindles and 1440 cloth machines, most of which were British goods. There were 46 silk reeling factories and 13,062 silk machines, mostly of Italy and Japanese origin. In 1913, Shanghai's imported machinery rose to 2.197 million taels, accounting for 0.94% of Shanghai's total import value and 25.7% of the country's total imported

Fig. 33 Photo of a Tea House-Baoyuanxiang

machinery value. The number of foreign companies engaged in the import of machinery is also increasing. In 1913, there were nearly 30 such foreign companies in Shanghai, including 15 German firms, 11 British firms, and 3 American firms. The machines they operated involved military, civilian, production, and daily life, monopolizing the machine import market. There were about 20 Chinese firms, that also imported small machines and light industrial machines, benefiting from the introduction of Western equipment and technology, a number of famous modern Chinese enterprises or enterprise groups have emerged in Shanghai.

From the First Sino-Japanese War to 1913, a total of 86 new machine factories were established in Shanghai, manufacturing and imitating textile machinery, steam engines, internal combustion engines, silk reeling machines, embroidery machines, hand-cranked sock machines, lithographic printing presses, steel belt cigarette machines, etc. In 1919, Shanghai's total import value of machinery commodities was 10.03 million taels, accounting for 40.28% of the country's total imports of similar commodities. Among them, textile machine imports were the most, including carding, spinning, weaving, printing and dyeing machines, etc. Shanghai's total import value of textile machinery was 2.68 million taels, accounting for 71% of the country's total textile machinery imports. From 1895 to 1913, there were 43 newly established foreign-invested factories with a start-up capital of more than 100,000 yuan, a total capital of 23.2 million yuan, and an average start-up capital of 540,000 yuan per factory. The influx of foreign businessmen not only promoted

Fig. 34 Photo of the Silk King of Modern China-Xue Shouxuan

the modernization process of Shanghai but also plundered a large amount of profits. During World War I, while the European powers were busy with the war, Japanese and American businessmen took the opportunity to speed up their investment in Shanghai. From 1911 to 1921, there were a total of 1741 foreign-owned enterprises in Shanghai, of which 984 were Japanese, ranking first.

After the First Sino-Japanese War, the structure of export commodities showed a continuous decline in the proportion of raw silk and tea, with groceries becoming a new growth point. After the First Sino-Japanese War, the proportion of raw silk in Shanghai's foreign trade continued to decline, accounting for 39.5% of Shanghai's total exports in 1894, and dropped to 27.7% in 1913. Raw silk exported through Shanghai is mainly sold to France and the United States, accounting for 70% of Shanghai's total raw silk exports. In addition, the export trade volume of tea has also continued to decline. Compared with tea from India, Japan, and Ceylon, Chinese tea is less competitive, and Russia, the main exporter of Chinese tea, has also begun to import from Ceylon and India. This led to a rapid decline in tea export trade. Although China's tea exports to Russia accounted for more than 50% of total export trade volume from 45% in 1894, China's tea exports to the United States fell from 22% in 1894 to 12% in 1913, and to the United Kingdom from 17 to 6%. As a result, the trade volume of tea exported through Shanghai decreased. However, the export trade of groceries developed rapidly during this period, including seeds, leather, beans, wool, straw hats, tobacco, mats, straw mats, and a small amount of cannabis. For example, before the First Sino-Japanese War, beans and seeds grocery exports accounted for less than 1% of Shanghai's total exports and grew to 11.7% by 1913. The exports of fur and groceries also increased from 8.4% of Shanghai's total exports before the First Sino-Japanese War to 14.2%, a relatively fast growth rate.

As for the structure of imported goods, cotton textiles remained the mainstream category in Shanghai's import trade. In 1894, out of the 13.79 million pieces of cloth imported into China, 13 million were imported through Shanghai. Cotton yarn was primarily imported from India, and most of the cotton yarn imported into Shanghai was re-exported, with only a small amount sold locally. The local consumption in Shanghai mainly consisted of high-end foreign fabrics, accounting for about 1/5 of Shanghai's imported foreign fabrics. In 1913, the import value of cotton textiles accounted for 43% of Shanghai's total import trade, making it the largest category of imported goods.

In addition, the import trade volume of new categories such as rice, sugar, coal, and kerosene also showed an obvious upward trend, especially the import of food products, which grew rapidly. In 1907, the import value of rice, sugar, aquatic products, and flour alone accounted for 23% of Shanghai's total imports. From 1900 to 1910, among Shanghai's imported goods, kerosene grew the fastest, increasing from 21 million gallons to 91 million gallons. Other categories such as ores, vehicles, machinery, dyes, chemicals, and electrical materials also saw notable increases, with these categories together accounting for 11.4% of Shanghai's total imports in 1913.

A noteworthy trend during this period was the rapid decline in the opium imports. In fact, the import volume of opium has been declining since the 1880s. This was due, on the one hand, to the increase in the supply of domestically produced opium, and on the other hand, to the rising prices of Indian opium. In the period from 1895 to 1900, the annual import volume of opium was about 50,000 piculs, which was lower than the 63,000 piculs imported in 1894. In 1906, China and Britain reached a treaty to limit the import of opium from India, reducing imports by 1/10 every year since 1908. In May 1911, China and Britain signed a treaty to ban opium, stipulating a complete ban on the opium trade by the end of 1917, including a ban on the import of opium from overseas and the cultivation of domestic opium. According to customs data at that time, the number of inbound and outbound vessels at Shanghai Port reached its peak in 1906, with 23,045 inbound vessels and 32,600 outbound vessels. By 1919, there were 8704 inbound vessels and 9132 outbound vessels at Shanghai Port. The number of inbound and outbound vessels has been significantly reduced.

5 The New Cultural Trends in Shanghai Fostered by the Development of Trade

Wars and the port system imposed by foreign powers reshaped the traditional economic landscape of China. In the early stage of the opening of Shanghai in 1843, the city had not yet shown its immense trade potential. Guangzhou held the position of China's central for foreign trade. However, with the outbreak of the Taiping Rebellion in 1851, the pattern of China's foreign trade began to change. The conflicts in the southern regions disrupted traditional trade routes, severely impacting Guangzhou's foreign trade. Many of the trades that were originally exported through Guangzhou began to shift towards Shanghai, forming new pathways for foreign trade. Additionally, the treaty port system played an indirect protective role, leading to a massive migration of population and business operations to Shanghai, which provided ample market elements for the city's rapid development in foreign trade.

In 1861, the opening of ports in Zhenjiang, Jiujiang, and Hankou fundamentally transformed the traditional trade routes in the Yangtze River basin, particularly in the middle reaches. The region gradually evolved into the hinterland of Shanghai, facilitating exponential growth in Shanghai's import and export trade. After the First Sino-Japanese War, the opening of more ports, along with advancements in shipping, railroads, and telecommunications, led to a swift growth in Shanghai's foreign trade. Amid escalating tensions from the war, Shanghai transformed from a relatively isolated local town into the center of modern China's foreign trade. Influenced by the influx of Western material civilization, the coexistence of Chinese and foreign communities, and a lifestyle that emulated Western lifestyles, a modern civilization that integrated modernization and Westernization emerged in Shanghai, completely overturning the traditional lifestyles of Shanghai residents.

5.1 Influx of Foreign Goods: New Things Are Emerging

Shanghai, recognized as the birthplace of lifestyle transformation in modern China, was the first to establish a modern urban lifestyle. Numerous products of Western modern civilization, including modernized innovations, urban facilities, and industrial goods, were initially settled in Shanghai before gradually disseminating across the nation (Fig. 35).

For example, after the opening of Shanghai, with the influx of foreign merchants, new-style hotels were established along Yangjingbang (now Yan'an East Road) to meet the accommodation needs of travelers and businessmen. In 1846, the British businessman Astor House Richard built a hotel near the Bund on Gongguan Road (now Jinling East Road). This hotel, known as the Astor House Hotel, was the first modern hotel in Shanghai and featured not only guest rooms but also recreational facilities such as a ballroom, poker room, billiard room, and bar. Subsequently, a French-style inn called Micali appeared on Cathedral Street in the French Concession.

Fig. 35 Photo of Astor House Hotel

In the early twentieth century, the Huizhong Hotel, located on Nanjing East Road, already had six stories. Additionally, the tallest buildings in Shanghai, the earliest rooftop gardens, the first use of electric lights, and the first hydraulic elevator all appeared within these new-style hotels. The emergence of these new-style hotels not only facilitated the foreign trade activities of Shanghai but also greatly enriched the residents' lives (Fig. 36).

As soon as Shanghai became a trading port after the Opium War, many Western missionaries, merchants, and travelers introduced the newly invented camera to the city. In 1852, a foreign merchant named Hermann Hasbender started to operate photography and portrait coloring at the Longtai Foreign Firm located on Fuzhou Road. Subsequently, a Frenchman Legrand opened a photography studio on the Bund, which was the first photography studio in Shanghai. In 1876, nearly ten photography studios were established by the Chinese, including Su Sanxing, Rishun, Shitai, Tongxing, Huaxing, Hengxing, Yichang, and Gongfang, had emerged in the area from Guangdong Road to Nanjing Road. Among them, Su Sanxing was originally established in Hong Kong and relocated to Hankou Road in Shanghai in 1870, which was famous for photographing celebrities. At the end of the nineteenth century, the leading famous photography studios in Shanghai included Baoji, Yaohua, Zhizhen, and Baochang, collectively known as the "Four Heavenly Kings" of the photography industry. At the Paris Exposition in 1900, a photo exhibited by Yaohua won an award,

Fig. 36 Yaohua won an award at the Paris Exposition in 1900

making it the only awarded photography studio from China at the world expo in the Late Qing Dynasty.

Shanghai was the first city in China to have telephones. In 1876, the Bell telephone was patented, and it was introduced to Shanghai in 1877. In 1881, the establishment of the Great Northern Telegraph Company by Danes in Shanghai facilitated the development of telephone service in this city. In 1898, the Shanghai Mutual Telephone Company imported automatic telephones from Sweden and the United States, marking the settle of modern telephones in Shanghai. This provided a good start for the development of telephone services and greatly facilitated both external and internal communications in Shanghai (Figs. 37 and 38).

In 1917, Shanghai had already begun to take shape as the largest city in the Far East. This year, the Shanghai Grand World Amusement Park opened, the South Shanghai Sports Stadium was completed, the Xianshi Store officially opened at the intersection of Nanjing Road and Zhejiang Road, and a tram line was established between Yangjingbang (now Yan'an East Road) and Lao Zhaqiaoshilu (now Fujian Road). Additionally, many aspects of Western industrial civilization and technological achievements were successively introduced to Shanghai. In 1865, Nanjing Road witnessed the existence of gas streetlights, horse-drawn carriages, trains, automobiles, bicycles, electric lights, and trams. Additionally, municipal equipment such as garbage trucks, fire alarms, hydrants, sprinklers, and alarm clocks, various machines like weaving looms, textile machines, and steam engines, and everyday goods such as

Fig. 37 Photo of a bound-foot woman riding a bicycle in 1905

Fig. 38 Photo of a Telephone in 1910

sewing machines, Western soap, wool fabric, umbrellas, clocks, paper, toothbrushes, needles and threads, scales, cotton fabric, blankets, buttons, and towels began to flow into Shanghai before the 1870s, quickly dominating the consumer market.

5.2 *Prioritize Foreign Things: Western Cultures Gradually Infiltrated*

As foreign goods were distributed and accepted, the embodied Western lifestyle had a profound impact on the citizens of Shanghai, greatly altering various aspects of their daily lives, including clothing, food, housing, and transportation.

5.2.1 The Dress Culture

The period of 1843 to 1910 marked the beginnings of modern dress culture in Shanghai. Influenced by Western cultural trends, there was a noticeable Westernization in dress styles. In the late Qing Dynasty, although most men's dress still adhered to the traditional Chinese styles, a minority began to wear Western-styled dresses such as top hats and leather shoes in addition to their traditional clothing like skullcaps, long gowns, and riding jackets. There were also various adjustments made regarding sleeve width, the length of the long gown and riding jacket, collar heights, and types of buttons. While these changes might have not been accepted by the majority at that time, they represented a significant leap in the dress culture of Shanghai residents.

The changes in women's clothing are much more significant and rapid compared to those for men. In the late Qing Dynasty, the cheongsam worn by women in Shanghai typically featured a stand-up collar, a right-over-left closure, a loose fit, long sleeves, straight cut from top to bottom, no slits, and a wide hem. With the integration of Western fashion elements, the cheongsam gradually evolved while being embraced by more women, undergoing various modifications such as the introduction of lapels, ruffled collars, V-neck designs, sleeveless and ruffled sleeves, shortened lengths, and a more fitted waist. Notably, these changes have become more pronounced since the 1920s.

Apart from the cheongsam, one of the most significant markers of change in women's dresses was the emergence of new-style fashions. Suits and overcoats gradually gained acceptance, while skirts became the new favorite among urban women. Capes, western-style coats, jackets, swimsuits, and various styles of hats and scarves all became part of women's fashion, which exhibited a vibrant and ever-evolving landscape. Since 1911, women's skirts have undergone substantial changes influenced by Western fashion elements. The wrap-style skirts gradually transformed into pull-over skirts, giving rise to diagonal skirts, tower skirts, and bell-bottom skirts. The sewing techniques and designs tend to be simple, gradually abandoning elements of traditional women's skirts.

Moreover, with the implementation of the New Deal in the late Qing Dynasty, various girls' schools emerged, most of which were modeled after Western institutions. The students' dresses incorporated many Western fashion elements, moving away from a single style and strict standards. Changes included shorter sleeves, higher pant legs, narrower waists, and higher heels, leading to a gradual Westernization of attire. Overall, the changes in dresses in this period were mainly manifested as fashionable, personalized, highlighting curves, which represented a significant break from traditional Chinese social and cultural ethics.

5.2.2 The Dietary Culture

Since the opening of Shanghai in 1843, changes in the dietary industry can mainly be observed in three aspects.

First, the industrial and commercial development in Shanghai after its opening facilitated the expansion of the local food industry. This primarily included three types of establishments: small to medium-sized restaurants that offered easy dishes or potluck along with a few stir-fried dishes; medium to large-sized restaurants that focused on "HE CAI" (mixed dishes) and stir-fried dishes; and large renowned restaurants that specialized in high-end signature dishes and banquet services. By this time, Shanghai's local cuisine had already reached a relatively high level of development.

Second, in the late Qing Dynasty, restaurants from other regions continuously entered Shanghai. The first to arrive were restaurants serving Anhui cuisine, followed by those offering Suzhou and Wuxi cuisine, which became known for their Taihu Lake Boat Meals. By the end of the Qing Dynasty and the early Republic period, Shanghai had gathered 11 different types of regional specialty restaurants.

Third, with a significant number of foreigners beginning to settle in Shanghai after the establishment of the Shanghai concessions, Western food was brought in. In 1853, the first Western restaurant, J. Lewellyn & Co. Ltd "Shanghai Medical Hall", opened in Shanghai. In 1860, the RICHARDS HOTEL began offering accommodation for customers, with the meals prepared by British chefs and many of the ingredients sourced from abroad.

By the 1870s, there were a number of Western restaurants located in Shanghai, though initially, the patrons were predominantly foreigners. However, by the 1880s, some residents began to view dining in Western restaurants as a fashionable trend, leading to the adoption of a separate dining system. In 1897, the Cosmopolitan Butchery opened, specializing in German cuisine, and it attracted a considerable number of ordinary people who came to enjoy delicious Western dishes. Along with Western cuisine, some previously uncommon ingredients, such as onions, cauliflower, potatoes, and cabbage, also were brought to Shanghai, appearing in local markets by the early twentieth century (Fig. 39).

Moreover, Western beverages also began to make their way into Shanghai. In the 1850s and 1860s, businesses established by Western such as the Farr Brothers &

Fig. 39 Photo of Cosmopolitan Butchery

Co., Evans & Co., H. Peel & Co., and the Empire Brewery, were already producing carbonated drinks, soda water, and beer. In 1892, the British businessman-owned Aquarius was established specializing in the production of distilled water, soda water, mineral water for dining, lemonade, and carbonated drinks, all of which became quite popular. Overall, since the opening of Shanghai, the development trend of the food industry has primarily been characterized by the continuous fusion of local cuisine and foreign dishes, while Western food gradually became the fashion pursuit by Shanghai residents.

5.2.3 The Residential Architecture

With the opening of Shanghai, Western architectural structures, construction techniques, and imported building materials began to infiltrate the traditional buildings. The earliest buildings incorporating Western elements in Shanghai were the British Consulate (built in 1849) and the Gimson Chamber of Commerce (built in 1865). These buildings integrated the colonial architectural style characterized by verandas, typically featuring square floor plans and heights of one to two stories, constructed mainly of wood or brick-wood combinations. Initially, these independent residential buildings were predominantly inhabited by foreigners themselves.

In September 1853, the Xiaodaohui Association revolted in Shanghai, resulting in chaos that caused a mass exodus of refugees from the county town and into the concessions, breaking the previous "separate living" status quo. To capitalize on this situation and gain more profits, developers began constructing commodity housing specifically for these refugees, which later became the Shikumen Li-Long residential

Fig. 40 Gongshun Lane (the earliest Shikumen Li-Long residential building in Shanghai)

building specifically designed for Chinese people. To save costs, developers initially built these Li-Long residential buildings with wooden structures. In less than a year, from September 1853 to July 1854, over 800 Li-Long residential buildings were built in the area now known as Guangdong Road and Fujian Road. However, due to the fire risk associated with wooden structures, the concession authorities later prohibited their construction. From 1870 onward, developers began to build Li-Long residential buildings using a brick-wood hybrid structure (Fig. 40).

Meanwhile, in the wake of the financial panic in 1870, the conglomerate Dent & Co. went bankrupt, leading to the fragmentation and auction of its vast land holdings. Such events occurred frequently and spurred the renewal of architectural styles in Shanghai. Following the completion of the Neoclassical HSBC Building (1874) and the Deutsch-Asiatische Bank Building (1878), the previously popular colonial-style buildings with verandas were no longer constructed. Instead, a diverse array of architectural styles emerged, in sync with vogues in England. After the First Sino-Japanese War, Japan began to establish factories in Shanghai, increasing the Japanese population. This period saw the construction of a significant number of urban independent and commercial buildings in various styles, including French Renaissance style (e.g., the Danish Great Northern Telegraph Company Building, 1907), Neoclassical style (e.g., the Banque de l'Indochine, 1911), and Spanish styles (e.g., the Palace Hotel, 1906; Shanghai North Railway Station, 1907).

Overall, the evolution of residential architecture in Shanghai, from the early colonial-style Li-Long residential building with external corridors to the urban independent residences incorporating various Western elements in the 1910s, essentially represents a process of embracing Western architectural culture and technology. In other words, traditional Shanghai architecture gradually evolved into Western-style buildings.

5.2.4 The Transportation

In the opening of Shanghai, the main means of transportation were unicycles and sedan chairs. As the number of foreign residents in Shanghai gradually increased, various styles of Western-style two-wheeled and four-wheeled carriages emerged, which could offer improved travel efficiency.

In 1868, the first bicycle in China appeared in Shanghai, described as "one person sitting on the vehicle, with one wheel in front and another behind, using the tips of their feet to push off the ground and propel the wheel forward." However, the number of bicycles at that time was quite limited. Until 1897, there were only a few hundred bicycles in all of Shanghai, most of which were owned by foreigners residing in China and were not accessible to the general public as a mode of transportation. In 1874, the jinricksha, introduced from Japan, gradually became popular. To make it more eye-catching, the jinricksha was painted yellow, hence the name "Huangbaoche (rickshaw)." After a series of modifications, the speed and coverage of rickshaws significantly improved, further enhancing the travel efficiency of Shanghai residents. Additionally, rickshaws also became a means of livelihood for some of the lower-income citizens.

The "crown jewel" of transportation-automobiles-were introduced to Shanghai in 1901 by a Hungarian named Leinz. This marked the arrival of the first modern automobile in China-Oldsmobile Model R from General Motors Company. Following this, various luxury cars flooded the Bund in Shanghai, although at that time, automobiles were primarily enjoyed by foreigners.

Shanghai was one of the earliest cities in China to have trams. In 1905, the British-owned Shanghai Electric Construction Co., Ltd. was established and began laying tram tracks from what is now the Nanjing Road intersection to the Bund on Yan'an East Road. In 1908, the first tram line, operated by Jewish real estate magnate Silas Aaron Hardoon, officially opened, starting from Jing'an Temple and running to the Shanghai Club, covering a total distance of 6.04 km. This marked the beginning of modern public transportation in Shanghai. Overall, the transition from unicycles and sedan chairs to the emergence of Western-style carriages and rickshaws, as well as the introduction of modern transportation tools like bicycles, automobiles, and trams, fundamentally transformed the way people traveled in Shanghai and even across the country before the twentieth century. This modernization accelerated the urban pace of Shanghai and propelled the evolution of lifestyles among various social classes (Fig. 41).

Fig. 41 The first tram in Shanghai

5.2.5 The Lifestyle and Entertainment

After the opening of Shanghai, entertainment venues became increasingly popular, and the number of commercial theaters continued to rise. The first commercial theater in Shanghai, Sanya Theatre, was established in 1851. It served tea in the morning and staged Kunqu Opera in the afternoon, marking a shift from aristocratic leisure to mass entertainment. In 1866, Shanghai's first Peking Opera theater officially opened, and in 1884, the Dangui Tea Garden, built by Liu Weizhong, became the largest and most influential Peking Opera theater in Shanghai at that time. In 1908, the construction of the new stage at Shiliupu marked the transformation of Shanghai theaters from old-style tea gardens into modern drama theaters. A series of fashionable new plays and serial operas reflecting various social issues were staged, catering to the diverse spiritual and cultural needs of the people. In the same year, the Spanish man Antonio Ramos Espejo built Shanghai's first cinema using iron sheets, the Hongkou Grand Theatre, at the corner of Zhapulu and Haining Road, further integrating Western civilization through the medium of film.

In addition to theaters and films, foreigners in the concessions also operated various clubs that provided entertainment activities. The earliest Western club in Shanghai was the British Club, established in 1864, also referred to as the Shanghai Club. Inside the club, there were not only reception rooms but also large and small dining rooms, bowling alleys, billiards rooms, reading rooms, game rooms, and bars, offering a rich array of entertainment facilities. These clubs, along with the numerous operatic circles, shops, inns, taverns, teahouses, and bookstores, constituted a unique consumer space for the Shanghai residents, presenting a blend of Eastern and Western cultures and lifestyles.

In 1918, the Commercial Press officially established the Activity Film Department, which engaged in the production of films on a broader scale. The films produced at that time were categorized into five main types: scenic, current events, educational, modern drama, and traditional drama. Scenic films covered a wide range of famous landmarks across the country, current events films reflected social life at the time, and educational films primarily aimed to disseminate culture. In 1920, the Activity Film Department produced two traditional drama films (opera films) starring the renowned Peking Opera artist Mei Lanfang, namely "Chunxiang Nao Xue" (The Playful Choon Heong) and "Tian Nü San Hua " Fairy Gives Flowers to the Earth). Mei Lanfang himself directed both films. However, the modern drama films produced by the Activity Film department were mostly low-quality, dull, and poorly made, leading to a gradual loss of audience interest. Overall, after the opening of Shanghai, Shanghai not only became a hub for different types of Chinese opera but also saw the rise of Western-style cinemas and clubs. As a result, people's entertainment life was gradually becoming more Westernized.

5.3 *Subverting Traditions: Modern Concepts Are Emerging*

Since its opening, Shanghai has undergone extraordinary changes due to the impact of capitalist systems and concepts. These changes not only transformed Shanghai's status and image but also brought about a disruptive shift in the traditional concepts of the Shanghai residents.

5.3.1 The Consumption Concept

After the opening of Shanghai, new consumption trends swept through the Bund in Shanghai, leading its residents to gradually abandon traditional hierarchical consumption concepts and outdated consumption mindsets. They began to create and enjoy a brand-new urban lifestyle. In the streets and alleys of Shanghai, as well as in various aspects of social life, the phenomenon of "Prioritizing foreign things" was evident. Many people's social activities and daily lives became increasingly Europeanized, dining on Western cuisine, wearing suits and gold-rimmed glasses, watching movies, using electric lighting, taking photographs with cameras, and riding on trams. During the late Qing Dynasty, the term "Yang" (foreign) had become the most enchanting word in the minds of Shanghai residents. At the same time, Shanghai residents began to break free from the pursuit of frugality in their consumption concept, viewing luxury as a consumption goal. On one hand, they sought ways to earn money, and on the other, they indulged in extravagant and fashionable spending. Wealthy merchants engaged in ostentatious consumption, which directly guided the lifestyles of ordinary citizens. What began as envy gradually turned into imitation, and the pursuit of luxurious enjoyment became a popular trend.

5.3.2 The Consumption Patterns

Shanghai residents gradually broke away from the hierarchical concepts of the feudal aristocracy. Many high-end consumer goods that were once exclusively used by princes, nobles, and wealthy officials gradually entered the realm of ordinary citizens' consumption, due to the joint catalysis of modern industry and commercial trade. Items that once signified social status, such as clothing and utensils, began to be used freely regardless of wealth or social standing. The feudal order of social hierarchy that linked consumption to identity and status was continuously negated and eventually disappeared in the consumption practices of Shanghai people.

Not only did Western material goods directly enter people's lives, but they were also accompanied by a plethora of Western advertisements. This influx helped to popularize Western lifestyles and instilled Western ideologies and values. As early as 1907, the Kobayashi Company from Japan began advertising its Lion Brand Tooth Powder in newspapers, serving as a form of health education. This influence led to the production of China's first package of toothpowder and the first tube of toothpaste in Shanghai, and they soon became a household item, marking the beginning of a modern civilized, hygienic urban lifestyle. On April 4, 1912, the Shun Pao published book advertisements that introduced foreign economic and social systems, as well as English-Chinese dictionaries. This influx of new ideas through books undoubtedly contributed to enlightening minds and spirits and reshaping the populace. The periodical press and advertisements in modern Shanghai played a vital role in disseminating Western civilization, including modern Western lifestyles. Urban living increasingly became an aspiration for many. Overall, after the opening of Shanghai, Shanghai residents gradually developed a modern consumption mindset characterized by prioritizing foreign things, a penchant for luxury, and universal equality.

5.3.3 The Marriage Concept

Shanghai took the lead in advocating for freedom in marriage and simplified wedding ceremonies, marking a significant advancement in modern Chinese social civilization. Traditional marriage concepts, which emphasized blood ties and clan affiliations, gradually weakened. Instead, the Western-style marriage model of free love and independent choice of spouses began to change the marriage concept of Shanghai residents. Additionally, as the number of foreign residents settling in Shanghai increased, the custom of holding religious wedding ceremonies in churches was introduced. At that time, citizens yearned for simple weddings, yet many opposed the religious aspects of such ceremonies. As a result, a secularized civil wedding ceremony gained widespread acceptance and popularity. In this new format, a respected elder often served as the officiant, and the ceremony was held in public social venues rather than in churches. In the early twentieth century, civilized wedding ceremonies were quite prevalent in Shanghai.

5.3.4 The Values

In the rapidly developing commercial environment, amidst the atmosphere of merchants working round the clock and counting every penny, the value system of Shanghai residents gradually evolved, diverging from traditional Confucian views. A utilitarian value system began to take root. Due to the pressure exerted by foreigners at the time, the Chinese government also started to encourage people to engage in business to reduce the foreigners' exploitation of Chinese resources. From the perspectives of national self-improvement, safeguarding Chinese rights, and resisting Western commercial plundering, Shanghai residents gradually recognized the importance and necessity of establishing a profit-seeking mindset. The public began to embrace a new value system that regarded making profits as completely respectable, and worthy of vigorous advocacy and support. Pursuing profit not only helped individuals become wealthy but also served as a guarantee for national prosperity and rejuvenation. Money, once viewed by scholars as tainted with mercenary motives, was no longer looked down upon in the Huangpu River area. The utilitarian value system gradually gained recognition.

5.3.5 The Life Philosophy

As an opened trading port, Shanghai has created a social environment characterized by the convergence of Chinese and Western cultures, leading to the gradual formation and enhancement of an open-minded awareness among its residents. This openness was primarily manifested in their acceptance of new things, such as moving from naïve curiosity to embracing electric lighting and shifting from disapproval to appreciation of tap water. Shanghai residents gradually became accustomed to these new things that surpassed their previous imagination, ultimately accepting and utilizing them. It was this open mindset and awareness that enabled these new things to swiftly integrate into everyday life, catalyzing the emergence of a modern lifestyle among Shanghai residents. Furthermore, a sense of public norms gradually took shape among Shanghai residents. After the establishment of the Shanghai concessions, a large number of modern management methods were introduced, along with a series of regulations. Through the constraints of public norms, Shanghai residents began to abandon their previous casual, unrestricted lifestyles, which often lacked hygiene awareness. This guided them in transitioning from an agrarian way of life to a modern urban lifestyle.

Chapter 2
The Convergence of East and West (1919–1949)

1 Introduction

The Bund, the most charming area of Shanghai, bears witness to the city's historical depth, economic prosperity, and cultural, inheriting the vein of urban civilization. In 1844 (the twenty-fourth year of the Daoguang Emperor's reign in the Qing Dynasty), the Bund was designated as a British concession, becoming a true portrayal of the international settlement in Shanghai's ten-mile stretch. This marked the beginning of modern Shanghai's urban development, as well as the old Shanghai concession and the entire city's modern era.

After the Opium Wars, China's control over foreign trade transitioned from the Qing Dynasty to Western merchants. Shanghai, which was forced to open, took only a short decade to surpass Guangzhou, becoming the largest trading hub in modern China. The flourishing of the comprador system provided a new form of foreign trade advantage. The development of land transportation further promoted the breakdown of trade barriers. In response to the impact of Western goods, Shanghai's national industry rose, leading to the initiation of the national goods movement…

2 Foreign Firms and Compradors

2.1 The Rise of Foreign Firms

The name "Suzhou Creek" originated after the opening of Shanghai to foreign trade. Some adventurous foreign immigrants sailed from Shanghai upstream along the Wusong River, reaching Suzhou and subsequently naming the waterway "Suzhou Creek. "In 1848, the Shanghai Daotai Lin Gui signed an agreement with the British Consul in Shanghai on the expansion of the British concession, officially naming the

© Fudan University Press Co., Ltd. 2025
W. Shengqiao, *Century of Shanghai Trade*,
https://doi.org/10.1007/978-981-96-8701-5_2

Fig. 1 The symbol of Shanghai's urban history—The Bund

Wusong River section "Suzhou Creek" for the first time. From then on, the name "Suzhou Creek" gradually spread (Fig. 1).

From the early nineteenth century to the 1930s, Suzhou Creek remained a primary shipping route connecting Shanghai to nearby towns and villages, mainly due to the underdeveloped land transportation network compared to the water routes. Large volumes of consumer goods, fuel, and raw materials for factories relied on water transport. Shanghai's earliest modern shipbuilding, flour, textiles, silk weaving, chemicals, metallurgy, machinery, and even the factories for the processing of water, electrical, and coal equipment, gradually emerged along both banks of Suzhou Creek (Fig. 2).

In 1845, the Shanghai Daotai announced the "Shanghai Land Regulations," delineating the area north of Yangjingbang (present-day Yan'an East Road) and south of Lijiazhuang (present-day East Beijing Road and Yuanmingyuan Road) for British merchants to lease land and build houses, which later became known as the concession. The following year, the western boundary was established at Boundary Road

Fig. 2 Old Bund streets

(present-day Henan Middle Road).In 1848, the British Consul in Shanghai, Rutherford Alcock, reached an agreement with the Shanghai Daotai, Lin Gui, to extend the concession northward to Suzhou Creek and westward to a straight line between Zhoujingbang and the Su Residence along the banks of Suzhou Creek (present-day Middle Xizang Road).

In July 1854, Britain, France, and the United States established the International Settlement. In 1862, the French Concession separated from the International Settlement, and in 1863, the British and American concessions formally merged into the Shanghai International Settlement. Within the concession, foreigners invested in public utilities, established schools, and published newspapers. The concession authorities were responsible for municipal construction and issued a series of administrative regulations for managing the concession. The concession also became a window for Chinese people to understand and learn about Western culture and institutions. The Bund is a symbol of Shanghai and the starting point of the city's modernization. It extends from the west bank of the Huangpu River in the east to the sidewalks on the west side of Zhongshan East First Road and Zhongshan East Second Road in the west, from Dongmen Road in the south to the southern bank of Suzhou Creek in the north. The waterfront stretches for 2.6 km, making it the most iconic and classic urban landscape area in Shanghai, as well as the most important public activity space in the city center.

After Shanghai was opened as a commercial port, foreign banks, commercial firms, associations, and newspapers began to congregate there. The Bund quickly became the financial center of the entire country and even the Far East. In August 1943, the Bund was handed back to the Wang Jingwei puppet government by the Shanghai International Settlement, marking the end of its century-long concession period. The Bund has always been regarded as a landmark building and a symbol of Shanghai's urban history.

In 1843, a group of British merchants followed their first consul, George Balfour, to this unfamiliar city. At that time, the banks of the Huangpu River were natural shoals. During low tide, the water receded to the center of the riverbed, exposing a large expanse of the shoal. During high tide, the water covered the shoal again. The Huangpu River, being Shanghai's main waterway, had swift currents, necessitating the use of towlines for boats traveling upstream. Over hundreds of years, the footprints of the trackers created a winding path along the banks of the Huangpu River, known as the "Towpath." This towpath became the earliest road on the Bund.

To the west of the towpath lay farmland, dotted with scattered thatched cottages amid the crisscrossing ditches and fields. Though it appeared desolate, experience and intuition told these foreign merchants that this place was an uncut "jade." After repeated negotiations with the Shanghai Daotai, eight foreign firms were the first to settle on the Bund (Figs. 3 and 4).

Fig. 3 The Bund in the 1850s

Fig. 4 Historical view of the Bund

In the 23rd year of the Daoguang Emperor's reign (1843), before the British Empire established a concession in Shanghai, it first designated the riverfront area of the Bund as the anchorage for its ships. On November 29, 1845, in the 25th year of the Daoguang Emperor's reign, the "Shanghai Land Regulations" were passed, designating 830 mu of land west of the Bund as the British concession. Subsequently, the colonial authorities built the British Consulate at Lijiazhuang (also known as Lijiachang). Shortly thereafter, along the southern bank of the Huangpu River, adjacent to the British Consulate, foreign firms such as Sassoon, William Forbes&Co, Russell & Co.,Dent & Co. and Tianchang & Co. began to establish their presence.

> Angang Dai (Professor of History at Fudan University): "Foreign firms that entered China were called 'yanghang' by the Chinese. These firms were the first to set foot here after the opening of the port in 1843. The buildings along the Bund were essentially all foreign firms."
>
> Changlin Ma (Research Fellow at the Shanghai Municipal Archives): "At that time, after trade began, many foreign firms started renting land and constructing buildings in Shanghai. Jardine Matheson was the earliest, having rented land on the banks of the Huangpu River as early as 1842, followed closely by other foreign firms."
>
> Xiuli Zhang (Researcher at the Shanghai Academy of Social Sciences Institute of History): "Its development was very rapid. By 1850, there were already more than 40 foreign firms. The early foreign firms were characterized by their integrated operations, engaging in trade, shipping, exchange, and insurance."

The long-term policy of isolation led to national poverty and weakness. After the opening of Shanghai, foreign settlers, primarily from Britain, the United States, and France, began to establish their blueprint for concessions on this land to achieve their goal of invading Shanghai and ultimately annexing the entire country. Foreign firms were the bridgeheads for these colonial powers first entering Shanghai.

"Since the opening of the port, the prosperity of this region has grown day by day. Carriages are closely packed, and those entering the market are almost dazzled by the sights. It is rapidly surpassing famous towns such as Guangdong and Hankou." In 1876, Qing scholar Ge Yuanxi described the bustling scene of Shanghai after the opening of the port in the preface to his "Miscellaneous Notes on Travels in

Shanghai." He meticulously recorded the names of over a hundred foreign firms and illustrated them.

In his writings, he recorded a total of 18 foreign firms in the prime area of the Bund.

Today, the Jardine Matheson Building may no longer stand out, but it boasts a distinguished past. From comprehensive import and export trade to dock shipping, from constructing railways to investing in factories, Jardine Matheson's influence permeated almost every field during its more than a century-long presence in Shanghai.

> Angang Dai (Professor of History at Fudan University): "Early foreign firms were all-encompassing, engaging in all sorts of businesses, including smuggling opium. As long as there was profit to be made, they would do it. Gradually, as more foreign firms emerged, they began to compete with each other, leading to specialization and division of labor."

2.1.1 Jardine Matheson & Co.

Jardine Matheson & Co. is the most renowned long-established British trading firm, once the largest British conglomerate in the Far East, engaging in trade with China during the Qing Dynasty. Jardine Matheson was founded on July 1, 1832, by two Scottish British men, William Jardine (1784–1843) and James Matheson (1796–1878), in Guangzhou, China. Jardine Matheson played a crucial role in the early development of Hong Kong, earning the phrase "There was Jardine Matheson before there was Hong Kong." It was also the first European company to establish itself in Shanghai and the first foreign company to set up in Japan.

In its early years, Jardine Matheson primarily engaged in the trade of opium and tea in China. When Lin Zexu implemented the opium ban in 1839, the founder of Jardine Matheson, William Jardine, personally lobbied the British government in London to go to war with the Qing Dynasty. He also strongly advocated for seizing Hong Kong from the Qing Dynasty as a trading post.

In its early years, Jardine Matheson primarily engaged in the trade of opium and tea in China. When Lin Zexu implemented the opium ban in 1839, the founder of Jardine Matheson, William Jardine, personally lobbied the British government in London to go to war with the Qing Dynasty. He also strongly advocated for seizing Hong Kong from the Qing Dynasty as a trading post (Fig. 5).

Jardine Matheson & Co. was one of the first three foreign firms to enter Shanghai. Its former Shanghai headquarters is located at the corner of Beijing East Road and the Bund, across the street from the original Shanghai People's Broadcasting Station, at 27 Zhongshan East First Road on the Bund. This building is one of the significant structures in the Bund architectural complex and is a nationally protected cultural heritage site.

Jardine Matheson & Co. was founded in Guangzhou in 1832 by British merchants. After the opening of Shanghai in 1843, merchants from Britain, the United States, Germany, Japan, and France successively came to Shanghai to establish foreign firms, chasing after enormous profits. Statistics show that by 1852, there were 41 foreign

Fig. 5 Jardine Matheson & Co. in the Late Qing Dynasty

firms in Shanghai, with British firms being the most numerous, totaling 27. By 1859, Shanghai had 62 foreign firms, with Jardine Matheson being the oldest and most renowned. In the 1880s, Jardine Matheson not only enjoyed a prestigious reputation in Shanghai but was also known as the "King of Foreign Firms" worldwide. In the late Qing Dynasty, early foreign firms amassed initial capital through smuggling and trading opium, engaging in the trade of goods and opium between China, India, and Britain. Jardine Matheson, also known in its early days as Magniac & Co., was the world's largest opium dealer.

In 1837, the company owned 12 fully armed opium smuggling ships. By 1840, when Viceroy Lin Zexu of the Guangdong and Guangxi provinces seized 20,000 chests of opium in Guangzhou, 7000 of them belonged to Jardine Matheson & Co. The two founders of Jardine Matheson were subsequently expelled by the Qing government. After the Opium War, opium dealers from various countries established their main bases in Hong Kong, where armed opium ships were anchored at ports. In 1843, Jardine Matheson made a comeback and set up a branch in Shanghai. For a considerable period in Shanghai, Jardine Matheson's main business remained the opium trade. In 1874, the British-owned Woosung Railway Company, under the pretense of road construction, forcibly built the Woosung Railway. This railway company was owned by Jardine Matheson. In July 1876, the railway from Old Shooting Range (present-day Wujin Road, North Henan Road) to Jiangwan was opened to traffic, attracting crowds of onlookers. Some locals, lacking scientific knowledge, were terrified of this massive machine and threw bricks at the train, demanding the Qing government dismantle the railway (Fig. 6).

In 1844, the first land auction in Shanghai, China, saw Jardine Matheson & Co. as the buyer. At that time, Jardine Matheson's competitors in Hong Kong included other

Fig. 6 The Cold Storage Company established by Jardine Matheson & Co.

trading companies such as Dent & Co. and Sassoon & Co. After 1872, Jardine Matheson abandoned the opium trade in China and gradually diversified its investment activities. Besides trade, the company invested in building railways, docks, various factories, and mines in mainland China and Hong Kong, and operated businesses in shipping, banking, and other industries. In addition to constructing China's first railway, the Woosung Railway, in Shanghai in 1876, Jardine Matheson also installed China's first elevator and introduced various machinery and industrial equipment. After 1912, Jardine Matheson's company headquarters were located in Shanghai.

In 1920, Jardine Matheson & Co. established the Jardine Cold Storage Company on the Shanghai waterfront. In 1921, it consolidated all its silk-spinning enterprises to form the Jardine Spinning Bureau, with the Jardine Packing Factory as its subsidiary. Additionally, Jardine Matheson invested in the construction of the Kowloon-Canton Railway and the Shanghai-Wusong Railway, and founded a shipping company to control coastal and Yangtze River inland transport in China. The company also built docks, warehouses, storage facilities, and a brewery. The Jardine Packing Factory on North Suzhou Road was one of the most important logistics hubs along Suzhou Creek at that time, serving as the starting point for much of the old Shanghai's logistics and express deliveries (Fig. 7).

Entering the twentieth century, a new wave of renovations and expansions of old buildings began along the Bund, and Jardine Matheson & Co. was no exception. The new Jardine Matheson Building was constructed starting in 1920 and completed in November 1922. Designed by British architect Si Jingseng of Moorhead & Halse and constructed by the Chinese contractor Yu Chang Tai Trading Co., the building covers an area of 2100 m^2 with a total floor area of 14,300 m^2. The building's exterior is styled in the architectural fashion of the British Renaissance revival (also described by some as New Classical Conlinist architecture). It features a reinforced concrete

Fig. 7 The Jardine Packing Factory on North Suzhou Road

frame structure. The exterior walls are built of granite, and the seven-story building is adorned with Corinthian columns, square at both the top and bottom. The walls are made of rusticated stone blocks with horizontal lines, presenting a solid and stable appearance. This building is one of the early examples in Shanghai of using stone as the exterior wall material (Fig. 8).

The entire building has a "concave" layout, with the west side recessed and the east facade divided into three sections. The first and second floors form the first section, featuring Roman arches for the doors and long windows, with the exterior walls clad in large, rough-hewn granite slabs. The steps leading up to the main entrance are

Fig. 8 Jardine Matheson & Co. in Historical Times

paved with smooth stone blocks. On either side of the main entrance are large wall-mounted lanterns. Ascending the steps, one encounters two large steel-clad doors. Each side of the entrance features four arched steel windows spanning two stories. Between the windows on the ground floor and the second floor are 1-m-wide bronze-colored metal panels. The second floor is adorned with a stone-carved ram's head, and each window is equipped with canopies.

The third to fifth floors form the second section. The third floor features a stone balustrade balcony, supported and decorated by four massive Corinthian stone columns. Between the columns are balconies and stone railings (Fig. 9).

The fifth floor and above constitute the third section. The roof has a broad eave, and the top of the building features a large terrace. In front of the terrace is a balustrade with a stone screen in the middle, closely attached to which is a dome. At the center of the dome, there is a flagpole. Unlike a bank, the building does not have a public banking hall, but each office is designed and decorated in a luxurious manner.

The eaves on the sixth floor are quite broad, and the roof features a 2-m-high stone wall. The south and north exterior walls of the building have identical windows, balconies, columns, and decorative carvings. The ground floor walls and floors are paved with marble, while the corridors on the upper floors have mosaic floors, and the offices feature waxed wooden strip flooring. The original rooftop was a terrace with a balustrade in front and a stone screen in the middle. Above the center, there was a dome, divided into three sections, with a flagpole on top. On both sides of the terrace, there were also stone screens and domes, all intricately carved with figures, animals, and sailing ships.

Fig. 9 Completion ceremony of Jardine Matheson & Co. on November 15, 1922

After the outbreak of the Pacific War, the Jardine Matheson Building was forcibly taken over and occupied by the Japanese Mitsui & Co. In 1946, Jardine Matheson resumed operations, but business was no longer as prosperous as before. Due to the decline in business, the company had to lease the building to various tenants, including the Cheong Hing Shipping Company, Overseas Aviation Company, Hong Kong Airlines, as well as the offices of the First Commercial Secretary, Financial Counselor, and Press Office of the British Embassy.

After 1949, most of Jardine Matheson & Co.'s assets and businesses in mainland China were nationalized. In 1954, the company's last office in China was forced to close, and the headquarters was relocated to Hong Kong. In 1955, the building was managed by the Shanghai Housing Bureau and used by the Shanghai Foreign Trade Bureau and its affiliated units. In 1961, Jardine Matheson was first listed on the Hong Kong Stock Exchange, where it was oversubscribed more than 50 times. In 1983, two additional floors were added to the top of the building, altering its original design and covering the original terrace, balustrade, stone screen, and dome. In 1984, Jardine Matheson moved its place of incorporation from Hong Kong to Bermuda, and in early 1990, it transferred the listing of the company and many of its subsidiaries from Hong Kong to Singapore or London. Having witnessed significant changes over a century, Jardine Matheson shifted its focus away from Hong Kong just before its return to China. Nevertheless, Jardine Matheson still maintains substantial business operations in Hong Kong through its subsidiaries, which include Hongkong Land, Dairy Farm, Mandarin Oriental Hotel Group, Jardine Pacific, and Jardine Motors. The company's investments span various sectors, including construction (Gammon Construction), real estate (Hongkong Land), shipping (Hong Kong Air Cargo Terminals, Jardine Airport Services, Hongkong International Terminals), retail (Wellcome Supermarkets, 7-Eleven, Pizza Hut, Maxim's Catering), investment banking, hotels (Mandarin Oriental), and insurance, employing over 100,000 people. Jardine Matheson also has investments in Southeast Asia and the United Kingdom. Despite most of its business operations remaining in Hong Kong, the company's operational headquarters are no longer located there (Fig. 10).

At the end of 2009, Rolex's flagship store moved into 27 Zhongshan East First Road on the Bund. The Rolex store, located in the ground floor retail area, is its largest flagship store globally, covering an area of 1000 m^2. Prior to moving in, a significant investment of 80 million yuan was made for internal renovations. This project aimed to restore the historical appearance of the Jardine Matheson Building, reviving its former glory from the old Shanghai era.

After the restoration of the entire building at 27 Zhongshan East First Road on the Bund, some of the original features of the old structure have been preserved. Ascending the nearly 4.9-m-wide main staircase inside the building, you'll find that the stair steps, wainscoting, balustrade bases, and the intermediate and entire platform areas are all decorated with marble. The staircase is also covered with bronze non-slip

Fig. 10 Landscape restoration of the exterior of the Jardine Matheson Building

Fig. 11 Night view of the Jardine Matheson Building Today

panels. The cast iron balustrade features intricately embedded scroll-shaped wrought iron designs. In the wine cellar on the second floor, the weathered old walls have been completely preserved (Fig. 11).

Some of the wall plaster has fallen off, revealing the exposed steel pipes underneath. On the third floor, the ancient wooden floors, charming old glass windows, and vintage movable door shutters evoke a sense of the building's 90-year-old history. In the presidential room on the third floor, an old crystal chandelier catches the eye. Although some of its lights are no longer functional, it still exudes a sense of antiquity. One cannot overlook the mosaic floors in the corridors. Many of the small floor tiles have retained their original bricks, and the green "bricks" are actually inlaid with jade.

In the modern history of Shanghai, Jardine Matheson & Co. was undoubtedly a powerful presence. From comprehensive import and export trade to dock shipping, from constructing railways to investing in factories, over more than a century of its presence in Shanghai, Jardine Matheson's influence permeated almost every field. Shanghai, this Eastern metropolis, enabled Jardine Matheson to establish its dominance as the "King of Foreign Firms."

2.1.2 William Forbes & Co.

William Forbes & Co., established by Scottish expatriates in China, began using Shanghai as its base in 1844, engaging in various international trades, including opium and tea. After Tianjin was opened as a treaty port, the company quickly set up a branch there. The Shanghai office was located on Heba Road in the British Concession (now Tai'erzhuang Road) and managed by William Forbes and others. William Forbes & Co. primarily dealt in the import and export of raw silk, tea, paper, timber, and hardware. Alongside Jardine Matheson and Russell & Co., it was one of the first foreign enterprises to establish a presence in Shanghai (Fig. 12).

Shanghai's Dianchi Road is a small street near the Bund. In 1908, the British firm William Forbes & Co. built a row of consequently named Forbes Road at that time. The building at 100–110 Dianchi Road, designed by the architectural firm Tonghe, was completed in 1908. The William Forbes & Co. building is a typical example of Queen Anne-style architecture, featuring exposed red brick walls with white lime mortar joints, horizontal bands at different levels, and precise brickwork with neat joints. The building is three stories high (four stories including the attic), with the

Fig. 12 William Forbes & Co.

Fig. 13 Original site of William Forbes & Co., Now a Protected Historical Building

corner section being four stories high. Originally, it had a conical metal roof, which has since been replaced with a flat roof (Fig. 13).

> Xiuli Zhang (Researcher at the Shanghai Academy of Social Sciences Institute of History): "Among the foreign firms, some dealt in dyes, some in medicinal herbs, some in machinery, and others in daily necessities. The types of businesses varied. One of the more famous companies was the German firm, Waibel & Co., which almost monopolized the import of dyes into China."
>
> Changlin Ma (Research Fellow at the Shanghai Municipal Archives): "Later on, Shengchang & Co. primarily focused on exporting machinery, reflecting a division of labor. In the early days, they dealt in silk and tea, but later expanded into hardware, including chemical dyes, and a variety of other products."

2.1.3 Swire Group

Swire Group, second only to Jardine Matheson & Co. in influence in modern China, traces its origins to John Swire & Sons, founded in 1816.The company primarily operated in the shipping industry (Fig. 14).

In 1867, it established the China Navigation Co. Ltd with a nominal capital of £1 million. In 1872, it founded the China Navigation Company, becoming one of the three major shipping companies alongside Jardine's and Russell's shipping companies. It opened the Shanghai-Hong Kong route and, in 1875, added the Yangtze River route, subsequently expanding its coastal routes in China and international routes. Beyond shipping, Swire Group also diversified into other sectors. In 1881, it acquired large tracts of land in Quarry Bay on Hong Kong Island and established the Taikoo Sugar Refinery, which began operations in 1883.

Fig. 14 John Swire

Swire Group has an inseparable relationship with trade in China. 150 years ago, the Swire family crossed the ocean to the Far East, establishing the China Navigation Company, which eventually became one of the leading passenger and freight transportation companies along China's coastal and inland waterways. This development enabled Swire Group to dominate the Chinese trade market (Fig. 15).

In fact, since the early 1850s, John Swire & Sons had been shipping British wool and cotton textiles from Liverpool to China, entrusting foreign firms in Shanghai to sell them. However, this indirect approach was only a temporary measure. Therefore, John Swire decided to partner with Richard Shackleton Butterfield, a wool merchant from Yorkshire, England, to establish their own trading firm for China. Swire Group officially opened on December 3, 1866, in the old Fletcher & Co. building at the corner of Fuzhou Road and Sichuan Road, managed by one of John Swire's partners, William Lang.

Fig. 15 Opening announcement of Swire Group in 1866

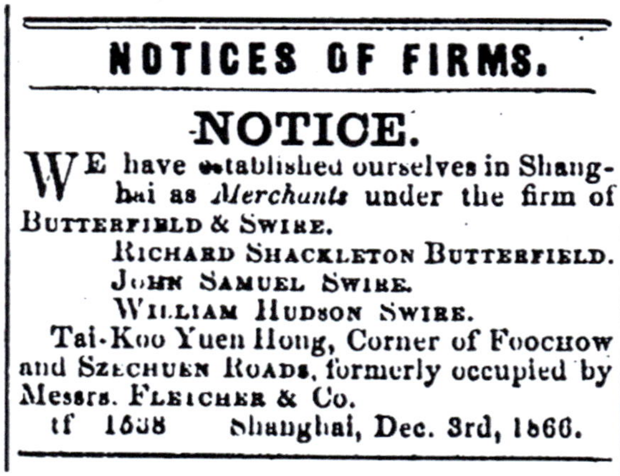
NOTICES OF FIRMS.

NOTICE.

WE have established ourselves in Shanghai as *Merchants* under the firm of BUTTERFIELD & SWIRE.

RICHARD SHACKLETON BUTTERFIELD.
JOHN SAMUEL SWIRE.
WILLIAM HUDSON SWIRE.

Tai-Koo Yuen Hong, Corner of FOOCHOW and SZECHUEN ROADS, formerly occupied by Messrs. FLEICHER & Co.

tf 1638 Shanghai, Dec. 3rd, 1866.

As an agency, Swire Group primarily engaged in commodity trade. However, beyond this, Swire Group also served as the Shanghai agent for a new British ocean shipping company, Blue Funnel Line, which was founded in 1866 by Alfred Holt, a friend of John Swire in Liverpool. In fact, it was through business dealings with Blue Funnel Line that John Swire began to conceive the idea of operating shipping services on the Yangtze River. Swire foresaw that Shanghai, connected by the "golden waterway" of the Yangtze River, would become a hub for the distribution of products from the vast Yangtze River basin and around the world. Consequently, he shifted his investments from trade to the shipping industry. This transition transformed the company from a single trading firm into a conglomerate centered around Swire Group and China Navigation Company (Figs. 16 and 17).

Fig. 16 Swire Group Office Building in 1923

Fig. 17 The Busy Bund of the French Concession in the 1920s, Featuring the Swire Group Office Building, Large Warehouses, and Taikoo Dockyard

Due to the continuous expansion of its business, Swire's fleet operated extensively along China's coastal and inland waters. With a significant number of company ships, the onshore facilities became insufficient; in Puxi, there were only three floating docks. Consequently, Swire Group expanded its dock facilities in Pudong. By 1882, it had built the Huahong Dock in Pudong, in addition to the existing Old Taikoo Dock and the Blue Funnel Dock. Thus, Swire Group's China Navigation Company established a total of three docks on both sides of the Huangpu River. After 1949, the Huahong Dock in Pudong was incorporated into Shanghai Port's First Stevedoring District and renamed the Dongchang Road Dock (Figs. 18, 19, 20 and 21).

The shipping business created new commercial opportunities. Due to the increasing trade of importing sugarcane from Java and the Philippines, along with the existing markets in China and Japan, Swire Group purchased large tracts of land in the coastal area of Quarry Bay on Hong Kong Island and established the Taikoo Sugar Refinery Company. The construction of the Taikoo Sugar Refinery soon began, and it commenced operations in 1883, becoming one of the largest and most advanced facilities of its kind in the world at that time. Even today, Taikoo Sugar holds a significant market share in China and can often be found in supermarkets and restaurants.

In its early years, Swire Group served as a banking agent at several small coastal ports in China. The Taikoo Banknotes issued by Swire Group were once widely used as currency in Shantou, South China. These banknotes came in various denominations and were printed by Waterlow & Sons, a company in London specializing in banknote printing, to prevent counterfeiting. The issuance and redemption of these banknotes were strictly managed by the Swire Group's Shantou branch. In Guangdong Province, the Taikoo Banknotes circulated as cash until the 1930s (Fig. 22).

Fig. 18 Interior view of Swire Group Office Building in Shanghai, 1912

Fig. 19 The Bund in Shanghai, 1890

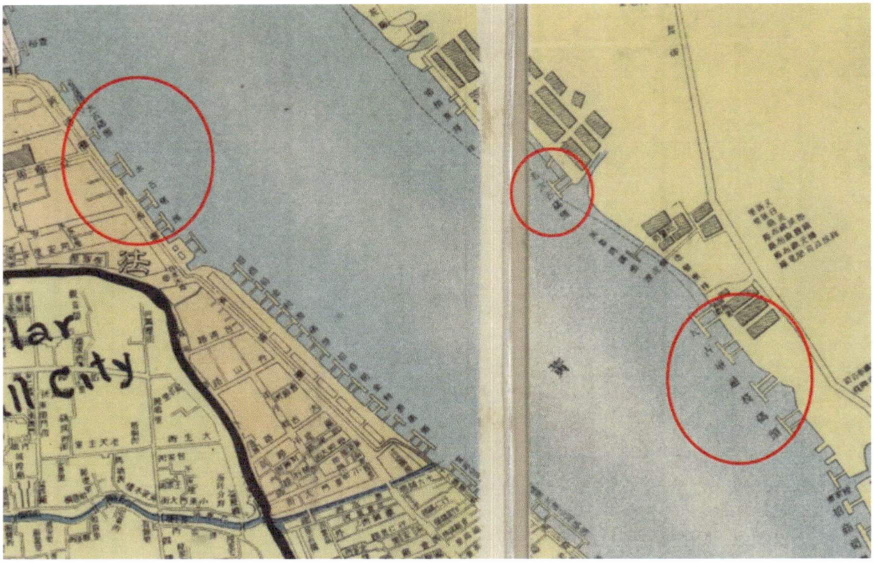

Fig. 20 The Three Taikoo Docks on Both Sides of the Huangpu River Marked on the 1913 Map of Shanghai Concessions by the Commercial Press

Fig. 21 The Former Site of the Swire Group Office Building Today

Fig. 22 Banknotes issued by Taikoo Bank

Due to its expanding business, Swire Group established branches or offices from the Yangtze River region to the Northeast of China. The company's total capital grew to £1.8 million, and it owned 614 acres of real estate, accounting for 9% of all British-owned property in Shanghai. In 1934, Swire Group built a mansion called Hazelwood for its taipan (chief executive) at the intersection of Route P. Legendre (now Xingguo Road) and Avenue Haig (now Huashan Road), at the boundary of the International Settlement and the French Concession. The mansion was designed by Scottish architect Clough Williams-Ellis. Interestingly, Williams-Ellis never visited Shanghai; he simply sent the designs from Scotland and remotely supervised the construction progress through monthly reports and photographs.

By the 1930s, Swire Pacific has become one of the leading shipping and trade companies in Shanghai and even in the Asia–Pacific region. Together with Jardine and Sassoon, Swire Pacific is one of the three giants of British commercial and foreign banks. But a catastrophe is slowly approaching.

After the "July 7 Incident" in 1937, the Sino-Japanese War broke out. At first, Swire was still protected from the flames of war because of its British status, but by the end of 1941, when Japan started the Pacific War, the foundation of Swire's nearly seventy years in China was almost destroyed. In November 1937, all the Chinese territory in Shanghai fell, because the British and American public concession and the French concession gathered foreigners, envoys and businessmen from all over the world, the Japanese army did not dare to act rassly in the concession, but the situation was in danger, and the living space of Chinese and foreign enterprises was also in danger. In order to prevent the Japanese from pursuing, dozens of ships were scutched in the Yangtze River between Shanghai and Nanjing as obstacles to slow the Japanese advance on the waterway, and the Yangtze waterway became narrower. However, Swire had no intention of retreating to protect itself, and insisted on maintaining service by sending tugboats and barges to and from the Yangtze River to the Shanghai Concession, in an effort to maintain the water transport network of wartime China. Each time the vessel approached the obstacle, it would approach the shore to unload cargo and passengers, then transfer to land transport. After crossing the obstructed waters by road, it would then transfer to another fleet to continue its journey. Together with other foreign airlines, they supported shipping in the lower reaches of the Yangtze River during the war.

In December 1937, as Japanese forces approached Nanjing, a large number of Chinese and foreign refugees crowded onto the Swire steamship for evacuation. Among them, the "Huangpu" was considered one of the last vessels to assist in the evacuation of Chinese and foreign personnel from Nanjing. The ship was not only packed with a large number of refugees fleeing the war but also carried a batch of priceless Chinese artworks that had just returned from an exhibition in Britain, eventually making a successful withdrawal to Hankou. During the war against Japanese aggression, Swire steamships continued to operate with Shanghai's foreign concessions and Hong Kong, China, as their hubs, striving to maintain normal services along the coastlines of North and South China, as well as the Yangtze River and the inland river routes in South China. They shuttled between various locations to sustain passenger transport and material exchange. On the morning of December 8, 1941, the Japanese forces launched surprise attacks on Pearl Harbor and regions including Hong Kong, China, engaging in undeclared warfare and rapidly moving into several foreign concessions in Shanghai and Tianjin (Fig. 23).

After the Japanese surrender in August 1945, Chinese and foreign companies returned to Shanghai, hoping to get their assets back from the Japanese as soon as possible. The political and commercial landscape at that time was extremely complex, with various forces vying for business interests. The significant devaluation of currency led to financial turmoil, and the rampant activities of gangs in Shanghai caused serious concerns about public security. Swire reported to its London headquarters "Labour movements have become the norm in Shanghai, with gangs often fighting and using various means to annex a number of public utilities and industries."

In the later period of the Liberation War, with the continuous victory of the People's Liberation Army, foreign-funded enterprises in China have moved their corporate funds abroad according to the situation. Generally speaking, although foreign-funded enterprises are in a state of decline at this time, they still play an important role in economic activities because of their long-term monopoly of certain industries. From February 1947 to January 1948, foreign capital accounted for 44.4% of Shanghai's import and export trade. In 1948, there were 223 coastal ships in Shanghai, of which 167 were owned by British capital, most of which were owned by Swire. The Financial and Economic Commission of the CPC Central Committee made the

Fig. 23 The sunken ships along the Huangpu River in 1938

same description of China's economic situation in 1950, believing that foreign ships would still play an important role in international trade and coastal shipping, and that imperialism still had great control over China's trade and transportation, and even Shanghai's public utilities.

2.1.4 Defag Corporation

Shanghai Tang from the twentieth century to the 1940s was the fashion vane of old China. In the 1920s, young female students who love beauty often wore a white front shirt, narrow waist and wide sleeves, and black silk dress shoes. They held books in their hands and walked gracefully on the Shanghai Beach, becoming a beautiful scenery at that time. In the 1930s, Chinese cheongsam was suddenly popular in the Bund, which was popular among young and middle-aged women because it could fully reflect the curvy beauty of eastern women. At that time, the main fabric of the Chinese cheongsam on the Bund was the Yintan limbo with blue as the keynote. Yintan Lingshu was loved by young and middle-aged women in Shanghai in the 1930s and 1940s for its non-fading quality (Fig. 24).

Yindanshilin cloth is produced by Defag Foreign Bank, which was founded by German Dehn in Shanghai in the 1920s, and Yindanshilin is the name of a reduction dye, which is the transliteration of German Indanthrene. Cloth dyed with this dye is not only bright in color, but also durable in color. It is precisely because of the use of this special dye that the Yintan limbo produced by Defag is very popular. The use of life scenes in advertisements can make consumers have a sense of closeness to advertisements, effectively alleviate consumers' rejection of advertising, so that

Fig. 24 An advertisement for Dufour's indigo dyed cotton fabric

consumers can identify with products in a casual state. At the same time, people generally have a herd mentality in their daily life, and the life scenes in advertisements can have a demonstration effect on potential consumers and induce them to take purchasing behaviors. Because of this, many advertisements attach great importance to the life of the advertising scene, and the Yindansilin advertisement is no exception.

2.2 The Appearance of Comprador

With the rise of foreign firms, a new type of occupation—comprador appeared. Known to Shanghainese as "chaff ferry," a transliteration of the Portuguese word for "comprador," comprador came between Chinese and foreigners to make deals. The description of the comprador in the "Shanghai Travel Bamboo Branch Poems" is "The name "Kang Baidu" is no small matter, associated with the Ningbo and Xiangshan regions. Upon meeting someone, they proudly proclaim their excellence, ranking themselves among the top tiers of foreign companies."

Comprador is a special class of brokers, with dual identities of employees of foreign firms and independent businessmen. As employees of foreign firms, comprador is protected by foreign forces and is not subject to Chinese laws. As independent businessmen, comprador can also buy and sell goods on the mainland on behalf of foreign firms, lease houses and purchase real estate.

Xiong Yuezhi (Researcher of the Institute of History, Shanghai Academy of Social Sciences, Distinguished Professor of Fudan University): The comprador played a role in connecting China and the West, and played a role as a bridge in the contact. Because of the language barrier between China and the West, someone had to be able to communicate between the two sides, so the comprador came into being.

Fan Weiguo (Researcher, Institute of Economics, Shanghai Academy of Social Sciences): The earliest comprador was mainly from Guangdong, because before modern times, the Qing government opened to the outside world mainly in Guangzhou, and the foreign trade was presided over by an authorized organization called Thirteen Banks. After the opening of the port, Shanghai surpassed Guangzhou and became the largest treaty port in China, so the comprador in Shanghai became probably the largest team of comprador in modern China.

Dai Angang (Professor of History, Fudan University): Now comprador is known as the bridge and link between China and foreign trade. This assessment is objective. Comprador is an indispensable group of people in China's early Sino-foreign trade. In the past, we thought they were all traitors, but they were not. They were the first group of enterprising Chinese who were willing to face the world and meet the challenges.

After the Opium War, the comprador system changed with the development of foreign firms. The common interests of comprador class and foreign businessmen make them a very unique group in Chinese history, and they become a tool for Western countries to invade and control China politically and economically. These comprador classes not only deal with the import, export and storage of money, but also participate in business operations and commodity transactions, and often carry out purchasing and marketing business deep into the mainland on behalf of foreign firms. Negotiate prices with Chinese merchants, conclude trading contracts, and gain the trust of both parties in the receipt and payment of goods by virtue of their position. They are becoming the face of foreign trade with China.

With the increasing of comprador capital, comprador bourgeoisie gradually formed. Most of the comprador capital comes from the commissions received by the comprador. In an instant, "gold can be found with bare hands." In addition, by operating a foreign bank, the comprador will lend money to the foreign bank and earn interest together with the bank.

Picture 25, taken in June 1931, is a group photo of Du Yuesheng, the boss of Shanghai Qing Gang, and celebrities from all walks of life. The one in the middle was Yu Qiaqing, a famous businessman from Shanghai who was a comprador at that time. He was not the biggest businessman in Shanghai, but he became president of the China General Chamber of Commerce. Even Du Yuesheng should respect him. Five years after this photo was taken, one of the busiest roads in Shanghai was named after him. What kind of talent did Yu Qiaqing have that made him so prominent in the Band?

Yu Shunwei – Son of Yu Qiaqing (interview materials): Because his rural family is difficult, so after studying for a few years, he was introduced to Shanghai, then into the pigment company. He came to the company at the age of 19, the boss gave him shares, and he grew step by step. He also made his own paints and traded.

Wu Songdi (Professor, Institute of Historical Geography, Fudan University): I have been to the home of Yu Qiaqing, who is from Cixi, Ningbo. Yu Qiaqing's family is so poor that he entered Shanghai barefoot.

Fig. 25 A large group photo of Yu Qiaochi with Du Yuesheng and others

> Fan Weiguo (Researcher, Institute of Economics, Shanghai Academy of Social Sciences): Yu Qiaqing had a nickname at that time called the barefoot fairy, how did this nickname come about? When he was an apprentice, once it rained, he took off his pair of cloth shoes, wrapped them up, and went home barefoot. He was reluctant to part with these shoes, and a pair of new shoes got wet. He was from Ningbo, and he was also from a very poor background. In the past, people who were very young to Shanghai students were relatively poor, rich people would not come out so young.

Yu Qiaqing (1867–1945), a native of Cixi, Zhejiang Province, was a patriotic national capitalist and a magnate in the shipping industry in modern China. In 1881, Yu Qiaqing, who was only 14 years old, was introduced to Shanghai and became an apprentice in the Ruikang paint shop on Wangping Street. Because he worked hard and was good at attracting business, he was quickly appreciated by the boss, and became a street runner and responsible for contacting the business. Peers on Wangping Street competed to hire Yu Qiaqing with high salaries, while the shop owner tried to retain her with raises and dry stock. Since 1892, he has served as comprador of Texang Lulin, Sino-Russian Daosheng Bank and Dutch Bank. Since 1898, he participated in negotiations with the French Concession Office in the Siming case. In 1906, he initiated the organization of the Chinese Team of the Wanguo Business League, opened the Siming Bank in 1908, and then organized the Nanyang Quanye Association and served as vice president. He founded Ningshao Shipping Company, Sanbei Shipping Company and Hong 'an Shipping Company successively.

Fig. 26 Yu Qiaqing

The three companies had more than 30 ships with a total tonnage of more than 91,000 tons, which was the crown of domestic private shipping at that time (Fig. 26).

Yu Qiaqing's early career involved finance, shipping, real estate, mining and many other industries, from the beginning was a speculative businessman. As far as Yu Qiaqing's method of investing in real estate is concerned, he has early understood the so-called "Lay eggs behind closed doors" method." If he has used official forces to intervene in land acquisition in the name of establishing public facilities, after the construction of public facilities, he can use the attached land to develop real estate or mortgage for profit." "To enclosure land in the name of public welfare, and then divide part of the land for profit, or change the use of the land to build houses for profit, this strategy of collusion between government and business to develop real estate, Yu Qiaqing used it freely at that time."

During the 1911 Revolution, Yu Qiqing was very supportive of these anti-Japanese activities. He provided some meeting places for the anti-Japanese activists and often donated money to them to solve their financial difficulties. Not only that, Yu Qiqing is also very active in charity. He often paved roads and establish schools, so the public reputation is excellent. In 1920, he co-founded the Shanghai Stock Exchange and served as its chairman. He also served as chairman of the All China Association of Industry and Commerce and the Shanghai General Chamber of Commerce. During the May 30th Movement, in the name of the May 30th Event Committee of the Shanghai General Chamber of Commerce, he arbitrarily modified the terms of negotiation to the imperialists and proposed to stop the strike. During the Anti-Japanese War, he organized the Sino-Italian shipping Company in Shanghai, and served as the president of the Shanghai Refugee Relief Society, handling the grain and obtaining profits.

> Ma Changlin (Shanghai Archives Research Institute): He was able to speak pidgin English, which was understood by foreigners and not very standard, and he mainly got acquainted with foreigners. Later, a foreigner thought that he was very clever, so he went to Lulin Foreign Trade, first as a street walker, then as a deputy comprador, and then as a general comprador. So he developed slowly.

> Fan Weiguo (Researcher, Institute of Economics, Shanghai Academy of Social Sciences): Because the threshold of comprador is relatively high, the first is to understand the procedures and rules of import and export trade, the second is to understand foreign languages, and the third is to be a solid businessman. Comprador should be guaranteed by someone, and the guarantee also requires a certain market relationship, so foreign firms will hire people to be a comprador, so comprador became a scarce resource at that time, and it also gained relatively high profits in trade.

Siming Public Office, founded by Ningbo people, named after Ningbo Siming Mountain, is an organization similar to the hometown association, which has won the support of Ningbo people. In 1898, the French Concession Bureau, relying on its prerogative, forcibly expropriated and sent troops to demolish the walls of the Siming Office in the name of road construction. The young and energetic Yu Qiaqing and her fellow villagers rose up in revolt and encouraged the laundry workers to go on strike.

> Ma Changlin (Shanghai Archives Research Institute): Yu Qiaqing raised his social popularity through this incident. At that time, he was only in his thirties. This was the first time, and the second time was the incident in 1905 that made him even more famous.

The Siming Public Office incident and the court case, so that Yu Qiaqing constantly appeared in the public, and fully showed its talent, gradually, he became a well-known person in the Bund.

In 1906, Yu Qiaqing went to Japan for investigation, and he decided to develop industry after returning home. In 1908, he and a group of Ningbo residents in Shanghai set up the Siming Bank. In 1909, Yu Qiaqing began to invest in the shipping industry, and successively established Ningshao, Sanbei and Hong 'an Shipping Companies, which operated the routes from Shanghai to Ningbo and Shanghai to Hankou, and gained huge profits, becoming the first private shipping enterprise in China at that time. In 1924, Yu Qiaqing was elected the president of Shanghai General Chamber of Commerce.

> Li Tiangang (Professor of Philosophy, Fudan University): Many of the comprador became national capitalists in Shanghai and became the first merchants. The first batch of industrial capital investment, let alone investment in real estate, retail sales, became industrial capitalists.

> Ma Changlin (Shanghai Archives Research Institute): Yu Qiaqing himself was a compran, and later he also invested in many enterprises, including the Ningshao Shipping Company

and the Sanbei Shipping Company. He served as the president of the General Chamber of Commerce, and after he had gained a certain social status, he became closely related to politics and the regime. Before the Revolution of 1911 broke out, he also supported Chen Qimei, and Yu Qiqing was also a minister of meritorious service during the Revolution of 1911.

In the turbulent times of the early twentieth century, in order to seek a stable business environment, the merchant class had to seek political shelter, and so did Yu Qiaqing. He changed from time to time, participating in different regimes and political events and showing completely different political attitudes. Support Shanghai's recovery during the Revolution of 1911; In the May 30th Movement, boycotting British goods, advocating domestic goods and raising funds to maintain strikes; However, he gave financial support to Chiang Kai-shek when he launched the "April 12" counter-revolutionary coup and became the political businessman behind Chiang Kai-shek.

Ma Changlin (Shanghai Archives Research Institute): When Chiang Kai-shek was in Nanchang, Yu Qiaqing went to Nanchang specifically to see Chiang Kai-shek, in fact, there is a little like our popular "first name" meaning, so after Chiang Kai-shek arrived in Shanghai, Yu Qiaqing of course as a support for Chiang Kai-shek's regime was valued. Later, he and Chiang Kai-shek, especially during the Anti-Japanese War, he still took some actions against Chiang Kai-shek's anti-Japanese regime, or did some support. Including in Chongqing, he bought many vehicles from abroad to support the transportation of the Anti-Japanese War. So Yu Qiaqing is also a famous person and his experience is very complicated.

On April 26, 1945, Yu Qiaqing died of illness in Chongqing. From a poor child in the countryside, to a big comprator in Shanghai Beach, and then to a political businessman with good hands and eyes, Yu Qiaqing's life trajectory is interspersed with the development of early Shanghai trade, which confirms each other.

Dai Angang (Professor of History, Fudan University): China's early trade, especially Shanghai's early trade, could not do without comprador.

Fan Weiguo (Researcher, Institute of Economics, Shanghai Academy of Social Sciences): Comprador played a very important role in foreign trade from the 1870s to the beginning of the Republic of China, that is, in the early twentieth century. If they leave the comprador, Chinese businessmen can't get imports. And Chinese exporters can hardly export their goods directly without the comprador. So the comprador actually has an advantage in the Chinese market and an advantage in foreign trade relations.

The development of Shanghai trade is inseparable from the financial industry, and when talking about the comprador giants of the old Shanghai financial industry, we have to mention the Xi family. After the Opium War, when Shanghai was opened to foreign businessmen, Xi Yuanle, from the Dongshan Xi family in Dongting, moved to Shanghai with his family. After Xi Yuanle arrived in Shanghai, with the strong capital of his family, his eldest son Xi Suxuan and his fourth son Xi Sugui successively set up a bank and managed it well.

In the later period of Tongzhi in the Qing Dynasty, the two brothers successively set foot on the road of comprador. Xi Suxuan joined the British Macquarie Bank (the predecessor of Standard Chartered Bank), and Xi Sugui, who understood English, entered HSBC through the strong recommendation of his uncle Shen Eryuan, starting from the bottom of the "floor runner" (that is, salesman).

In 1874, facing the crisis of coastal defense, the Qing government asked HSBC to borrow money for Fujian and Taiwan defense, which amounted to 2 million tairs of silver. This was the first time that the Qing government borrowed money from a foreign bank. Wang Huaishan, the comprador at that time, had no bottom in his heart-he was afraid of offending the court if he did not borrow money; If the Qing government borrows money from banks, when will it be able to recover such a large sum? Can British bosses agree? If the bank doesn't collect the money, the comprador will be in trouble. After thinking about it, he found the street runner Xi Sugui as a substitute to contact Tianjin.

Shrewd Xi Sugui thinks that the count makes demands on HSBC, which can improve the relationship between HSBC and the count. Tianjin was the seat of Li Hongzhang, the minister of the North Ocean and Xi Sugui had seen the current events clearly when he came to Tianjin that Sino-french War was imminent so that the Qing Dynasty must purchase much ordnance, if HSBC couldn't borrow money, the Qing Dynasty would borrow from other foreign banks. After repeated negotiation, Xi Sugui finally succeeded in borrowing the money and because of the project, Xi Sugui had shown his courage and talent so that he had become the HSBC comprador.

Xi Sugui became a comprador of HSBC Bank, and was also appreciated by the Qing Dynasty ministers Li Hongzhang and Zuo Zongtang. In order to get a huge loan, they competed to draw Xi Sugui, Li Hongzhang also specially wrote to the court, for him to sponsor the official position, Xi Sugui obtained two titles red top flower wing, and donated a post of intendant. He relied on his connections with the Qing Dynasty and his status as a comprador at HSBC to achieve success one way or another. From 1874 to 1890, the Qing government borrowed 17 loans from HSBC, most of which were handled by Xi Sugui alone, so he got a lot of commissions, and HSBC's business was also booming, and he was even more generous.

At that time, in order to obtain liquidity, banks in Shanghai often borrowed money from foreign banks and then used it. Some of the money was lent out to small and large firms for profit, and since Xi Sugui signed off on HSBC's loans, almost all of them begged him to buy shares or hire people he introduced as assistants. At the same time, Xi Sugui extensively invested in the money industry, silver buildings, pawns, gold, but also in Pudong and Nanjing Road, Fengyang Road area to buy a lot of real estate. Xi Sugui died in 1905 and on the day of the memorial, from the Bund to the Xi's home on Fengyang Road, white cloth tents were set up at various intersections along the way, altanyi road sacrifices were set up at the gates of Chinese and foreign merchants and some foreign banks, and the public concession patrol also armed escort the funeral procession through Nanjing Road. At that time, Xi Sugui was the only comprador who could enjoy such treatment after the death of the Bund (Fig. 27).

Xi Sugui has five sons, the eldest son Xi Yucheng inherited his father's business as HSBC bank comprador; The second son Xi Yukun was the manager of Yingkou Qing Dynasty Bank and Xi Yukun's son Xi Dexun was the deputy comprator of American Commercial Express Bank; The third son Xi Yuguang successively served

Fig. 27 Xijia Garden, Julu Road, Shanghai

as the comprador of Baoxin Bank of the United States, the deputy manager of the Shanghai Branch of the Ministry of Household Bank, and the associate manager of the Shanghai branch of the Qing Bank. Xi Yuguang's son, Xi Demao, served as the comprator of Huayi Bank, the director of the Central banking Department and the general manager of the Bank of China, while another son, Xi Debing, was the director of the Shanghai Central Mint; The fourth son, Xi Yumi, was a comprador at Taiwei Bank; The fifth son Xi Yukui successively served as manager of Hankou Branch of Qing Bank, deputy comprador of HSBC Bank, Comprador of Sumitomo Bank, and Comprador of British Commercial Bank.

Many other children of the Xi family have served as managers, deputy managers and other senior staff in Chinese government-run and private banks, and the Xi family has accumulated huge sums of money to open banks, yarn Industry Bank and Huifeng Bank. In addition to the financial sector, business activities also cover other fields. Like Xi Chunyuan's Xi Huafeng silk stack and Xi Shouyu's Dalen Silk Bureau, they are well-known in the Shanghai silk industry. Xi Shouyu also became the president of Shanghai Xuelong Corporation, becoming the leader of the Shanghai silk industry. For example, Xi Decan invested in Fufeng flour Mill, Xi Yucheng invested in public cotton mill and Pudong beach, Xi Suxuan is also engaged in real estate management in many places.

According to statistics, from the end of the nineteenth century to the beginning of the twentieth century, more than 20 banks and foreign firms of great influence were set up in Shanghai by foreign investors. Among them, 23 members of Xi's family (including his son-in-law) successively served as comprador in 13 foreign banks, and 5 members of Xi's family served as comprador in two foreign banks, which is unique in modern China. The rich and powerful Xi family became a financial family in Shanghai Beach, and even foreign media called it "the first financial family in modern China".

3 Concession and Trade

3.1 The Free Economy of the Concessions

Shanghai's eclectic architectural style makes the city full of unique charm. The formation of these Shanghai architectural styles cannot be separated from that special era. After Shanghai opened a port, a special area appeared along the Huangpu River, which was the concession. For a long time in modern times, the municipal structure of Shanghai was divided into three boundaries and four districts, including the Chinese boundary, the public concession and the French concession. At that time, Shanghai's trade was mainly conducted in the concession area.

> Fan Weiguo (Researcher, Institute of Economics, Shanghai Academy of Social Sciences): The Shanghai concession is a product of the treaty system. After the signing of the Treaty of Nanjing, Shanghai opened its port, which included the terms of concession land. Therefore, in 1845, the British consul in Shanghai and the Shanghai Daotai signed a charter of Shanghai Lease, which was the fundamental system of the concession.

> Xiong Yuezhi (Researcher, Institute of History, Shanghai Academy of Social Sciences, Distinguished Professor, Fudan University): The concession is of vital significance to the development of Shanghai's trade. At first the concession was merely a place leased to foreigners for business. The sovereignty of this place is still Chinese, and it was originally stipulated to be a Sino-foreign division. The concession is for foreigners only. Chinese are not allowed to live here. Therefore, at the beginning, the Chinese in the concession went in to buy vegetables, sweep the floor and help as domestic servants, but the Chinese were not allowed to buy land and build houses here. It's called the Sino-foreign division.

The development of the concession during the period of the Huayang Branch Office was extremely slow. However, war broke out a few years later. In 1853, the army of the Taiping Heavenly Kingdom crossed the Yangtze River, and the rich Jiangnan became the battlefield. Coupled with the occupation of Shanghai by the Small Knife Society, a large number of fleeing people poured into the concession, and the population of the concession increased from less than 300 people before 1853 to 20,000. By the end of the Taiping Rebellion in 1864, the population of the concession had reached a record 500,000.At that time, the concession had one advantage: Xiao Dao Hui did not fight the concession, and the Taiping Heavenly Kingdom did not fight the concession too, so the concession became a precious place to avoid war. These war-driven refugees brought three things with them: first, a lot of money; The second is the talent, there are many people originally business and they came to Shanghai to do business; The third was labor, and there were those who were neither very rich nor in business, but who brought labor and stimulated the development of consumption in the concessions.

The administration of the concession does not interfere too much with the market entities, and thus the market entities gain a kind of economic freedom. That is, what to run, what to do, what to invest in, no one to control, and this kind of economic freedom is relatively speaking in the late Qing Dynasty especially valuable.

Xiong Yuezhi (Researcher, Institute of History, Shanghai Academy of Social Sciences, Distinguished Professor, Fudan University): As a result, we see so many enterprises crowded in the concession that the best large companies we see engaged in trade are all in the concession.

3.2 *The Prosperity of the Banking Industry*

In order to meet the needs of the expansion of trade, Western invaders have penetrated into various fields related to it. Among them, opening banks in China has become an important means for them to realize the interests of aggression in China. The first foreign bank was established in Shanghai in 1847. More than 100 years after the founding of New China in 1949, imperialists opened dozens of banks in Shanghai, and most of these banks chose to settle in the Bund.

Xiong Yuezhi (Researcher, Institute of History, Shanghai Academy of Social Sciences, Distinguished Professor, Fudan University): Shanghai was the first to develop trade, is related to trade, because to buy and sell must have a relationship with finance. Buy with money and sell with money in circulation. Therefore, after the formation of the Shanghai Trade Center, the financial center will soon follow.

In the research materials of the modern history of Shanghai, it was once believed that the earliest foreign Bank in Shanghai was the Macquarie Bank (which opened a branch in Shanghai in 1857), but in fact the first foreign bank in Shanghai should be the Oriental Bank.

Fan Weiguo (Researcher, Institute of Economics, Shanghai Academy of Social Sciences): The earliest foreign bank was the Oriental Bank, which landed in Shanghai in 1847, and then a large number of British, French, German, Russian, Japanese and American banks were established in Shanghai. Most of these banks were also built in the concession, so the Shanghai Finance Street was dominated by foreign banks, and the largest and most imposing building on the street was the British bank HSBC.

The Bank was originally a British royal chartered Bank with its head office in Bombay, India, formerly known as the Bank of Western India, and later merged with the Bank of Ceylon in Ceylon (now Sri Lanka), renamed the Oriental Bank. In 1845, he moved his head office to London. At that time, Britain was trying to expand its trade with China, and as a financial fortress for British imperialism to invade China, Oriental Bank opened branches in Hong Kong (1845) and Shanghai (1848).It obtained huge profits from Britain's trade with China, including the opium trade, by

Fig. 28 Liru Bank

handling international exchange. As a chartered bank, Oriental Bank received special protection and support from the British government in playing the functions of a colonial bank, and the Royal Charter even granted it the "qualification of issuing bank" in China. According to records, in the 1850s, most of the banknotes in circulation in Shanghai were issued by Oriental Bank (Fig. 28).

> Dai Angang (Professor of History, Fudan University): So first there was business, then there was finance. Finance is to serve business, and of course finance also promotes business. So Shanghai's financial industry has a very vivid picture, so we can understand why Shanghai is a financial center. It has been a financial center for more than a hundred years, and Shanghai has been a port for more than a hundred years. China's largest port, but also China's first trade port, naturally become the first financial center.

4 The Break of Trade Routes

4.1 Shanghai Railway Old North Station

The prosperity of Shanghai's foreign trade largely benefits from the superior port transportation environment. Shanghai's location at the midpoint of China's mainland coastline and the mouth of the Yangtze River, coupled with the Yangtze Delta's Huangpu River, the Grand Canal and the spiderweb of Jiangnan waterways, give it an unrivalled port advantage. However, with the continuous development of trade, foreign businessmen in Shanghai began to seek the development of land transportation.

At 200 Tianmu East Road in Shanghai, there is a building with British classical architecture, which is known to old Shanghainese as the most familiar but "Old North Railway Station", which is where the Shanghai-Nanjing Railway Station was once located. In 2004, the Shanghai Railway Museum was rebuilt on the original site, which has quietly told the history of China's railways for many years.

After the defeat in the Sino-Japanese War of 1894–1895, Zhang Zhidong, the then Governor of Huguang and Liangjiang, proposed twice to build the Shanghai-Nanjing Railway. However, the Qing government built the Songhu railway first, and then built the Shanghai-Nanjing railway. The Shanghai-Nanjing Railway was built by the Qing government with loans under the pressure of Britain, and it was also the most wasteful railway injected with capital at the end of the Qing government. The Shanghai-Nanjing Railway started construction in April 1905 and was officially opened to traffic in April 1908 (Fig. 29).

Li Tiangang (Professor of Philosophy, Fudan University): Railway transportation was very important after the twentieth century, because it opened up the communication lines of the whole of China outside the Jiangnan water towns.

Xiong Yuezhi (Researcher, Institute of History, Shanghai Academy of Social Sciences, Distinguished Professor, Fudan University): When we talk about canals, we're just talking about different directions, north–south directions, and railways can also take into account the problems of the highlands. If there are mountain roads, flat roads, and high and low roads, the railway can break through these restrictions. So the construction of railroads was very important for transportation, for commerce.

The Old North Railway Station, or Shanghai North Railway Station, was located at the intersection of Tianmu East Road and Baoshan Road in the present Jing'an

Fig. 29 Shanghai Old North Railway Station

District. From 1950 to 1987, it was called Shanghai Railway Station, until the Shanghai Railway Station (new passenger station) was completed. After the new Shanghai Railway Station was built, the station was habitually called the North Railway Station or the Old North Railway Station by Shanghai people. Today, the red-and-white British classical style building was restored to 80% of its original scale in 2004, and was built on the original site of the Shanghai Railway Museum.

After the completion of the Shanghai-Nanjing Railway in 1908, the Shanghai Railway Station was set up at the entrance of Baoshan Road on Jie Road (now Tianmu East Road).The original station house consisted of six bungalows, two of which were used as waiting rooms. The following year, a four-story office building was built in front of the station. This office building is designed by the British. The outer wall of the ground floor is built with Qingdao stone, and the first floor and above are all built with steel columns and beams. The walls are built with red bricks, decorated with light colored strip inlaid stone, marble columns and arched doors and Windows. This building was called "beautifully constructed and majestic" at that time, and people took it as the symbol of Shanghai Railway Station.

In December 1916, Shanghai-Nanjing Railway and Shanghai-Hangzhou Railway were connected, and Shanghai-Nanjing Railway Shanghai Station became the terminus of the two roads, renamed Shanghai North Railway Station. In 1932, the Japanese imperialists provoked the "The Incident of January 28", and the four-story office building of the Shanghai-Nanjing Railway Bureau was destroyed in the war. After restoration the following year, it was again damaged by Japanese bombing in the August 13 Incident in 1937. It was repaired after the victory of the Anti-Japanese War (Fig. 30).

In December 1987, after the official opening of the new railway station in Shanghai, the usual lively Shanghai North Railway Station was retired and gradually forgotten in people's minds. However, from 1909 to 1987, the old railway station with a history of nearly 80 years has carried countless wind and rain in history and countless guests from south to north, playing an indispensable role in the history of Shanghai.

In August 2004, on the occasion of the 55th anniversary of the establishment of the Shanghai Railway Bureau, the Shanghai Railway Museum was opened on the site of the old North Railway Station, and is now the Shanghai Science Popularization Education base. In December 2017, it was selected as the first batch of national primary and secondary school students' research practice education bases and camps by the Ministry of Education.

Like the railway past: The outdoor plaza evokes the image of an early railway station, with its bulky steam locomotives and timber-framed platform canopy. The 4-story main building of the museum is built in accordance with the original construction of the Shanghai-Nanjing Railway Station in 1909 with 80% of the proportion, reproducing the British classical style of the Shanghai Railway Station.

Guided by the scientific concept of development and with historical materials and objects as the main carrier, Shanghai Railway Museum displays the history of Shanghai and East China Railway for more than 100 years since the railway entered China in the 1860s and 1970s, highlighting the changes and development of railway

Fig. 30 Shanghai Railway Museum

productivity. The museum is divided into 6 parts, with more than 50 exhibition items and nearly 1000 exhibits. There are precious old railway equipment, old equipment and historical pictures, as well as knowledge and fun for the audience to participate in the popular science projects.

4.2 Wusong Railway

In 1849, the China Gazette published an article advocating the construction of railways in China to expand foreign trade in China, which mentioned the construction of two railways in Shanghai, one extending to Hangzhou and the other to Suzhou. Subsequently, the foreign businessmen in Shanghai and the British consul separately requested the construction of a railway between Shanghai and Suzhou, but both were rejected.

Therefore, the British changed their strategy and built a railway from Zhabei in Shanghai to Wusongkou without the consent of the Qing government, named Wusong Railway.

> Wu Songdi (Professor, Institute of Historical Geography, Fudan University): This railway was built without government approval, and after it was built, the Chinese people also watched the fun, and there were objections. As a result, two of the spectators were crushed to death

without care, and the people rose up and attacked it. They became angry and began to make trouble, and later it was dismantled.

The Wusong Railway is a section of the Songhu Railway, China's first operating railway. It's a narrow-gauge railway from Wusong Wharf to Shanghai County, named for the winding Wusong River. The railway was built by the British capital Group headed by the British Capital Group and opened to traffic in 1876, with a total length of 14.5 km. The following year, the Qing government redeemed and demolished it. Twenty years later (1897), the Qing government rebuilt the Songhu Railway with official funds, and the line roughly followed the original direction, extending to the end of Henan North Road, with a total length of 16.09 km, and resumed operation in 1898.

On July 3, 1876, when the Jiangwan section of the Songhu Railway was officially opened to traffic, as China had never had a railway before, spectators on both sides of the track "stood like walls". In the following 100 years, the Songhu Railway witnessed the rise and fall of glory and disgrace after the opening of Shanghai, and also endured the baptism of the battle of Songhu. The Songhu Railway is the first railway officially put into operation in China. At that time, maritime materials were transported to the city through the Songhu Railway, which made important contributions to the economic and social development of Shanghai.

With the change of The Times and the development of Shanghai's urban transportation, this "predecessor" of China's railway is gradually withdrawing from the historical stage. After the opening of the light rail Mingzhu Line in 2000, the southern section (Old North Station - Jiangwan) and the northern section (Hejiawan - Wusong Bridge) of the former Songhu Railway have been dismantled. At present, only the middle Jiangwan-Hejiawan part, as a branch line of the Shanghai-Nanjing Railway, is still "exerting waste heat".

In 1872, the terminus of the first phase of the Songhu Railway was located in Jiangwan Town. In 1874, the railway was built by the British merchant Jardine Matheson. On July 3, 1876, the section from Tianhou Palace North (now the intersection of Henan North Road and Tanggu Road) to Jiangwan was officially opened to traffic. On December 1, 1876, the Songhu Railway, China's first railway with a total length of 14.5 km, was completed and opened to traffic. In the 21st year of Guangxu (1895), Zhang Zhidong, Governor of the Two Rivers and Minister of South Ocean Trade, proposed twice to the Ymen of the Prime Minister of the Qing government to build a military railway between Wusong - Shanghai - Jiangning, thinking that the construction of this road is "beneficial to commerce, fundraising, and coastal defense three ends", and suggested that this road is divided into five sections. Take "Wusong to Shanghai, Shanghai to Suzhou, Suzhou to Zhenjiang, Zhenjiang to Jiangning and Suzhou to Hangzhou as a section, raise a section of money, that is, do a section of the road", and propose a budget and fundraising methods. At that time, the Qing government was defeated by Japan in the Sino-Japanese War, forced by the national public opinion, announced the implementation of the policy of "implementing real government", indicating that it would change its attitude of delaying the construction of railways in the past. In the 22nd year of Guangxu (1896), the Qing government ordered Liu Kunyi, the governor of Liangjiang after the Sino-Japanese War, to make "strength preparations" for Zhang Zhidong's proposal to build a railway from Wusong to Jiangning. Later, Zhang Zhidong and Zhili Governor Wang Wenshao will play Wusong to Jiangning railway assigned to Sheng Xuanhuai presided over the railway company. Approved by the Qing government and instructed to "first repair Songhu, after building Huning". Accordingly, the Songhu Railway between Wusong and Shanghai was rebuilt.

On December 1, 1896, the Railway Corporation was formally established in Beijing under the supervision of Sheng Xuanhuai, and an office was set up in Shanghai. The railway Corporation will soon move its headquarters to Shanghai because of the Songhu Railway. At the beginning of the establishment of the railway Corporation, the Qing government transferred the surplus money from the construction of Luhan Railway to the construction of Songhu railway. The Songhu Railway was the first railway in Jiangnan built by the Qing government with official funds.

Guangxu twenty-third year (1897) January 26, Songhu railway started, by Sheng Xuanhuai personally in Shanghai to supervise the construction, and hired the German Xileba presided over the construction of the road. The line generally follows the direction of the original Wusong railway, using part of the old subgrade. The following year (1898), the entire line was completed on June 18, June 19 inauguration ceremony, July 16 officially opened for business. The construction cost of the whole line is 925,800 silver taels. Until the thirty years of Guangxu (1904), when the Shanghai-Nanjing Railway was merged into the "Songhu Branch Line", the railway company invested a total of 1.099 million silver tael before and after. After the Songhu railway merged with the management of Huning Railway, after many years of operation and expansion, the line and station equipment have been greatly changed.

During the "1228 Songhu War", all station houses along the Songhu Railway were destroyed and the line Bridges were bombed. After the armistice, the line was restored, but the station houses along the line were not rebuilt until 1934, and passenger and cargo traffic gradually returned to pre-war levels. After the fall of Shanghai in 1937, Japanese soldiers repaired the damaged lines of the Songhu railway. In April 1939, Huabei Transportation Co., LTD. (Huatie for short) was established, and the Songhu Railway was renamed Wusong Line. On the eve of the victory of the Anti-Japanese War, China Railway dismantled a section of the Wusong Line from 10 km north of Hejiawan to Cannon Taiwan. After the victory of the War of Resistance against Japan, the Railway Bureau restored the section from Hejiawan to Wozao Bang. In May 1949, when the Kuomintang troops were trapped in Shanghai, the Zhanghuabang Station was set on fire by the routed troops, and all 24 tracks and 42 groups of switches in the station were destroyed, and all railway machinery and equipment were looted and lost.

From 1949 to 1962, Songhu Railway continued to handle suburban passenger transport business. In 1962, Shanghai buses use large buses, Shibei bus line extended to Wusong Town and Shanggang A factory, the line is basically parallel to the Songhu railway, plus Songhu railway passenger and freight trains on Zhabei, Hongkou urban level crossing people and vehicles pass interference is larger, by the relevant departments of Shanghai and railway Bureau agreed, Passenger trains on the Songhu branch line stopped running in early 1963. Subsequently, the section from Hejiawan to Baoshan Road of Songhu Railway was used as a freight transport line.

It is said that in less than a year after the Wusong Railway was opened to traffic, the number of passengers exceeded 160,000, and the fare at that time was half an ocean for the upper seat, twenty-five cents for the middle seat, and 120 yuan for the lower seat. The Wusong Railway was dismantled by the Qing government after a year of operation, until 1896, at the request of Sheng Xuanhuai, the minister of Railways at that time, the railway was rebuilt and renamed as the Songhu Railway. Songhu Railway is China's first operating railway, after more than a hundred years of wind and rain, in 1997, dismantled, in the sea of change, the Songhu Railway has witnessed the ups and downs of Shanghai after the opening of the port, and Shanghai has been together for 140 years. To commemorate this railway, the site of Jiangwan Station of Songhu Railway is now preserved at the intersection of Wenshui East Road, Guangji Road, Shanghai.

Today, in the square at the exit of the former Tiantong Temple station, a commemorative sculpture composed of steel rails and wheels is erected; The Wusong town station was built by the relevant departments of Shanghai Baoshan District according to the original appearance, and then stood again in the former site of the Wusong Railway Wusong Town station, paved with a section of steel rail, placed an old steam locomotive, and wooden board room waiting room, Wusong station sign and isolation wood fence... Visitors from all over the country are welcomed free of charge (Fig. 31).

Fig. 31 Landscape of the memorial site of Wusong Town Station

4.3 Shanghai-Nanjing Railway

According to the Historical records of Qing Dynasty Diplomacy, in July and October 1895, Zhang Zhidong, the governor of Liangjiang, proposed twice to the Ymen of the Prime Minister to build the Shanghai-Nanjing Railway. In 1903, Sheng Xuanhuai, the superintendent of the Railway Corporation, signed a loan contract with the British merchant Jardine Matheson, successively borrowing a total of 2.9 million pounds. In April 1905, construction of the Shanghai-Nanjing Railway began (Fig. 32).

Dai Angang (Professor of History, Fudan University): At the beginning of the twentieth century, the economy of the Yangtze River Delta had a relatively great development, which was caused by two factors. The first was that after the Treaty of Shimonoseki, foreign investment could more easily invest in China. The second was that after the Treaty of Shimonoseki, China had a slogan called "saving the country through industry", which enhanced national strength through industry, economy and trade. The Shanghai-Nanjing Railway is in the context of saving the country by industry, that is, in the context of expanding foreign investment, that is, in the context of both, borrowing money from foreigners, China built its own railway.

On April 1, 1908, the Shanghai-Nanjing Railway was opened to traffic. The Chinese were nominally assigned to preside over affairs, but the real power of management was in the hands of the British. The Shanghai-Nanjing Line starts from Shanghai Railway Station, passes Kunshan, Suzhou, Wuxi, Changzhou, Danyang, Zhenjiang and other cities, and terminates at Xiaguan, Nanjing, with a total length of 311 km.

Fig. 32 Shanghai-Nanjing Railway Station in Shanghai

4.4 Shanghai-Hangzhou Railway

The Shanghai-Hangzhou Railway is a railway from Zhabei District of Shanghai to Shangcheng District of Hangzhou, Zhejiang Province in China. It was started in 1906 and completed in 1909, with a total length of 189 km and a total of 36 stations. It is connected with Shanghai-Nanjing Railway, and together with Zhejiang-Jiangxi Railway, Hunan-Guizhou Railway and Guizhou-Kunming Railway, it forms an east–west railway trunk line in central and southern China. It is a part of the main East–west trunk line along the southeast coast of China, and it is also a transportation trunk line connecting Jiangsu, Shanghai and Zhejiang provinces.

On July 24, 1905, in order to resist the looting of Zhejiang railway rights by Britain and the United States, more than 160 people such as Tang Shouqian and Zhang Yuanji, on behalf of Zhejiang Province, gathered in Shanghai Xuanqiao Foreign Affairs Bureau and decided to set up a commercial office of Zhejiang Provincial Railway Co., LTD. (referred to as Zhejiang Road Company) to set up a provincial railway. In 1905, the survey and design of the Shanghai-Hangzhou Railway began. In August 1907, the Jiangshu Railway Line was completed and opened to traffic, ending the history of Hangzhou without a railway. On August 13, 1909, the Hufeng and Hangfeng sections of the Shanghai-Hangzhou Railway were connected, and the Zhejiang section of the Shanghai-Hangzhou Railway was completed and opened to traffic.

In 1905, in order to resist the imperialist invasion and regain the construction right of Zhejiang railway, Tang Shouqian and Zhang Yuanji established Zhejiang Railway Company with the support of the Zhejiang Fellow Countrymen Association (which was the foundation of the revolutionary organization of the Restoration Society in the late Qing Dynasty) and took the post of prime minister to build the Shanghai-Hangzhou Railway. Since Gongchen Bridge was a Japanese concession at that time, where commerce was developed and economy was prosperous, Tang Shouqian's initial design drawing was to place the terminus of the Shanghai-Hangzhou Railway at Genshan Gate, and prepare to lay a branch line from Genshan Gate to Gongchen Bridge. Tang Shouqian was satisfied with this idea, but he never expected that his design only focused on the economy, but ignored the political factors.

That year, Tang Shouqian's beloved husband Ma Yifu returned from a study tour in Europe and America. Although Ma Yifu was only in his 20s at the time, Tang Shouqian enjoyed chatting with him. One day, Ma Yifu came to the soup home as a guest, when Tang Shouqian was discussing railway design drawings with his staff, he asked his son-in-law to also come to the discussion. Who knows Ma Yifu after a look but a drawing torn in half. "Why is that?" The staff was horrified. Ma Yifu seemed a little excited, he said: "China's man-made railway should think about the Chinese people." why Instead of stopping at Yangshi Street (now Jiangcheng Road) in the downtown area and laying a branch line to Nanxing Bridge to facilitate the connection between land and water and the future southward extension of the railway, should we stop at Genshan Gate and lay a branch line to Gongchen Bridge Concession to facilitate the Japanese?" The staff looked at each other and finally looked at Tang

Shouqian. Tang pondered for a moment and felt that Ma Yifu's words made sense. Worthy of being his beloved husband, he gave them a vivid political lesson. Tang Shouqian not only did not rip the drawings as rude, but also changed the Genshan Gate into a freight station according to Ma's plan, and set the terminal station in the north end of the Yangshi Street city (that is, today's Hangzhou City Railway Station, after the Shanghai-Hangzhou Railway was opened in 1909, the construction of 20 m of bullet stone road near the railway station was the first automobile road in Hangzhou).

For the first time, the train thundered from Shanghai to Hangzhou, along the Disha River, and entered the city station. The noise was as great as the power of the people. After the ceremony, more people still gathered at the city station and refused to disperse for a long time. Tang Shouqian sat in the car to hear the public singing a new folk song: "The railway twists and turns and stretches far into the distance. It has two branches, one to Shanghai and the other across the Qiantang River. Peculiar limbs flew, surpassing the dragon and phoenix, as if delivered to Kua 'e to chisel the female wall."

On August 13, 1909, the entire Shanghai-Hangzhou Railway was opened to traffic. The planned Shanghai-Hangzhou railway originally started from Shanghai, through Fengjing, Jiashan, Jiaxing, Tongxiang, Chang 'an direct to Hangzhou, which is a relatively straight line. However, by chance, Tongxiang all walks of life believe that the railway to pass through farmland, cemetery, housing, so the monster noise will destroy their feng shui, so resolutely refused to purchase land, and was strongly opposed by the local landlord gentleman.

However, Haining people from all walks of life and the upper echelons were surprisingly open-minded and welcomed the railway very much. Wu Xiaolu, Xu Hangbin (a member of the league and a senator), Xu Shenru and others believed that if the railway passed through Haining, it would be a great good thing. So they vigorously promoted the Shanghai-Hangzhou railway from Jiaxing curve south, through Xiashi, Chang 'an, Linping to Hangzhou. After changing course, it formed a large bend of about 80 degrees with a radius of about 440 m at Kip Shek. Such drawings, submitted to Zhejiang railway superintendent Tang Shouqian there is difficult to be approved. So Xu Liuliang thought of a way to draw two drawings of the railway route from Hangzhou to Fengjing in Zhejiang Province, one is from Hangzhou to Xiashi, and the other is from Xiashi to Fengjing. When the two drawings are seen separately, the curvature is not large, almost straight line. After reading the drawings, Tang Shouqian thought that the railway route southward plan was very feasible and approved.

At that time, the construction of the section of the Shanghai-Hangzhou railway from Fengjing to Shanghai was undertaken by Jiangsu Province, and the section from Fengjing to Hangzhou was undertaken by Zhejiang Province. In order to facilitate the early completion of the Xiashi section of the railway and avoid problems, Xu Liuliang constructed the Zhejiang section of the railway from both ends at the same time, one end from Hangzhou to Xiashi, and the other from Fengjing to Xiashi, to minimize the possibility of further changes in the direction of the railway. After the opening of the Shanghai-Hangzhou Railway, the convenience of transportation led to the prosperity of Xiashi, and soon the Haining county government moved from the ancient town of Yanguan to the northeast end of the county, which is now the Haining urban area.

After the completion of the Shanghai-Hangzhou Railway, it has played a great role in promoting the economic development of Zhejiang, especially Hangzhou and Jiaxing, and greatly promoted the economic and cultural exchanges between Shanghai, Jiaxing and Hangzhou. It can be said that the Shanghai-Hangzhou Railway, together with the Shanghai-Nanjing Railway, laid the foundation for the Yangtze River Delta region to become the most prosperous area in modern China. Regrettably, from 1937 to 1945, the Shanghai-Hangzhou Railway was occupied by the Japanese and became a transportation line for the Japanese invaders to plunder China's wealth. Even today, we can still see the artillery towers left by the Japanese occupation era along the Shanghai-Hangzhou Railway.

After the victory of the Anti-Japanese War, the Shanghai-Hangzhou Railway returned to the embrace of the motherland. After liberation, the Party and the government invested a lot of money to transform the Shanghai-Hangzhou Railway, and the railway began to enter a period of rapid development. On April 1, 1980, the Shanghai-Hangzhou Line began to use internal combustion engines to pull passenger trains. At the end of 1991, the transformation of the double line of Shanghai-Hangzhou Railway was completed. On the morning of December 27, 1991, the opening ceremony of the double line of Shanghai-Hangzhou Railway was held at Chang 'an Railway Station. In 2005, the Ministry of Railways carried out the electrification and expansion of the Shanghai-Hangzhou Railway. In September 2006, the electrification expansion was completed, and a train left every six minutes on the Shanghai-Hangzhou Railway, and the travel time between Hangzhou and Shanghai was reduced from more than 150 min to less than 90 min. April 18, 2007, Shanghai-Hangzhou line for the first time to operate the harmony number of EMU—since then, Shanghai-Hangzhou railway into the ranks of China's modern railway trunk line (Fig. 33).

5 The Rise of the Domestic Movement

5.1 Hongsheng Match Factory

The invasion of a large number of foreign goods has had a great impact on China's traditional native goods. Zheng Guanying wrote in "Prosperous Times Crisis": "cloth, yarn, lace, socks, scarves into China, and needlework unemployment; Kerosene, foreign candles, and foreign electric lamps entered China, and the cypress trees in several provinces in the southeast were abandoned as useless; Foreign iron, foreign needles, and foreign nails were inserted into China, and most of the men who built them had nothing to do…".

> Li Tiangang (Professor of Philosophy, Fudan University): Foreign goods are imported, they are distributed in Shanghai, after the distribution of the market, there is a profit, the retailer will raise money, set up their own factories, and then the foreign businessman is the same,

Fig. 33 Shanghai-Hangzhou Railway Railway Bridge across Suzhou River

> the foreign businessman used to be a seller, but after he made profits, he converted, reduced the cost of goods and then produced in Shanghai, so immediately began to develop industry. They sell a commodity, make a profit, implement local production, and create a new industrial category.
>
> Ma Changlin (Research Curator, Shanghai Municipal Archives): After the trade, because the ship was coming, there were some initial repairs, including processing and processing factories, and that is the factory we see. Around 1850, there were already more than a dozen repair yards in Shanghai. In addition, the silk processing of the initial trade was that foreign traders purchased cocoons and processed them locally. Later, foreign investors set up a silk processing plant in Shanghai, which also became one of the varieties of Shanghai's industrial construction. On this basis, cotton mills were developed and cotton was processed locally, so this was another influence.

In the face of the impact of foreign goods, the national industry in Shanghai has risen, and a number of national capitalists have emerged. Match King Liu Hongsheng is one of them. Liu Hongsheng was born in Shanghai into a family of comprador. At the age of 17, he entered St. John's University, and at the age of 21, he became a coal salesman at the Shanghai Kaiping Mining Bureau. He started as a porter and worked his way up to manager of the sales company of Kaiping Coal Mine in Shanghai. In addition to being a comprador, he also joined hands with the Shanghai Yitaixing Coal company to start a business of selling coal by himself. In just a few years, Liu Hongsheng has gone from a poor college student to a millionaire.

Liu Hongsheng actually has no big background. Although he studied at St. John's University, a missionary school, he already felt that Chinese people were being bullied more by foreigners, but he could do nothing at that time, because he did not have the ability in all aspects of the economy to start his own business. He later told people that he had no way, only one way, relying on foreigners.

Dai Angang (Professor, Department of History, Fudan University): Zheng Guanying made a very vivid statement, that is, the beginner of business war is an outsider. That is, to engage in business warfare with outsiders, I began to learn the skill of business warfare from foreigners, and when I learned the skill, I used this skill to engage in business warfare with foreigners.

Matches, the older generation called it "foreign fire", as the name suggests, it is an exotic product. During the Daoguang period of the Qing Dynasty, Westerners gave matches to the Chinese emperor as the highest gift. Since then, foreign brands such as Sweden's Phoenix brand and Japan's Monkey brand have entered the Chinese market in large numbers as commodities. In order to recover their rights and interests, some national capitalists set up industries and produced modern chemical products.

On October 1, 1920, Liu Hongsheng invited Du Jiacun and seven other people to raise 120,000 silver dollars to establish a private Hongsheng match factory, which was located in Shimen Tang, outside Xumen, Suzhou, which backed the canal and was convenient for transportation and conducive to modern enterprise production. Hongsheng Match Factory with Suzhou Beisi Tower as the trademark, is the representative of Suzhou modern industry, it produces Dingjunshan, pagoda and other trademarks of matches, and at that time dumped in China Sweden match competition. The factory has 757 employees and implements a 10-h working day (Fig. 34).

In addition to the Hongsheng match factory, Liu Hongsheng also founded China Wool Textile Factory, China Match raw Material Factory, Northwest Wool washing long, Guizhou Cement Factory, Lanzhou Northwest Wool Textile Factory and so on. For several decades, Liu Hongsheng was famous throughout the country with many titles such as "King of Coal", "King of Matches" and "King of Wool textile".

In 1956, the private enterprise Hongsheng technology match Factory and Zhongnan Match Factory and other four enterprises merged, reorganized into the public–private joint venture Hongsheng Match Factory. In 1966, it was renamed Suzhou Match Factory. In 1992, the factory and Suzhou Xinhu village jointly established Suzhou Hongsheng Match Factory Co., LTD. In July 1998, Hongsheng Match Co., Ltd. disintegrated. After 2000, most of the factories of Hongsheng Match Factory became part of the green belt, and only one house in the Republic of China period stood by the bank of the moat, which is now a scenic spot in the ancient city of Suzhou.

5.2 *Ying Chang and China*

Ocean Fire once held more than 80% of the Chinese match market. In particular, Swedish and Japanese companies are very strong, and under their dumping, many domestic matches have lost money for years and are in a difficult situation. Liu Hongsheng clearly knew that in the face of internal troubles and foreign attacks, at

Fig. 34 Public–private joint venture Hongsheng Match Factory

this time, only consistent external, quell the price war, is the only way to protect themselves and their domestic counterparts.

The Great China Yingchang Jie Stele on the west side of Heping Road in the western Section of Zhenjiang City is a witness to the history of that time. Greater China Yingchang Jie is the predecessor of Zhenjiang Match Factory, the current address is in Zhenjiang City Jinshan Road 18. Its predecessor was Zhenjiang

Yingchang Match Factory, founded in 1920, in January 1956, the implementation of public–private partnership, renamed Zhenjiang Match Factory. After liberation, it was at an advanced level in the national match industry.

In 1920 and 1921, Shao Erkang, the founder of Shanghai Yingchang Match Company, and Chen Jintang, a Japanese Chinese, set up Yingchang Match Factory and Suisheng Match Factory in Zhenjiang. Yingchang Match factory has a capital of more than 200,000 yuan, more than 200 houses, 660 workers, more than 50 machines and equipment, and 720 matches per day. The size of Suisheng Match factory is similar to Yingchang Factory. Matches are mainly sold to Jiujiang, Wuhu, Hankou and Shanghai. After the May 30th Massacre, shops refused to sell Japanese matches, and the Suisheng Match Factory closed in 1928.

In August 1928, Liu Hongsheng published the famous "Report Match Trade Book" and proposed the merger of several Chinese and Yingchang match factories. In 1930, Shanghai Yingchang Match Company, Shanghai Zhoupu Zhonghua Match Co., Ltd. and Suzhou Hongsheng Match Company merged to form Greater China Match Co., LTD. Zhenjiang Yingchang Match Factory is under the jurisdiction of Greater China Match Co., LTD.

In Liu Hongsheng's letter to his peers, he detailed several advantages of the merger of the domestic match industry, from which it can be seen that Liu Hongsheng united his domestic counterparts, formed a price alliance, and jointly resisted the idea of foreign fire. However, because Chinese matches are taxed higher than Swedish matches, the final price is at a disadvantage.

In November 1929, Liu Hongsheng established the National Match Federation composed of 52 match factories across the country. They mobilized workers to boycott foreign goods, jointly signed a petition to the Nanjing government, asking for tax assistance to the domestic match industry, and control imported matches to support domestic products.

After the establishment of Greater China Match Co., LTD., it merged with other companies in the same industry and expanded its scale. It has not only resisted the dumping of foreign matches, but also greatly improved the production technology and management, established a set of centralized management systems for production, sales and finance, and unified product specifications. It has set up a special technical class to study and solve the big problem that the match head is easy to get damp, so that the quality of the match meets the Swedish famous brand standard.

The merger brought hope to the crisis-plagued match industry and attracted others. On January 1, 1931, Jiangxi Jiujiang Yusheng Match Company was merged with a net asset value of 457,351.87 yuan. In 1932, Lu Xiaobo's Mussen match factory in Zhenjiang was also merged… In 1934, the Greater China Company had an annual output of 150,000 boxes of matches, accounting for about 15% of the total output of matches in the country, accounting for 50% of the output of matches in Jiangsu, Zhejiang, Anhui, Jiangxi, Hubei and Hunan, becoming the largest national match enterprise at that time. Its successful operation broke the situation of the unification of the ocean fire in China and grew the ambition of the Chinese people.

5.3 *Beauty Brand Cigarettes*

Mr. Liu himself is trying to lower the price of matches. He collaborated with Meili, a famous brand of cigarettes in Shanghai at that time, and printed cigarette advertisements on Greater China matchboxes. This added an extra stream of advertising revenue, allowing the product to regain competitiveness.

Liu Hongsheng also founded the China Wharf Company, Shanghai Cement Factory, Huafeng Enamel Factory, Zhanghua Plush textile Factory, Dahua Insurance Company, China Enterprise Bank. From "King of Matches" to "King of enterprises", Liu Hongsheng has witnessed the growth and development of Chinese national enterprises with 20 years of struggle.

In the 1930s, the domestic cigarette market in major cities was very competitive, and the "Three guns" and "Pirates" brands produced by the United Kingdom and the United States flooded the market, and domestic cigarettes were almost uninterested. In order to save the crisis, the boss of Shanghai Huacheng Tobacco company, which produces beautiful cigarettes, came up with a clever plan to hide a small portrait of Liang Shan 108 in each cigarette box, while stating that those who set a complete set of Liangshan heroes can go to Huacheng company agents in exchange for gold. As soon as the advertisement came out, the public rushed to buy the beautiful brand cigarettes, and the sales of the products skyrocketed (Fig. 35).

Some buyers set up 36 Liangshan Tiangang stars but how also not set up 72 earth star some people have 107 hero pictures, but also lack a, and what they lack is "Baoxing will Han Tao" this one. So some people began to buy the whole beauty brand cigarettes, and even some agents opened the whole box of cigarettes to look for them one by one, and then cleverly sealed them for sale, but they could not find Han Tao's portrait. As a result, "smoking looking for Han Tao" became the mantra of people at that time, spread very widely, beautiful brand cigarettes rely on this stunt in the market to gain a firm foothold.

Later, people learned that there was no "Yum General Han Tao" portrait in the cigarette. But they are still willing to buy Meili brand cigarettes, because the smoke of this kind of cigarettes is not worse than that of foreigners, and the price is cheap, of course, people are happy. Huacheng company's high reward is obviously a trick to hide the sea, and finally make their own enterprises in the cracks to seize a place.

Meili brand cigarette marketing is very successful, Meili brand cigarette advertising let the whole country know the old Shanghai popular star—Jiang Meiying. As a local girl in Shanghai, born in a rich and scholarly family, she has been gentle and elegant since childhood, and has become a great beauty when she grows up. Soon she was discovered by the director and shot the first commercial, which promoted her popularity to every corner of Shanghai, becoming the first beauty in the eyes of Shanghai people at that time.

> Li Tiangang (Professor, School of Philosophy, Fudan University): Foreign goods hit local goods, such a situation is only one or two decades, and then Shanghai's national industry will rise. Whether it is government-run or commercial, Shanghai itself, or overseas Chinese, the overseas Chinese businessmen who set up in Shanghai soon began to rise. They also

Fig. 35 Advertising picture of Beauty brand cigarettes

produce foreign goods of the same quality as England and Japan, or even cheaper, which we call domestic goods.

Fan Weiguo (Researcher, Institute of Economics, Shanghai Academy of Social Sciences): In modern China, especially after the Republic of China, a movement of domestic goods was launched, and a large number of domestic goods were exported to Southeast Asia. In the Southeast Asian market, Japanese industrial products and Chinese industrial products have formed market competition, and sometimes China's domestic goods have quite a market there.

Li Tiangang (Professor, School of Philosophy, Fudan University): The 1920s was a stage in which Shanghai's modern industry, including industry, commerce, trade, real estate and finance, was fully established. During this period, Shanghai's economy developed very well. I think it was a golden age of Shanghai's economic development. The 1930s was no longer the golden age of Shanghai, and the Japanese bombing immediately blew up a large number of Chinese industries in Shanghai, and Shanghai suffered a devastating blow during the "August 13 Songhu War of Resistance", and only the concession part was retained.

6 Trade in the Island Period

6.1 The Background to the Formation of Silos

After the "July 7 Incident" in 1937, the nationalist government began an all-out war of resistance, and the whole of China was reduced to a battlefield, and China's foreign trade declined rapidly. In Shanghai, until the eve of the outbreak of the Pacific War, Shanghai's foreign trade gradually recovered and developed and prospered after a short decline.

Xiong Yuezhi (Researcher of the Institute of History, Shanghai Academy of Social Sciences, Distinguished Professor of Fudan University): Although Japan occupied the territory of China, the Ministry of Industry and Bureau inside the concession was still in operation, and the economic and cultural life inside the concession was still the same, which formed the phenomenon we call the island, that is, the war outside was noisy, but it was still a peaceful place.

The 4-year period from the fall of Shanghai in November 1937 to the outbreak of the Pacific War in December 1941 is commonly referred to as the "Shanghai Island Period". On the evening of November 12, 1937, Shanghai fell in bitter wind and rain. After the Japanese army captured the four suburbs of Shanghai, that is, Hongkou District, Yangpu District and part of Zhabei District in the non-concession areas, as well as the Pudong area on the other side of the Huangpu River, due to political considerations, they did not continue to occupy the public settlement in the Puxi area of Shanghai, the French Concession and the cross-boundary road building area between the two concessions. This has created conditions for Shanghai's foreign trade in the special form of "isolated island".

On December 8, 1941, the Pacific War began when Japan attacked the U.S. Navy at Pearl Harbor. The Japanese troops then entered the Shanghai Public Concession, the French Concession and the area where the two concessions crossed the boundary to build roads. At this time, this special form of "island" also disappeared (Fig. 36).

During the isolated island period, due to the relatively stable political and social environment of the Shanghai Concession, many refugees poured into refuge, and the population of the concession suddenly increased. According to statistics, the population of the two Shanghai concessions before the war was less than 1.7 million. By early 1940, the population of the concession peaked at more than 5 million. After experiencing a brief downturn in the isolated period, with the influx of capital

Fig. 36 Shanghai in the isolated island period

flow, people flow and logistics, coupled with the relative stability of social order and the smooth flow of internal and external traffic, the financial industry, real estate industry, light industry and entertainment industry developed rapidly, and there was an unexpected abnormal prosperity.

Dai Angang (Professor of History, Fudan University): Because the concession was guaranteed, the Japanese did not dare to enter the concession. In this way, the wealthy people throughout most of China who had fallen into the hands of the Japanese invaders took refuge in the concession, and they carried their gold and silver treasures into the concession. There are so many gold and silver treasures gathered in a small space in the concession, and money always changes into money, money begets money, and we need to find ways to invest.

Ge Tao (Researcher, Institute of History, Shanghai Academy of Social Sciences): This internal trade is profitable, because during the war, especially in such a special environment as Shanghai, all parties are in great need of materials, so whether it is to do foreign trade or do inland trade, it is a very profitable way to make money, and a lot of money is invested in this aspect at this time.

Xiong Yuezhi (Researcher at the Institute of History, Shanghai Academy of Social Sciences, Distinguished Professor at Fudan University): I have seen records that if you go to book a hotel during the island period, you often have to book it a week in advance, otherwise you can't book it. For quite some time, 80% of the country's light industrial products were provided by Shanghai. The factories are still operating, even more than before, this is a very special period of abnormal prosperity.

6.2 *Domestic and Foreign Trade in the Isolated Island Period*

With the maritime navigation of Britain, the United States, France and other countries, the Shanghai Concession was able to continue to maintain the relative freedom of overseas traffic and import and export trade, and the economic relations between the Shanghai Concession and the outside world were also continued. By October 1938, the water traffic affected by the war had been basically restored, and Shanghai immediately resumed its status as a national trading center, as can be seen from imports. At this stage, the total value of Shanghai's imports increased from 508 million yuan in 1937 to 3.41 billion yuan in 1941. The total export value increased from 404 million yuan in 1937 to 1.929 billion yuan in 1941. At the same time, foreign investment in Shanghai continues to rise. Before the outbreak of the Pacific War, the investment of Britain and the United States in Shanghai accounted for 72.6% and 64.9% of their total investment in China, respectively. While China's military and people were in dire straits, British and American businessmen were making fortunes in China.

Xiong Yuezhi (Researcher at the Institute of History, Shanghai Academy of Social Sciences, Distinguished Professor at Fudan University): The Japanese have adopted a very special thing towards Shanghai, that is, they have closed it but not completely closed it. Because Japan was a country with a shortage of strategic materials, there was a war going on at that time, and the war had a lot of things that needed to go through special channels from other places. For example, some materials need to be obtained from the United States and Britain, which adopted sanctions against Japan during the war confrontation. Those things are not available through normal channels, but through the third party, the concession, they can be obtained from the United Kingdom and the United States, and Japan can then obtain such strategic materials from other channels. Therefore, the Shanghai concession has become an indirect channel for the Japanese to obtain something, which makes them adopt a sealed attitude towards the concession, which is a very wonderful phenomenon.

During this period, the central and western parts of the Public Concession and the French Concession were flooded with capital and people; According to statistics, in December 1938, there were nearly 4 700 factories here, 10 times the number before the war, and by 1939, the city had 1 705 new factories, of which the traditional textile industry recovered the fastest. According to the statistics of the Shanghai Cloth Factory Association at that time, by 1939, Shanghai's textile industry alone had set up 823 new factories and workshops, adding 23,200 machines and producing 1.42 million pieces of cotton cloth per month.

Due to the recovery of traffic, rich people from all over the world have taken refuge in the Shanghai Concession, and the department store retail industry has shown an unusual prosperity; Retail sales in Shanghai have more than doubled since the pre-war period, and there are almost daily customers. The most famous department store retail giant Yongan company around 1939, the average daily turnover of more than one million yuan, each employee receives an average of about 60 customers a day. By 1941, the company's turnover had increased nearly five times compared with 1938, and its profits had surged 11 times.

6.3 Entertainment Life in the Isolated Island Period

Cinemas have also sprung up, "full of customers" often hanging high in the door, "in the two concessions, there are 28 large and small movie theaters, which are not included in the Hongkou area and the movie theater attached to the game field." Since then, due to the great demand, some new cinemas have been built, such as the Queen's Theatre, which was completed at the end of 1941 with a capacity of 2 000 people, the cost is very large, and in order to achieve the spectacular, another pagoda has been built next to it. As the traveler Vania Oakes described in her diary, "the life of the American and English seems to be exactly the same as before 1937, and they eat, dance, and drink more than before." Most of them are employed by big companies and their salaries are paid in dollars or pounds, so with the devaluation of the Chinese currency, their happy life is back." Flourishing Xiafei Road is full of White Russian jewelry shops, restaurants, dance venues, brothels… Although this bustling area is called "Little Paris", it has actually become "St. Petersburg".

This period also set off a wave of widespread use of radio. On the one hand, the Shanghai concession in the isolated island period was in the area of Japanese occupation, on the other hand, it kept the old order. So this is both the most advanced position and the safest place. The station in question is not a radio station, but a communication station that transmits messages through Morse code. Since the late 1920s, radio technology has gradually been introduced to China, and the public has seen the technology that can instantly transmit messages thousands of miles away. Some well-off young people with knowledge will be more radio as a means of making friends similar to the current network, in the vast radio network to find friends with the same hobbies, which was definitely a fashion at that time.

After the fall of Shanghai, the forces of all sides either entered or retreated to the concession, and the concession entered a complete island period. The Communists, the Nationalists, the British, the Americans, the French, the Soviets (including some exiled former Russian nobles), the Germans… It is no exaggeration to say that the whole world's spy network sends and receives telegrams by radio in the concession. However, this is not all the radio stations in the concession; in fact, the number of radio stations used by the intelligence agencies is only a small part of the total number of radio stations, accounting for the vast majority of radio stations, are commercial stations. The main reason for the rise of commercial radio was that Shanghai was home to almost all the resources that could be bought and sold in China. Although the outside of Shanghai was occupied by the Japanese army, both domestic cargo ships and European and American ships could still sail into the Huangpu River to dock in the concession area for loading and unloading, so trade did not stop. In addition to weapons trading, wartime materials such as clothing, medical equipment, food and drugs can be traded, which is also the conditions for negotiations between the Ministry of Industry and the Japanese government at that time (Fig. 37).

This is why businesses keep radio stations in the concession, because transactions will be required at any time, and if there is no immediate means to do so, how can it

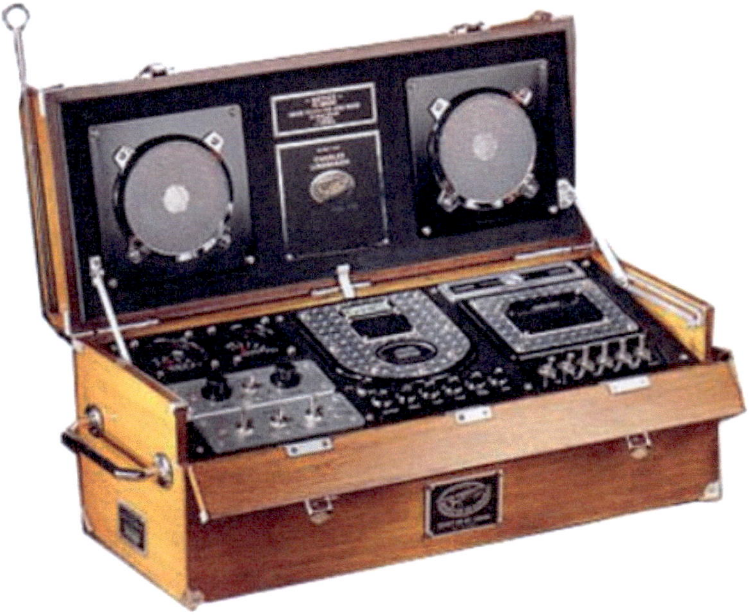

Fig. 37 Radio stations during the island period

be done? At the same time, it can be seen that the financial and trade development of Shanghai had completely surpassed that of other Chinese cities.

In addition, there is another important reason for the existence of radio station, that is, at that time there were still a lot of speculation and investment opportunities in Shanghai, many Chinese businessmen and officials are retreating to the west, but the investment of assets can not stop. Interestingly, when the Shanghai Concession entered the island period, it was precisely because of the large amount of capital investment that the Shanghai stock market maintained a high point until the Japanese army occupied the concession after the outbreak of the Pacific War and stopped stock trading. The performance of the Shanghai stock market during the entire island period was extremely amazing.

The abnormal prosperity of the island economy has allowed Shanghai's trade to persist. For more than a decade, people have been in a state of panic due to constant wars. Although it is difficult, Shanghai's domestic and foreign trade has not been interrupted. On May 27, 1949, Shanghai was liberated. With the acceptance of the people's government and the realization of public–private partnership, Shanghai's trade development entered a special historical stage.

Chapter 3
Forging Ahead (1949–1990)

1 Introduction

On May 27, 1949, Shanghai was liberated. The newly established people's government was warmly welcomed by the people of Shanghai. From then on, the rule of imperialism, feudalism, and bureaucratic capitalism in China's largest city came to an end, and Shanghai ushered in a new era. However, for the newly established people's government, they inherited a Shanghai that was full of problems and in need of development. At the same time, Western capitalist countries led by the United States imposed an economic blockade on the new China. Faced with internal and external difficulties, Shanghai's trade began to move forward in adversity.

2 The Challenges of a New Beginning

2.1 Establishing a Trade System

On May 27, 1949, Shanghai was liberated. The people of Shanghai, who had experienced years of war and suffering, warmly welcomed the People's Liberation Army and embraced a new life (Figs. 1 and 2).

Shanghai was the largest economic center in the Far East at that time, as well as the international trade center, financial center, shipping center, and the largest foreign trade port of old China. However, Shanghai was also the place where imperialist interests in China were most concentrated, and Shanghai's trade was mainly controlled by foreign capital and bureaucratic capital. The liberation of Shanghai put an end to the monopoly of foreign and bureaucratic capital and opened a new chapter for Shanghai's trade.

© Fudan University Press Co., Ltd. 2025
W. Shengqiao, *Century of Shanghai Trade*,
https://doi.org/10.1007/978-981-96-8701-5_3

Fig. 1 People's Liberation Army entering Nanjing Road

2.1.1 Establishing Foreign Trade Control

Before and after the founding of the People's Republic of China, with the liberation of major port cities such as Tianjin and other parts of the country, many foreign and Kuomintang commercial institutions requested to trade with us, and we also needed this kind of trade in order to quickly restore and develop the national economy. However, the old bureaucratic capital and private foreign trade institutions were either paralyzed or on the sidelines, and were not foreign trade institutions in the true sense. They were completely unable to adapt to the needs of foreign trade work under the new situation. In order to adapt to the new situation, the central government formulated foreign trade strategies and policies and accelerated the pace of establishing a controlled foreign trade system. After liberation, Shanghai also gradually established a corresponding controlled foreign trade system in accordance with the unified deployment of the central government.

2.1.2 Implement Import and Export License System

In order to implement the policy of controlling foreign trade, the implementation of the import and export license system is an effective measure and an important guarantee. By implementing import and export license management, we can develop import trade in an orderly manner, restrict and prohibit the import of goods that can be produced domestically, and use limited foreign exchange for the import of

Fig. 2 Parade celebrating the liberation of Shanghai on Nanjing Road

materials urgently needed by the country, so as to concentrate on promoting the recovery and development of the national economy. Before the founding of New China, the various liberated areas had already tried the license system to strengthen foreign trade control. After the founding of New China, the Central Ministry of Commerce gradually unified and improved the import and export license system in order to establish a system of controlling foreign trade.

The Ministry of Commerce issues specific import and export regulations, classifying imported goods into four categories: permitted imports, centralized purchasing and sales imports, prohibited imports, and licensed imports; similarly, exported goods are also classified into similar four categories. It is stipulated that both state-owned enterprises and private or foreign-funded enterprises must apply for a license from the local foreign trade administration or its branch when conducting foreign trade business. The application must include the name, specifications, quantity, price, country of import or export, and time of the goods, for review by the foreign trade administration or its branch. Only after obtaining the license can foreign trade enterprises engage in import and export business, and goods without a license will be treated as smuggling. The foreign trade administration and its branches issue import and export licenses based on various factors such as government policies, laws and regulations, national economic plans, and specific circumstances. This system is comprehensive and strict, applying to all goods rather than just some; not only private foreign trade enterprises and foreign-funded enterprises, but also state-owned foreign trade enterprises need import and export licenses, otherwise they will be dealt with as illegal smuggling. By implementing the import and export commodity license system, the government effectively controls foreign trade.

2.1.3 Implementing the Foreign Exchange Settlement System

Strengthening the management of foreign trade settlement is an important means to ensure the implementation of the centralized control foreign trade policy. As early as April 1949, before the establishment of the People's Republic of China, the North China People's Government issued the "Interim Measures for Foreign Exchange Management in North China" and its implementing rules. Soon after, East China, Central China, and South China also successively issued interim measures for foreign exchange management with basically the same content and their implementing rules. During the period of economic recovery, due to different local conditions and a lack of management experience, the Central People's Government did not formulate a unified foreign exchange management method. In June 1950, the People's Bank of China issued a notice on "Amending the Interim Measures for Foreign Exchange Management and Following the Instructions for Implementation and Transfer to Subordinate Units", recognizing the interim measures for foreign exchange management previously issued by various major administrative regions and correcting any inappropriate provisions, thereby unifying some regulations.

In the early days of the establishment of the People's Republic of China, the main content of the foreign exchange management system was:

① Foreign exchange management is handled by the People's Bank of China designated by the People's Bank of China; banks with good foreign exchange credibility that have branches or representative offices abroad can, after approval by the People's Bank of China, act as agents for the Bank of China to buy and sell foreign exchange on behalf of clients.

② The Bank of China is the designated foreign exchange trading center, and the daily exchange rates are posted by the Bank of China after being approved by the

People's Bank of China based on market conditions. Foreign exchange transactions must be based on these rates, and all off-exchange transactions are strictly prohibited.

③ Except for barter trade as stipulated by the state, the foreign currency proceeds from exported goods must go through the foreign exchange settlement procedures. All foreign exchange must be deposited in the Bank of China in exchange for foreign exchange certificates, which can be withdrawn in Chinese yuan according to the exchange rates or sold within the trading center.

④ Import and export enterprises that purchase foreign exchange certificates or apply to the Bank of China for foreign exchange conversion must hold import licenses or submit foreign exchange application documents approved by the Bank of China for freight charges, commissions, insurance, etc. Later, the State Council issued the "Interim Measures for the Allocation and Use of Foreign Exchange," and the Ministry of Foreign Trade formulated specific "Interim Measures for the Management of Foreign Exchange for State-owned Foreign Trade Companies" and "Interim Measures for the Application of Foreign Exchange for Private Factories and Importers," further improving the foreign exchange management system. The implementation of the foreign exchange settlement system unified the foreign exchange management systems issued by various regions, brought the operation and management of trade foreign exchange under state ownership, and effectively ensured the implementation of the unified control system for foreign trade operations.

2.1.4 Implementation of Protective Tariff Policy

The protective tariff policy is a trade protection measure that imposes heavy taxes on similar imported products based on the market competitiveness of domestic products. It increases the cost of imported goods above the market price of similar domestic products, thereby protecting domestic industries. After the establishment of the People's Republic of China, in order to protect the weak industries of the new China, the Chinese government decided to implement a protective tariff policy. In January 1950, the State Council issued the "Decision on Tariff Policy and Customs Work," emphasizing that "customs tariffs must protect national production and must protect the competition between domestic products and foreign goods."

According to the tariff policy of the State Council, Shanghai Customs imposes export tariffs and adjusts tax rates on relevant export goods based on the actual situation of domestic industrial development and commodity supply and demand. For example, at the end of 1950, in order to restrict the export of certain products and guarantee domestic supply, Shanghai Customs imposed high export taxes on peppermint oil, pig bristles, tung oil, peanut oil, and other products. Starting from May 1951, the country implemented the "Customs Import and Export Tariff of the People's Republic of China" and the "Interim Implementation Regulations", classifying imported goods into four categories: necessities, needs, non-necessities, and luxuries, and imposing different tax rates. Starting from January 1952, Shanghai Customs implemented centralized taxation on goods imported by state-owned foreign trade companies from the Soviet Union and Eastern Europe. Starting from 1960, centralized taxation was also implemented on goods imported by the Foreign Trade General Corporation from Western countries. In 1967, the State Council decided to stop levying import and export tariffs on foreign trade companies and deposit the profits into the treasury. For imported goods with inconsistent pricing, tariffs are still levied according to the original regulations.

2.2 *Takeover and Transformation of Trade Institutions*

2.2.1 Takeover and Transformation of Old Customs

Customs is an important gateway and symbol of sovereignty for a country, and it plays an important role in foreign trade. In old China, which was semi-colonial and semi-feudal, the customs had always been under the control of foreign powers since its establishment. In the early morning of May 25, 1949, the battle to liberate Shanghai was intensifying. Ding Guitang, the highest-ranking Chinese member of the customs and former deputy director of the General Taxation Department of the Customs, led the staff of the General Taxation Department and the Shanghai Customs in a rebellion. The underground party members of the Shanghai Customs brought the red flag and secretly sewn slogans hidden in the Maritime Affairs Office to the sixth floor of the Shanghai Customs building. At 4:30 in the morning, the customs building hung up the first large red banner of "Welcome the People's Liberation Army to liberate Shanghai", and a red flag was raised on the tall clock tower by the Huangpu River.

Ding Guitang's uprising not only preserved the precious customs archives with a long history, substantial inventory, and a large number of customs ships, but also retained a large number of experienced customs personnel for the development of the new China Customs. After the liberation of Shanghai, Chen Yi and Xia Yan praised Ding Guitang on different occasions. In the words of Chen Yi, "Comrade Ding Guitang has made great contributions." Chairman Mao personally met with him and affectionately called him "Ding Customs" (Figs. 3 and 4).

> Zou Zengqiang (Executive Editor of "Shanghai Chronicles: Port Volume"): On May 27, 1949, Shanghai was liberated, and on May 30, the Shanghai Military Administration Council entered the Jianghai Customs. Before that, the control of our commodity inspection, identification, measurement, approval, import and export certification, etc. was in the hands of Western commodity inspection firms. In November 1951, Shanghai established the Commodity Inspection and Quarantine Bureau, which stipulated that all commodity inspections for imports and exports would be managed by the Shanghai Inspection and Quarantine Bureau. In 1952, Shanghai established the Shanghai Border Inspection Station, ending the history of Shanghai having a border without defense.

On May 30, 1949, the East China Military Administration Committee (hereinafter referred to as the Military Administration Council) sent military representatives Xu Xuehan and Jia Zhenzhi to officially take over Jianghai Customs, and at the same time, they respectively took over the Maritime Affairs Office, Junpu Bureau,

Fig. 3 The red flag flying at the Shanghai Customs building

Harbor Quarantine Station, and General Taxation Office. In December 1949, the State Council approved the "Provisional Organizational Regulations of the Customs General Administration of the Central People's Government," and in January and December 1950, it successively issued the "Decision on Tariff Policies and Customs Work" and the "Directive on the Principles of Establishing Customs and Adjusting National Customs Institutions." In accordance with the spirit of the above instructions, the new China Customs underwent reforms in terms of organization, personnel, etc., established a new customs system, and established the basic policies for customs work, stipulating that the new customs tasks are to implement taxation, regulate foreign trade goods, and combat smuggling. Kong Yuan was appointed as the first Director-General of the new China Customs (Figs. 5 and 6).

On February 16, 1950, according to the order of the General Administration of Customs, the Jianghai Customs was renamed as the Shanghai Customs of the People's Republic of China, with jurisdiction over the Wusong, Ningbo, and Wenzhou branch customs and postal support offices. On May 13 of the same year, the State Council of the People's Republic of China appointed Jia Zhenzhi as the first customs commissioner of Shanghai.

In April 1951, the State Council issued the "Interim Customs Law of the People's Republic of China," which provided clear regulations on the organizational structure, tasks and powers of the customs, the supervision of import and export goods, smuggling, and violations. In May 1951, in accordance with the trade protection policy

Fig. 4 Ding Guitang

stipulated in the "Common Program," the State Council also issued regulations such as the "Customs Import and Export Tariff of the People's Republic of China" and other important business regulations.

Following the principle of "complete takeover and gradual transformation," Shanghai Customs systematically reformed the old customs system: abolishing the old customs tax office system and establishing a system of division of labor under the collective leadership of the CPC Party group; clarifying responsibilities and tasks, lifting and transferring non-customs businesses, transferring the port operations of Shanghai, Ningbo, and Wenzhou and the river operations of Nanjing to the Ministry of Communications of the Central People's Government; transferring domestic parcel business inspection to the Shanghai Postal Bureau; discontinuing the collection of the Jinpu donation for imported foreign goods for domestic use; and ceasing the compilation of domestic trade statistics. Shanghai Customs put an end to its humiliating history as a semi-colonial and semi-feudal institution and transformed into a state administrative management agency under the control of the people (Fig. 7).

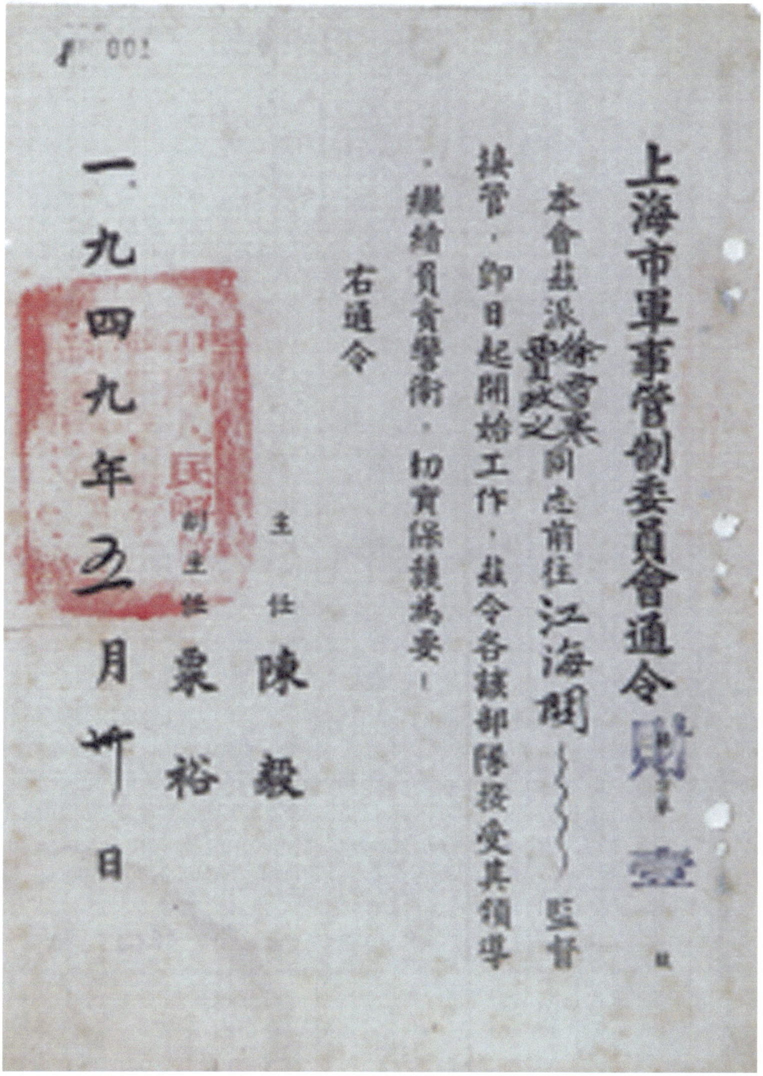
上海市軍事管制委員會通令 財 壹 號

本會茲派徐雪寒 賈振之同志前往江海關監督接管，即日起開始工作，茲令各該部隊接受其領導，繼續負責警衛，切實保護為要！

右通令

主任 陳毅

副主任 粟裕

一九四九年五月卅日

Fig. 5 Order for the Military Administration Council to take over Jianghai Customs

2.2.2 Reclaiming the Authority of Foreign Exchange Management

The management of foreign exchange is crucial for foreign trade. In China, foreign financial institutions and the monopolistic system of national bureaucratic capital banks, known as the "four banks, two bureaus, and one treasury," controlled the economic lifeline of old China. After the establishment of New China, the People's

Fig. 6 Jia Zhenzhi, the first customs commissioner of Shanghai Customs (middle)

Government completely abolished various privileges of imperialist countries in China, including those of foreign banks, and safeguarded China's sovereignty. At the same time, in accordance with the provisions of the "Common Program" adopted by the First Plenary Session of the Chinese People's Political Consultative Conference, which stated that bureaucratic capital should be confiscated and returned to the people, the People's Government took measures to confiscate the financial bureaucratic capital of the Nationalist government and took over the bureaucratic capital banks and insurance companies.

Shanghai is the center of major banks nationwide, where foreign banks and the headquarters of the Nationalist financial bureaucratic capital are mainly concentrated. Therefore, before entering Shanghai, relevant leadership agencies dispatched a group of cadres for training in Danyang, Jiangsu, to improve the policy level of the takeover staff. Shanghai was liberated on May 27, 1949, the Renminbi entered Shanghai on the 28th, and the Shanghai branch of the People's Bank of China was established on the 30th. At the same time, the People's Government began to handle and treat old financial institutions differently based on their capital nature. It took over the state bureaucratic capital banks, reorganized the Bank of China and the Bank of Communications into specialized banks, and relocated their headquarters to Beijing.

Although the People's Government took over the bureaucratic capital banks in Shanghai, foreign banks still had control over Shanghai's foreign exchange business. In order to restrict the foreign exchange operations of foreign banks, the People's Government explicitly stipulated that foreign banks must comply with the laws and

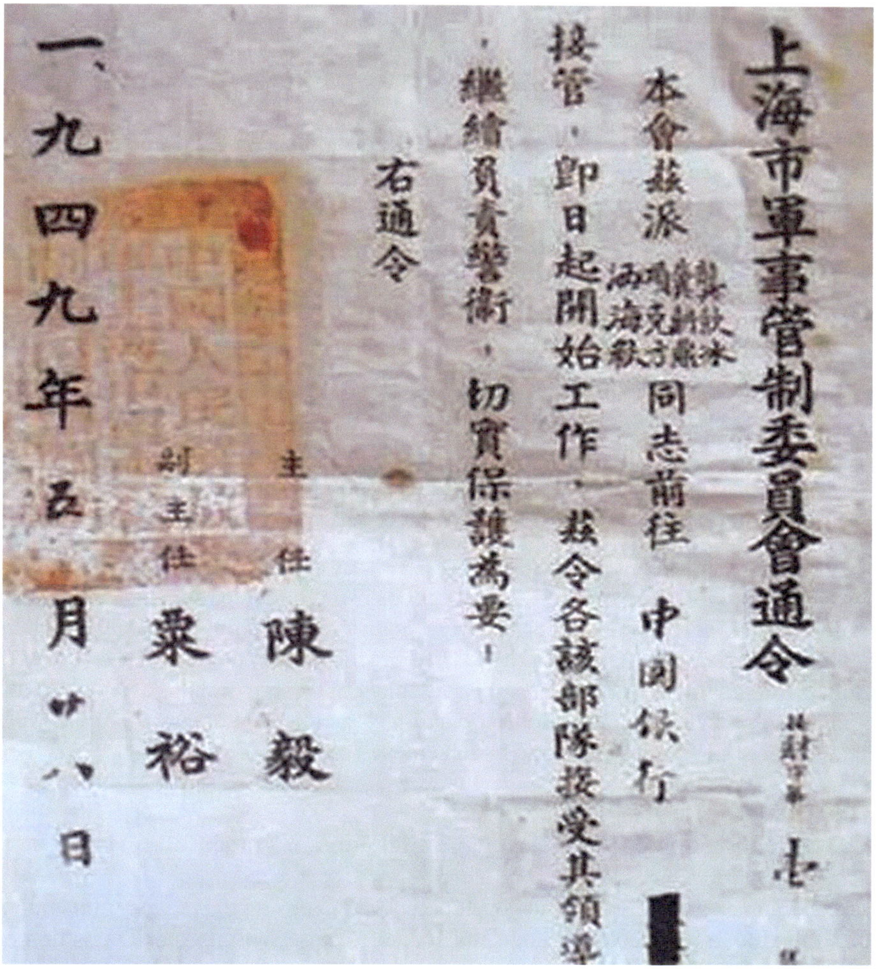
上海市軍事管制委員會通令

本會茲派 [illegible] 同志前往中國銀行 [redacted]
接管，即日起開始工作，茲令各該部隊接受其領導
，繼續負責警衛，切實保護為要！
右通令
主任 陳毅
副主任 粟裕
一九四九年五月廿八日

Fig. 7 Takeover order of the Bank of China issued by the Shanghai Military Administration on May 28, 1949

regulations of the Chinese government. They were allowed to engage in legal operations within the prescribed scope but were prohibited from engaging in unauthorized activities, such as evading funds, diverting foreign exchange, and other speculative illegal activities. The People's Government declared that it would provide legal protection for the legitimate operations and rights of foreign banks (Fig. 8).

At the same time, the People's Government designates reputable foreign banks to act as agents for the Bank of China in buying and selling foreign exchange, as well as handling foreign exchange transactions. These banks are supervised and guided by the Bank of China in their business operations. For example, they issue letters

Fig. 8 50 yuan banknote printed by the Shanghai Banknote Printing Factory in 1949

of credit through foreign banks to import necessary goods and utilize their lending business to support the export of Chinese goods. The Bank of China has established comprehensive agency contracts and representative relationships with HSBC and the Bank of America and their branches. These practices have played a certain role in China's foreign trade and facilitated the settlement of foreign exchange funds, as well as unified the management of domestic and foreign exchange business, reclaiming the autonomy of foreign exchange management.

2.2.3 Confiscation of Bureaucratic Capital Foreign Trade Enterprises

Bureaucratic capital emerged and developed in China during the process of its transformation into a semi-colonial and semi-feudal society. With its special position of holding state power, it monopolized the economic lifeline of old China and ruthlessly exploited the vast laboring people. Confiscating bureaucratic capital and transforming the ownership of bureaucratic capital into socialist public ownership is an important task of China's new democratic revolution (Fig. 9).

Shanghai was the most concentrated and important base of operation for bureaucratic capital in old China. In terms of domestic and foreign trade, bureaucratic capital owned a number of monopolistic trading companies, such as China Import and Export Corporation, China Cotton Corporation, and China Vegetable Oil Corporation. In the financial sector, the head offices or general management offices of bureaucratic capital and financial institutions, such as the central banks, Bank of China, Bank of Communications, China Farmers Bank, Central Trust Bureau, and Postal Savings and Remittance Bureau, which were mainly composed of bureaucratic capital, were all located in Shanghai. Therefore, Shanghai was the central hub of monopolistic finance in old China.

Fig. 9 Workers in the original bureaucratic capital factory counting materials, assisting the People's Government in taking over

After the establishment of New China, in accordance with the economic program of new democracy, the People's Government implemented measures to confiscate bureaucratic capital. By confiscating the state capital formed by the Kuomintang government and the private capital accumulated by the bureaucracy, along with the establishment of public-owned economy in the original base areas, a large-scale socialist state-owned economy was rapidly established.

After the liberation of Shanghai, the People's Government confiscated the Central Trust Bureau, China Silk Company, China Tea Company, China Vegetable Oil Factory, China Bristles Company, China Petroleum Company, Defu Cleaning Agency, Liwei Automobile Company, Yangzi Construction Company, and Fuzhong Company, among other bureaucratic capital, and established state-owned foreign trade enterprises on this basis. On June 13, 1949, Shanghai Trade Corporation was established, followed by the establishment of specialized companies in grain, flower yarn, coal industry, chemical raw materials, daily necessities, hardware equipment, medicine, local products, oil and fats, tea, fur, and silk, as well as China Import and Export Corporation and other domestic and foreign trade enterprises.

In order to meet the needs of unified dispatch of materials nationwide, the East China Trade Department reorganized all state-owned trade specialized companies in Shanghai into a national headquarters located in the East China region, unifying state-owned trade and dispatching materials. The East China Foreign Trade Corporation, with 11 subsidiary companies, was mainly composed of China Silk Company, China Tea Company, China Vegetable Oil Company, China Pig Bristles Company, China Fur Company, and others. This was the first generation of state-owned foreign trade enterprises in New China, providing favorable conditions for enhancing Shanghai's economic strength.

After the establishment of the Ministry of Foreign Trade by the central government in 1952, Shanghai's state-owned foreign trade enterprises were reorganized into six divisions: China Silk, Tea, Oil and Fats, Livestock Products, Local Products, and China Import. At the same time, banks, insurance companies, and shipping companies were also established as state-owned enterprises and institutions to assist foreign trade, thereby placing foreign exchange, insurance, shipping, customs clearance, warehouses, docks, and notary offices related to Shanghai's import and export under the control of the People's Government.

Private businesses engaged in import and export activities have always played an important role in Shanghai's foreign trade, and their activities are closely related to the political environment. As early as 1947, when the Kuomintang government strengthened import controls, private businesses found it difficult to conduct business and faced a tense and turbulent situation in Shanghai. Meanwhile, Hong Kong had no trade restrictions on imports and exports, making it easier to obtain industrial raw materials and promote finished products in Southeast Asia and overseas markets. Therefore, some larger private business entities transferred funds to Hong Kong, such as Wei Da Hua Hang and Nanyang Enterprise Company, by hedging foreign exchange in Hong Kong or establishing overseas branches. In 1948, as the Kuomintang government was about to collapse, they tried to transfer their funds as much as possible. Some private business entities collaborated with Hong Kong importers and exporters or directly established branches, such as Hong Fan Hang, which mainly exported feather and pig bristle, Ke Da Hang, which imported cocoa and coffee, Xin Hua Hang, which imported small commodities and cosmetics, and Da Mao Enterprise Company, which exported gauze. Many smaller private businesses that lacked the conditions to relocate to Hong Kong adopted a wait-and-see attitude and their foreign trade business generally declined. Of course, most private businesses chose to stay in Shanghai and wait for opportunities. In April 1949, the National Government's Import and Export Management Committee moved from Shanghai to Guangzhou, and Shanghai ceased issuing foreign exchange and import and export licenses. Shanghai's foreign trade came to a complete halt.

Protecting national industry and commerce is one of the three major economic principles of the New Democratic Revolution. In order to revive the Shanghai economy and promote foreign trade, the Shanghai People's Government implemented a policy of "utilization, restriction, and transformation" towards private businesses engaged in foreign trade, in accordance with the requirements of the New Democratic Revolution's economic principles. The government actively utilized the advantages of private businesses, such as their familiarity with market rules and existing business channels with foreign countries, and leveraged their positive role in foreign trade.

In the early days of the founding of New China, especially in trade with capitalist countries, private merchants played a special role. In the total trade volume with capitalist countries, the proportion of private merchants was 46.7%, 44.3%, and 37.5% respectively in the three years from 1950 to 1952, almost accounting for half of Shanghai's trade volume with capitalist countries, and always occupying an important position. It had a positive effect on breaking Western economic blockade and promoting urban and rural economy.

At the same time, the Shanghai People's Government also carried out cleaning and rectification of private and foreign-funded merchants engaged in import and export. In June 1949, the government stipulated in the "Interim Measures for the Management of Foreign Trade in the East China Region" and the "Registration Measures for Import and Export Traders" that merchants engaged in import and export must apply for approval from relevant institutions, obtain licenses, register with the industrial and commercial authorities, and then engage in import and export business. By the end of July, 1624 private foreign trade merchants had registered and obtained licenses. After qualification review, many private merchants were eliminated. In 1950, there were 1124 private import and export merchants in Shanghai, with 13,800 employees, accounting for 24.4% and 28.6% of the national total, respectively.

In 1952, the "Three Antis" and "Five Antis" movements were launched nationwide, and more than half of Shanghai's private import and export businesses were classified as seriously illegal or semi-illegal. The government adopted a policy of gradual replacement and restriction to transform them. After the "Three Antis" and "Five Antis" movements, there were only 785 private foreign trade merchants in Shanghai, with only 10,600 employees. The foreign trade volume of private merchants also continued to decline, from 359 million US dollars in 1950 to 299 million US dollars in 1951, and only 140 million US dollars in 1952, with the proportion dropping from 31.6% to 7.2%.

In order to strengthen the management of private businesses, under the leadership of the government, the Shanghai International Trade Industry Association for Import and Export Private Businesses was established in May 1951. It had 1070 members and merged with seven industry associations including the import and export industry, vegetable oil industry, sausage casing industry, rawhide industry, gauze industry, pig bristle industry, fur and oil bone industry, straw hat industry, and tea industry. Until the public–private partnership, this association became an important organization for the government to unite and manage Shanghai's import and export private businesses.

With the completion of the basic socialist transformation, the industry association lost its value and finally ended its historical mission in 1958.

2.2.4 Governing Foreign Import and Export Enterprises

Destroying imperialist economic control over China has always been a fundamental goal of China's modern democratic revolution. The Communist Party of China, early on in its establishment, proposed in the "Chinese Communist Party's Views on the Current Situation" to "correct the treaty tariffs, abolish various extraterritorial rights of the foreign powers in China, repay railway loans, and completely regain control." In the early 1930s, the party's documents repeatedly emphasized "not recognizing any political or economic privileges of imperialism in China" and that "the Soviet government will nationalize all economic lifelines controlled by imperialism." In order to ensure the supply of goods, the Central Committee of the Communist Party of China made the decision to allow foreign businesses to continue operating in China.

On the eve of the founding of the People's Republic of China, on February 16, 1949, the Central Committee of the Communist Party of China issued the "Decision on Foreign Trade," which clearly stated: "In order to conduct foreign trade, it should be allowed for those foreign commercial agencies who are willing to trade with the new China and willing to abide by the laws and regulations of the people's government to send representatives or designate agents to negotiate with us, and allow these representatives to establish offices at designated locations."

Prior to the establishment of the People's Republic of China, many foreign firms in Shanghai experienced a sharp decline or withdrew their investments, and many Chinese businessmen relocated to Hong Kong. According to statistics, in June 1949, there were still 376 foreign firms in Shanghai, which was half the number in 1938 and one-third less than in 1946. In 1950, there were 282 firms, 108 in June 1951, 90 by the end of 1952, 55 in 1953, 34 by the end of 1954, and only 22 in 1955. The remaining foreign firms in Shanghai were mostly British, with others being American, French, Soviet, German, and other nationalities.

The outbreak of the Korean War in 1950 marked an important turning point for foreign businesses in China. On December 16, 1950, the US State Department announced the freezing of Chinese assets in the United States. On December 28, the Chinese Government Council issued the corresponding order to freeze American public and private deposits, stating that "all property of the US government and US enterprises within the territory of the People's Republic of China shall be immediately controlled and inspected by the local people's government" and "all American public and private deposits in all banks within the territory of the People's Republic of China shall be frozen immediately."

On May 15, 1951, the Central Committee of the Communist Party of China issued the "Instructions on Dealing with American Assets in China," which outlined the basic principles for handling American enterprises in China. These principles stated that "those that have a significant impact on China's sovereignty and national economy and people's livelihood shall be expropriated; those with minor relevance or inconvenient to be expropriated shall be placed under trusteeship; those deemed necessary by the government may be requisitioned; general enterprises shall be subject to strengthened control to encourage self-cleanup and settlement... For a few American enterprises that do not pose major political or economic obstacles, conscious efforts can be made to retain some in Shanghai, Tianjin, and Guangzhou."

The Shanghai Municipal People's Government followed the policies and guidelines of the Government Council and, based on different circumstances, carried out rectification and cleanup of foreign firms in various ways, including military control, expropriation, trusteeship, transfer, and acquisition. The Shanghai Municipal People's Government militarily controlled American-owned companies such as Shanghai Electric Power Company and Shanghai Telephone Company. As a result, American businesses in China were essentially brought to an end.

After the United States openly seized my assets in the UK, we successively requisitioned British-owned companies in China, such as Shanghai Electric Power Limited, Shanghai Water Supply Limited, and Shanghai Gas Limited, from 1951 to 1952. From August 1951 to 1953, a number of foreign firms were transferred to relevant institutions in Shanghai. By early 1956, there were still 22 remaining. A group of long-established British enterprises began to propose transfers, and foreign firms that had developed in Shanghai after its opening gradually disappeared. Companies such as Jardine Matheson, Swire, and Hsin Chong continued to maintain business contacts with relevant departments in Shanghai through representatives or small-scale institutions after the transfer.

2.3 *Transformation and Expansion of Trade Partners*

2.3.1 Transformation of Trade Partners

After 1949, the world was divided into two major camps: one led by the Soviet Union, the socialist camp, and the other represented by the United States and Britain, the imperialist camp. These two camps were in opposition to each other.

In January 1950, China and the Soviet Union officially signed the Sino-Soviet Treaty of Friendship, and China-US relations reached a freezing point.

Xiong Yuezhi (Researcher at Shanghai Academy of Social Sciences, Distinguished Professor at Fudan University): Because Shanghai used to have frequent and deep connections with the European and American systems, after the two major camps became opposed, Shanghai's connections with Europe and America were cut off.

Ge Tao (Researcher at the Institute of History, Shanghai Academy of Social Sciences): The Korean War broke out in 1950, and our Chinese People's Volunteer Army went to Korea to participate in the War to Resist U.S. Aggression and Aid Korea. Western countries led by the United States imposed sanctions on our country in the name of the United Nations. After the sanctions, the pattern of trade in Shanghai, which had relied on overseas markets since modern times, came to an end.

In the early days of the founding of New China, capitalist countries led by the United States imposed an economic blockade on our country, especially after the Korean War, when the United States and other countries implemented a comprehensive economic blockade and froze our foreign exchange. Faced with a harsh international environment, our country actively responded, and one important manifestation of this was the transformation of our main trading partners. The main trading partners shifted from capitalist countries to socialist countries such as the Soviet Union and new democratic countries. There were also corresponding changes in Shanghai, which is China's main trading port.

Zou Zengqiang (Executive Editor of "Shanghai Chronicles: Port Volume"): Despite the embargo imposed by Western powers such as the United States, Shanghai's foreign trade was still developing, including trade with socialist countries such as the former Soviet Union and Eastern Europe, as well as Southeast Asia and Japan.

In 1950, the proportion of socialist countries in China's foreign trade volume was only 32.4%, which increased to 52.9% in 1951 and reached 72% in 1952. It remained above 70% until the late 1950s. Among these countries, the Soviet Union was of utmost importance. In 1950, the Soviet Union accounted for 29.8% of China's foreign trade volume, which increased to 41.4% in 1951 and further rose to 54.8% in 1952.

From 1950 to 1955, the Soviet Union provided China with 11 loans to purchase military supplies for the Korean War and domestic construction equipment. Starting from 1952, China imported a large amount of equipment and technology from the Soviet Union and Eastern European countries, mainly for the construction of the 156 key projects aided by the Soviet Union (Fig. 10).

Chao Gangling (Professor at Shanghai University of Finance and Economics, Vice President of Shanghai Commercial Economics Society): In the early 1950s, our main direction of imports was the Soviet Union because we had a Sino-Soviet friendship and received technical assistance from them, so many goods came from there.

Fang Huaijin (Central Committee Member of the China Democratic Construction Association, Standing Committee Member of the Shanghai Municipal Political Consultative Conference, Vice President of Shanghai Port Group): I remember when I was young, what imported goods could we taste? One was Mongolian sugar, produced by the Mongolian People's Republic, with a hint of milk flavor, not milk candy, but fruit candy. There was also Albanian wine, which we children wouldn't drink, cigarettes, and Iraqi honey dates. There were also some Korean food products, which were the imported goods we could see at that time and were related to our daily life.

Chen Zilei (Professor at Shanghai University of International Business and Economics, Vice President of the National Japan Economic Society, Vice President of the Shanghai International Trade Society, Deputy Secretary-General of the Shanghai Economic Society): Due to a lot of trade with the Soviet Union being border trade, mainly completed through the north, Shanghai used to be a port mainly responsible for maritime transportation and trade with Europe and some countries in Southeast Asia.

Poland was one of the first countries to recognize and establish diplomatic relations with New China. At the beginning of the establishment of diplomatic relations, the Polish government proposed the idea of jointly operating a shipping company with the

Fig. 10 Signing scene of the Sino-Polish Government Agreement

Chinese government. After nearly a year of consultations and negotiations, on June 15, 1951, the Sino-Polish Shipping Corporation was established. At the beginning of its establishment, Chairman Mao Zedong personally instructed to "do it well", Premier Zhou Enlai determined the company's name, and Vice Premier Chen Yun personally issued the company's business license.

Zhang Xiuli (Researcher at the Institute of History, Shanghai Academy of Social Sciences): At that time, because the Polish government was relatively friendly to China, the Chinese government and the Polish government jointly signed an equity equivalence, that is, each party held 50%, creating two Sino-foreign joint venture shipping companies.

Zhu Dezhang (General Manager of China-Poland Shipping Company): At that time, Poland was a strong maritime nation, with much stronger talent and technology in shipping compared to us. Our shipping conditions were relatively poor. In this situation, after cooperating with Poland, we created a maritime railway transportation line. It enabled us to timely transport some strategic materials urgently needed by our country and equipment for the construction of New China back.

Wu Qiyong, 88 years old, has been an old employee of China-Poland Shipping Company. From being an intern on the "Plaski" ship in 1957 to becoming the captain of the "Changxing" ship, most of his life has been connected with China-Poland Shipping Company.

Wu Qiyong (Former Captain of China-Poland Shipping Company): At that time, I was a crew member on the ship. Initially, our headquarters had Polish names, no Chinese names.

> The engine room was all Polish people, and we didn't understand anything. If we wanted to communicate with the people in the engine room, we had to go through someone who understood Polish to deal with them.

Due to economic blockade by Western countries, China-Poland Shipping Company faced extremely difficult development at its inception. In order to sail between China and Europe, all the company's documents were "disguised".

> Zhu Dezhang (General Manager of China-Poland Shipping Company): The international environment at that time exerted tremendous pressure and resistance on us. If our ships flew the five-star red flag, we definitely couldn't go out or come in. So at that time, we conducted foreign operations under the name of the Polish Ocean Shipping Company. The ships all flew the Polish flag.
>
> Wu Qiyong (Former Captain of China-Poland Shipping Company): At that time, there was a ship called "Bo 27" that was captured by Taiwan. Later, when we sent Chinese crew members, we were particularly careful about this matter because when they were captured, the crew members were dealt with by Taiwan.
>
> Zhu Dezhang (General Manager of China-Poland Shipping Co., Ltd.): Three Chinese crew members sacrificed their lives and were later recognized as martyrs. At that time, we also paid the price of life to ensure the smooth operation of the maritime railway line and to guarantee the transportation of some economic materials for our country.

China-Poland Company started with four old ships and operated the Asia-Europe liner transportation business, opening up the first transcontinental shipping route in New China. The much-needed construction materials and resources were continuously transported back to China through China-Poland vessels, and exported goods were also transported in large quantities to various parts of the world, strengthening China's connection with the world. In just over a year since its establishment, China-Poland Company transported equipment for 52 factories domestically and also carried scarce materials such as kerosene and rubber, making significant contributions to the early economic development of the country. The establishment, operation, and development of China-Poland Company have received the caring support of successive party and state leaders.

China-Poland Company was originally planned to operate in cooperation for 12 years. Due to pleasant cooperation and remarkable benefits, the two sides signed three contracts to extend the period. In 1976, China and Poland decided to implement indefinite joint venture.

Since the twenty-first century, with changes in the company's development strategy and fleet structure, as well as the establishment of globalized routes, China-Poland Company has become a leading enterprise in the field of global transportation of heavy equipment goods, and the role of the Chinese side has become increasingly prominent (Fig. 11).

Today, with the implementation of the national "Belt and Road" strategy, China-Poland Shipping Co., Ltd. has ushered in new development opportunities. Actively integrating into the process of "Belt and Road" construction, it adds momentum to the development of shipping economy.

Fig. 11 China-Poland Company's "Pacific" ship in operation

2.3.2 Expanding Trade with Southeast Asian Countries

In 1950, the Chinese government established bilateral trade relations with countries such as India, Myanmar, Pakistan, and Indonesia, and conducted civilian trade exchanges with some countries in Asia and Africa. In 1952, China took advantage of the opportunity created by the US embargo, which caused a sharp drop in rubber prices in Ceylon (Sri Lanka) and a domestic food shortage. On the basis of equality, mutual benefit, and fairness, China signed a five-year trade agreement with Ceylon for rice and rubber, achieving an important breakthrough in breaking the blockade. The China-Ceylon agreement stipulated a very large volume of trade, with China providing 270,000 tons of rice to Ceylon every year, equivalent to 60%-70% of Ceylon's annual rice imports, and importing 50%-60% of Ceylon's rubber production, which amounted to 50,000 tons per year. The central government decided that Shanghai would be responsible for implementing the China-Ceylon agreement, and thus Shanghai began its trade with Southeast Asia.

2.3.3 Expanding Trade Channels with Capitalist Countries

After the founding of New China, most Western countries followed the United States in imposing a blockade and embargo on China. Only Sweden, Denmark, Switzerland, and Finland established diplomatic and trade relations with China in 1950. In 1952, China signed a government-to-government trade agreement with Finland. In order to break the US embargo policy, China used various opportunities and channels to promote trade exchanges with Western countries, especially civilian trade relations.

In April 1952, during the International Economic Conference held in Moscow, the Chinese delegation had extensive contacts with business representatives from more than 40 countries in attendance. Trade agreements worth 200 million US dollars were signed with business representatives from 11 countries including the United Kingdom, West Germany, and Japan, dealing a blow to the US embargo policy. In the same year, China and Japan signed their first civilian trade agreement in June.

Subsequently, trade activities between China and Japan continued to thrive. In 1953 and 1955, China and Japan signed the second and third agreements on private trade successively. In 1953, Japan began to relax its embargo on China. In May 1957, the United Kingdom announced the relaxation of its embargo on China. Subsequently, countries such as France, West Germany, Italy, Belgium, and the Netherlands also gradually relaxed their embargoes, and trade activities between Shanghai and capitalist countries became increasingly active.

3 Forge Ahead in Exploration

3.1 Planned Management

In September 1956, the Communist Party of China held the Eighth National Congress, which formulated the basic tasks of commercial work during the second five-year plan period: continue to strengthen the acquisition and supply of industrial and agricultural products, expand commodity circulation, improve purchase and sale relations, continue to implement unified purchase and sale of major daily necessities; at the same time, selectively purchase certain industrial products and plan the organization of some free markets, continue to stabilize prices, further develop commercial networks, and facilitate the purchase and sale of goods by the masses. Starting from 1958, China began its second five-year plan, and the Party Central Committee put forward the general guideline of "working with great enthusiasm, striving to surpass others, and building socialism in a faster, better, and more economical way." Shanghai's trade advanced through continuous exploration.

With the basic completion of the socialist transformation of industry and commerce, China entered an era of highly centralized planned economy with public ownership as the mainstay. Correspondingly, foreign trade also adopted a highly centralized national monopoly system (Fig. 12).

> Chen Zilei (Professor at Shanghai University of International Business and Economics, Vice President of the National Association of Japanese Economy, Vice President of the Shanghai International Trade Association, Deputy Secretary-General of the Shanghai Economic Association): Under the planned economic system, we say that foreign trade is arranged by the state plan, which means that the production, supply, and sales are all operated by specialized import and export companies. After purchasing the products from the enterprises, they are

Fig. 12 In the spring of 1957, the first Canton Fair opened at the China-Soviet Friendship Building in Guangzhou

exported through trade. Therefore, it is all planned and arranged, so to some extent, the characteristics of a commodity economy are not very prominent.

Chao Gangling (Professor at the School of Business, Shanghai University of Finance and Economics, and Vice President of the Shanghai Commercial Economy Society): Under the planned economy, foreign trade companies decided what could be imported and what could not be imported. As a result, the imported goods at that time were very limited, mainly to meet the domestic demand for scarce raw materials or some foreign services.

In the early days of the founding of New China, the first five-year plan was implemented, and a large amount of construction materials needed to be imported from foreign countries, but it was difficult to obtain the required foreign exchange. In 1956, Yan Yijun, the special envoy of the Ministry of Foreign Trade stationed in Guangzhou, saw that the Guangdong foreign trade system had successfully held several small-scale material export exchange meetings, which gave him a bold idea: since the small-scale exchange meetings were going well, why not hold a larger one? (Fig. 13).

Yan Yijun (Former Secretary-General of the Canton Fair): After I came up with this idea, I sent a telegram to the Ministry of Foreign Trade, proposing to hold a China Export Commodities Fair. The Ministry of Foreign Trade obtained the approval of Premier Zhou and agreed.

In September 1956, the State Council approved the China Export Commodities Fair to be hosted by the China Council for the Promotion of International Trade, with

Fig. 13 Yan Yijun, the initiator of the Canton Fair, served as the Secretary-General of the 1st to 19th Canton Fairs

the venue set in Guangzhou. Subsequently, Yan Yijun suggested that the Ministry of Foreign Trade hold an export commodity fair in Guangzhou every year. Since then, the Canton Fair has stepped onto the world trade stage.

The Canton Fair is known as the "barometer" and "vane" of China's foreign trade. It has been held twice a year, without interruption, since 1957. The successful holding of the Canton Fair has provided the country with much-needed foreign exchange and supported China's foreign trade exports. It is not only a bridge for trade, but also a bond for enhancing friendship between China and people from all over the world. Premier Zhou Enlai personally guided the work of the Canton Fair on eight occasions (Fig. 14).

> Sun Yuanxin (Professor at Shanghai University of Finance and Economics): Two sessions are held each year, one in spring and one in autumn. The first Canton Fair had participants from 19 countries, mainly from Singapore, Hong Kong, and some other countries, totaling 19 countries. The transaction volume of the first Canton Fair was 80 million US dollars, which was relatively small.

> Chen Zilei (Professor at Shanghai University of International Business and Economics, Vice President of the National Association for Japanese Economics, Vice President of the Shanghai International Trade Association, Deputy Secretary-General of the Shanghai Economic Association): At that time, the products displayed domestically mainly consisted of several categories. One category was traditional handicrafts, another category was local specialty products, agricultural and sideline products, and so on. The only relatively large machinery was the Liberation brand trucks, so there were not many products that could be displayed. The focus was mainly on traditional and characteristic handicrafts and some local specialty products.

> Shi Liangping (Former Vice President of Shanghai Customs College, current Counselor of the Shanghai Municipal People's Government): For us Chinese people, the Canton Fair at that time indeed opened a window for China as a whole. It let us know what foreigners needed. By allowing some foreign products to enter, we realized that they would return these products to us at a higher price. But we also accepted it because we couldn't produce these things ourselves and they were not as good as what they made.

Fig. 14 In autumn 1957, business people negotiating the Liberation Automobile project at the second Canton Fair

During the planned economy era, under the overall leadership of the central government's "national chess game," the focus of China's foreign trade gradually shifted to Guangzhou, which is closer to Hong Kong, while Shanghai was designated as a "old industrial base" strategically. Under this strategic positioning, Shanghai transformed from a consumer city to a production city. Various high-quality industrial products were transported from here to the whole country.

Shanghai at that time, you couldn't do trade, so Hong Kong played a very important role. Because Guangzhou is closer to Hong Kong, it had many conveniences in this aspect, so it was reasonable to have export trade in Guangzhou at that time. And what was Shanghai mainly doing at that time? Shanghai was mainly a manufacturing base for Shanghai brand watches, sewing machines, bicycles, televisions, milk candies, malted milk, and beer.

Shanghai's heavy and light industrial products were renowned throughout the country. The whole country supported Shanghai's construction, mainly providing Shanghai with raw materials and agricultural products such as grain, cotton, and coal. At this time, a very important material exchange and circulation relationship was formed between Shanghai and the mainland, but this was not trade.

Shanghai's geographical location determines that it is definitely a trading center, but all its trading activities are actually restricted by planned economy, prices, and commodity allocation. In terms of foreign trade, Shanghai is also a port for imports and exports, so many goods still pass through Shanghai.

Yu Mingyang (Professor at Shanghai Jiao Tong University): At that time, in Shanghai, even if you wanted to do trade, you couldn't do it, so Hong Kong played a very important role. Because Guangzhou was closer to Hong Kong, it had many conveniences in this regard, so it was reasonable to place export transactions in Guangzhou at that time. And what was the main focus of Shanghai at that time? Shanghai brand watches, sewing machines, bicycles, televisions, milk candies, malt extract, and beer are mainly manufacturing bases.

Ge Tao (Researcher at the Institute of History, Shanghai Academy of Social Sciences): Shanghai's light and heavy industrial products are renowned throughout the country, and the whole country supports Shanghai's construction. The main support for Shanghai's construction comes from raw materials and agricultural products, such as grain, cotton, coal, etc. At this time, there was a very important material exchange and circulation relationship between Shanghai and the mainland, but this was not trade.

Wang Zhan (former Secretary and Director of the Party Group of the Development Research Center of the Shanghai Municipal People's Government): Shanghai's geographical location determines that it must be a trade center, but all its trade activities are actually restricted by planned economy, prices, and commodity allocation. In terms of foreign trade, Shanghai is also an import and export port, so many goods are still imported and exported through Shanghai.

3.2 Adjustment and Development

In 1958, China began its second five-year plan, and the Party Central Committee put forward the overall guideline of "encouraging enthusiasm, striving for the forefront, and building socialism with more speed and efficiency." After nearly 10 years of development in New China, Shanghai's foreign trade made significant progress, with the import and export volume reaching 695 million US dollars in 1958, including 629 million US dollars in exports, an increase of 51.6% compared to the previous year. The number of countries and regions to which exports were made reached an unprecedented 91. However, the following year, all indicators declined, and by 1962, exports fell to 553 million US dollars, only 75% of the export volume in 1959. From 1961 to 1963, the export volume remained below 600 million US dollars. With the improvement of the macro economy, Shanghai's foreign trade was able to recover, and the average annual growth rate of Shanghai's export trade from 1963 to 1966 reached 12.08%. In 1965, the export volume reached 757 million US dollars. From 1958 to 1965, Shanghai's import and export accounted for about 20% of the national total, and exports accounted for over 30%.

Shanghai's foreign trade work adhered to the principle of "economy serving politics and trade coordinating with diplomacy." From 1958 to 1965, Shanghai undertook 35 projects of economic cooperation and assistance with countries such as Vietnam, North Korea, Albania, Cuba, Mongolia, and Poland. In 1957, Shanghai's exports to socialist countries reached 315 million US dollars, accounting for 69.7% of Shanghai's total exports. In the 1960s, due to the deterioration of Sino-Soviet relations, Shanghai's exports to the Soviet Union rapidly declined from 351 million US dollars in 1959 to 50.96 million US dollars in 1965.

In response to the new changes, Shanghai strengthened its economic and trade relations with developing countries, Western Europe, and Canada. Starting from 1964, exports to capitalist countries exceeded those to socialist countries. The export trade to capitalist countries increased from 266 million US dollars in 1958 to 568 million US dollars in 1965. The proportion increased from 33.5% in 1958 to 68.1% in 1965. The export destinations to Western developed countries were Western Europe, Japan, and Australia in order. This was the second shift in the focus of Shanghai's foreign trade since its opening, from socialist countries such as the Soviet Union to Western capitalist countries.

In terms of the export product structure of capitalist countries, in 1958, industrial and mining products accounted for 11.8%, agricultural and sideline products accounted for 38.3%, and processed agricultural and sideline products accounted for 49.9%. By 1965, industrial and mining products had increased to 28.7%, agricultural and sideline products accounted for 25.3%, and processed agricultural and sideline products accounted for 46%. Overall, there have been significant changes in the structure of exported goods. During the "Great Leap Forward" period, the proportion of industrial products in exported goods grew rapidly, with more than half of the export products being industrial products in 1958, reaching 75.8% in 1960. From 1961 to 1965, there were changes in the structure of exported industrial products, with a decrease in the export of light textile products made from agricultural and sideline products and an increase in the export of heavy industrial products. This reflected the serious difficulties faced by agricultural production at that time and the improvement in industrial level. In terms of imported goods structure, the main imports were production materials such as steel, machine tools, trucks, and fertilizers. Due to the decrease in agricultural production, the import of grain and oil and other agricultural and sideline products increased during this period. From 1960 to 1965, the import of grain and oil ranged from 3.66 million US dollars to 5.5 million US dollars, an increase of more than ten times compared to the import of grain and oil of 300,000 US dollars in 1957.

In the early 1960s, the Shanghai Municipal Government decided, with the approval of the Ministry of Foreign Economic Relations and Trade, to use self-raised foreign exchange funds to import raw materials and process them into finished or semi-finished products for export, using the earned foreign exchange in a rolling manner. For example, imported cotton, woolen yarn, rayon, rubber, pulp, gold, silver, and gemstones were processed into cotton cloth, knitted cotton products, clothing, woolen fabrics, paper, tires, and handicrafts for export, not only earning foreign exchange through exports but also driving local industries.

3.3 *Unified External Relations*

Following the basic principle of "unified external relations" of the country, in the process of strengthening trade contacts with the mainland, the Shanghai Foreign Trade Bureau established offices in Jiangsu, Zhejiang, Anhui, Sichuan, Jiangxi, and other provinces to organize domestic sources of goods. In order to adapt to foreign aid work, in August 1961, the Shanghai Planning Commission established the Foreign Aid Office, which was reorganized into the Shanghai Foreign Economic Liaison Bureau and the Shanghai Branch of China Complete Equipment Export Corporation in 1965, implementing "one team, two brands" under the dual leadership of the Ministry of Foreign Trade and the Shanghai Municipal Government.

The high targets and exaggerated style during the Great Leap Forward naturally also affected the foreign trade industry. The proposed "big import, big export" policy led to the blind expansion of imports and exports beyond national capabilities. In order to achieve "big export", Even the exaggerated situation of "pointing to mountains to buy mines, pointing to rivers to buy fish" has emerged. In order to achieve "great progress," even overseas "warehouses are being cleared out" to purchase inferior goods that are stockpiled abroad. Shanghai has also put forward unrealistic targets, requiring a 20% increase in exports to the Soviet Union and Eastern European countries, and an 80% increase in exports to capitalist countries. The signed export contracts greatly exceed domestic production capacity, making it difficult to fulfill them. All of these have caused serious damage to foreign trade.

4 The Ups and Downs of Foreign Trade

4.1 Domestic Turmoil and Stagnation in Foreign Trade

During the "Cultural Revolution" that lasted for 10 years starting in 1966, international trade in the world was developing rapidly, and the Asian "Four Little Dragons" with their outward-oriented economies took advantage of this trend to rise. However, due to internal turmoil, China's economy was pushed to the brink of collapse, and its trade development suffered significant setbacks. During the ten years of the "Cultural Revolution," the annual average growth of Shanghai's export trade was 8.5%, far below the world's average annual growth of 17.3% in export trade. Shanghai's foreign trade and economic development faced difficulties and twists and turns under these specific historical conditions (Table 1).

4.1.1 Suffering from Impacts on Foreign Trade

In May 1966, the Cultural Revolution spread nationwide. The "Gang of Four" coveted the power of foreign trade and actively undermined the enthusiasm for foreign economic and trade activities with unfounded accusations. For example, they described flexible and proactive trade methods as "harming the country's rights and dignity." They banned the export of goods with traditional Chinese trademarks such as "Dragon Wind" and labeled them as "retro" and "old-fashioned." They criticized the import of small mechanical equipment and other goods as "worshipping foreign

Table 1 Total value of imports and exports of Shanghai's foreign trade (Unit: 100 million U.S. dollars)

Year	Total value of import and export goods in foreign trade		
	Total	import	Exit
1966	9.12	0.38	8.74
1967	8.89	0.47	8.42
1968	8.83	0.34	8.49
1969	8.92	0.16	8.76
1970	9.13	0.46	8.67
1971	10.39	0.58	9.81
1972	13.93	0.63	13.30
1973	23.96	0.80	23.16
1974	25.37	0.98	24.39
1975	23.28	1.08	22.20
1976	21.03	1.25	19.78

Data source "Historical Statistical Data on Shanghai's National Economy and Social Development: 1949–2000, Trade and Foreign Economic Volume", page 213

things." The foreign trade policies, principles, and achievements of our country since the founding of the People's Republic of China were strongly resisted and completely denied.

In the early stages of the Cultural Revolution, Shanghai's foreign trade suffered severe disruptions and impacts. The export trade remained at around 900 million US dollars, while the import trade was approximately 40 million US dollars. In 1969, the import volume was only 16 million US dollars, the lowest point in import trade since the founding of the People's Republic of China. Overall, from 1966 to 1970, Shanghai's foreign trade development was basically stagnant.

4.1.2 The Struggle Against Interference and Destruction of Foreign Trade

In the early stages of the "Cultural Revolution," when the "Gang of Four" interfered with and disrupted the foreign economic and trade front, Premier Zhou Enlai and Comrade Deng Xiaoping fought back with determination, making every effort to promote the development of foreign trade. For example, some people opposed the export of jewelry and other handicrafts. In response to this issue, Premier Zhou clearly stated at the Spring Canton Fair in 1967, "Many foreigners are willing to pay a high price to buy these things and appreciate them. What's wrong with us exporting these things to earn foreign exchange for the country?!" In addition, Premier Zhou repeatedly emphasized the importance and necessity of developing foreign trade. In October 1971, during a speech to representatives of national professional conferences on agriculture, commerce, foreign trade, and other fields, he pointed out, "We criticize relying on foreign exchange, but it doesn't mean we don't want foreign exchange; we mainly rely on the domestic market, but it doesn't mean we don't want foreign markets. Although we are developing our own machinery, the quantity and variety are not enough, and we still need imports. We also need to support our anti-imperialist comrades. From a political perspective, foreign trade also needs to develop."

In August 1975, when discussing the "Several Issues on Accelerating Industrial Development" drafted by the State Planning Commission, Comrade Deng Xiaoping also reiterated the necessity of expanding foreign trade. He pointed out, "If we want to import, we must export more things." "Traditional export products such as arts and crafts should be increased by all means." "In short, we need to export more things, bring back advanced and sophisticated technology and equipment, accelerate industrial technological transformation, and improve labor productivity" (Fig. 15).

Premier Zhou and Comrade Deng Xiaoping's fight against the disruptive actions of the "Gang of Four" in foreign trade played a great inspiring role for cadres and workers in the national economic and trade front. The vast number of cadres and masses in Shanghai's foreign trade front, with a patriotic heart, fully exerted their subjective initiative, and consciously made efforts to carry out foreign economic and trade activities, contributing their own strength to the development of Shanghai's economy and trade.

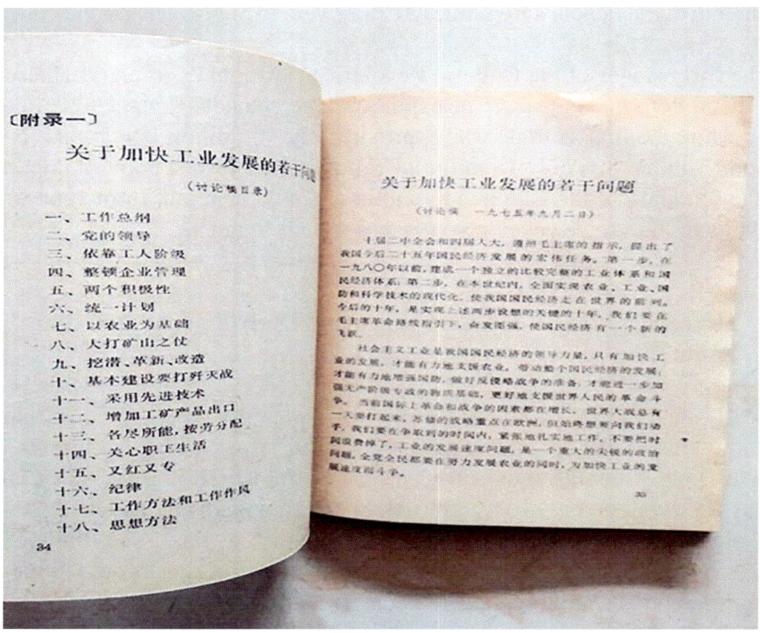
〔附录一〕

关于加快工业发展的若干问

一、工作总纲
二、党的领导
三、依靠工人阶级
四、整顿企业管理
五、两个积极性
六、统一计划
七、以农业为基础
八、大打矿山之仗
九、挖潜、革新、改造
十、基本建设要打歼灭战
十一、采用先进技术
十二、增加工矿产品出口
十三、各尽所能，按劳分配
十四、关心职工生活
十五、又红又专
十六、纪律
十七、工作方法和工作作风
十八、思想方法

34

关于加快工业发展的若干问题

（讨论稿 一九七五年九月二日）

35

Fig. 15 Draft of the "Several Issues on Accelerating Industrial Development" in 1975

4.2 Dramatic Changes in the International Situation and Foreign Trade Development

4.2.1 Improvement in Diplomatic Environment

In 1971, China regained its legitimate seat in the United Nations; in February 1972, U.S. President Nixon visited China; shortly after, Japanese Prime Minister Tanaka Kakuei's special plane also arrived at Beijing Capital Airport. Subsequently, China established diplomatic relations with Japan and the United States. The dramatic changes in the international situation have brought new development opportunities for China's foreign trade.

Xiong Yuezhi (Researcher at Shanghai Academy of Social Sciences and Distinguished Professor at Fudan University): Shanghai's trade with the Western world has been expanding continuously since Nixon's visit to China and the establishment of diplomatic relations in 1972. It has a great connection with Japan and gradually began to have connections with the United States. After the reform and opening up, the connections have become even more extensive.

Zou Zengqiang (Executive Editor of "Shanghai Chronicles: Port Volume"): After the establishment of diplomatic relations between China and the United States on March 18, 1979, the first American commercial ship, the Lelikex, arrived in Shanghai. On March 25 of the same year, Chinese merchant Liu Linhao set sail from Shanghai to Seattle, USA. Since then, trade between China and the United States has been increasingly strengthened and frequent. In 1983, regular container shipping routes between Shanghai and Europe, as well as Western Europe, were opened.

October 25, 1971, was a moment of great historical significance that can be recorded in the annals of Chinese history. With an overwhelming majority of 76 votes in favor, 35 votes against, and 17 abstentions, the 26th session of the United Nations General Assembly passed the proposal of 23 countries including Albania to restore all legitimate rights of the People's Republic of China in the United Nations and immediately expel the representatives of the Taiwan Kuomintang authorities from the United Nations and all its affiliated institutions. At this moment, every Chinese and people around the world who love peace and uphold justice cheered and rejoiced. This was a major breakthrough in our diplomatic work and had profound significance (Fig. 16).

On February 21, 1972, US President Nixon visited China and was welcomed by Premier Zhou Enlai and other Chinese leaders at Beijing Airport. On February 28, the "Shanghai Communiqué," which marked the establishment of diplomatic relations between China and the United States, was issued, and the relationship between the two countries entered a new historical period.

From September 25 to 29, 1972, Japanese Prime Minister Tanaka Kakuei visited China. On September 29, the "Joint Communiqué of the Government of the People's Republic of China and the Government of Japan" was signed, declaring an end to the abnormal state between the two countries and the normalization of Sino-Japanese relations.

Fig. 16 Restoration of China's legitimate seat in the United Nations in 1971

4.2.2 Changes in Major Trading Regions

The restoration of China's legitimate seat in the United Nations, as well as the establishment of diplomatic relations between China and the United States and China and Japan, greatly enhanced our country's influence and discourse power in the international community. This series of improvements in the diplomatic environment has provided opportunities for our country's economic development. The significant changes in the international situation and the emergence of favorable factors such as Western economic recovery have brought new development to Shanghai's foreign trade. During the period from the founding of New China to the beginning of the reform and opening up, Shanghai's important trading partners changed at different stages due to the influence of the diplomatic environment and political factors.

From 1949 to 1960, it was the heyday of Shanghai's trade with socialist countries such as the Soviet Union and Eastern Europe. From 1960 to 1977, it was a period of decline in trade. In 1950, the two countries signed a trade agreement, and the Soviet Union became China's most important trading partner in the early days of the founding of the country. From 1952 to 1960, Shanghai introduced technology and equipment from the Soviet Union and Eastern Europe, and transformed or built multiple projects such as steam turbine factories, smelters, and Shanghai shipyards. In the late 1950s, due to the deterioration of Sino-Soviet relations, trade between Shanghai and the Soviet Union and Eastern Europe plummeted, and trade volume decreased significantly.

In the early days of the founding of New China, due to the embargo and blockade imposed by the United States, Japan, Western Europe, and other countries, trade between China and the United States and China and Japan declined sharply. Starting from the early 1960s, as a result of the rupture of Sino-Soviet relations and the interruption of trade, Western capitalist countries such as the United States, Japan, and Western Europe gradually replaced socialist countries such as the Soviet Union and Eastern Europe, strengthening trade exchanges with Shanghai. Nixon's visit to China in 1971 became an important turning point in trade between Shanghai and Western capitalist countries. With the establishment of diplomatic relations between China and the United States and the normalization of relations between China and Japan, Shanghai's trade relations with the United States, Japan, Western Europe, and other countries grew rapidly and quickly became the most important trading partners. The easing of political relations created conditions for economic and trade cooperation, allowing Shanghai's foreign economic and trade activities to re-enter the capitalist market.

4.2.3 Expansion of Foreign Trade Scale

In the late period of the Cultural Revolution, due to various factors, Shanghai finally ended its long-standing stagnation in exports and actively developed foreign trade. At that time, all foreign trade companies organized capable sales personnel and focused on developing overseas trade, achieving significant progress. In terms of Shanghai's total import and export volume, it reached 1.038 billion US dollars in 1971, breaking the 1 billion US dollar mark for the first time. By 1977, the total import and export volume had increased to 2.321 billion US dollars, 1.68 times higher than the 867 million US dollars in exports in 1970.

During this period, Shanghai's trade with Western capitalist countries developed rapidly due to international and domestic political factors. In 1976, Shanghai's export trade with the United States, Japan, the European Community, and other developed countries reached 683 million US dollars, 2.04 times higher than the 225 million US dollars in 1970, and the proportion of Shanghai's exports increased from 25.8% to 34.47%. It is worth mentioning that from 1972 to 1976, Shanghai's cumulative exports to the United States reached 167 million US dollars, and in 1976, exports to the United States reached 62.26 million US dollars. Trade with Japan developed even faster, with exports increasing from only 51 million US dollars in 1970 to 182 million US dollars in 1976, an increase of 2.57 times. Exports to the Federal Republic of Germany, Hong Kong, and Australia also increased significantly.

4.2.4 Optimization of Import and Export Commodity Structure

Looking at Shanghai's export commodity structure, in 1975, the proportion of agricultural and sideline products in Shanghai's exports decreased from 63.92% in 1953 to 37.40%. Textile products and electromechanical instruments increased from

35.17% and 0.91% in 1953 to 48.86% and 13.74% respectively. In 1978, Shanghai's exports of sideline products decreased significantly, with textile products accounting for more than half of the exports, and by the mid-1980s, they accounted for over 60%. Exports of electromechanical instruments also increased significantly. Even in the mid-1990s after the reform and opening up, textile products and electromechanical instruments remained the main export products of Shanghai.

From the imported goods structure in Shanghai, in the 1950s and 1960s, hardware and dyes were the main imported products, such as seamless steel pipes, thin steel pipes, and cast iron. In the 1970s, with the huge changes in the international situation, the types of imported goods began to diversify, and some machinery and high-tech equipment gradually appeared. For example, in 1972, Boeing aircraft, artificial satellite communication ground stations, and synthetic fibers were imported from the United States; in 1973, machinery and complete sets of equipment such as petrochemicals, telecommunications, and electronic devices were imported.

5 The Epitome of the Era of Import and Export Goods

5.1 Maling Canned Goods: The "Top Performer" in Export Goods

When it comes to Maling Canned Goods, old Shanghai residents will be familiar with it. In an era where material resources were not abundant, canned goods greatly enriched people's menus, and Maling Canned Goods were undoubtedly among the best. Even today, you can still see the presence of Maling Canned Goods in major supermarkets in Shanghai. What is less known is that since the 1960s and 1970s, Maling Canned Goods have been exported to more than 70 countries across five continents, making them bona fide "best-seller" products among Shanghai's export goods (Fig. 17).

Zhao Zhifang is the former factory director of Shanghai Maling Canned Goods Factory. She joined the factory in 1962 and has experienced all stages of Maling Foods' transition from a planned economy to a market economy. When it comes to the popularity of Maling Canned Goods in the international market back then, Director Zhao speaks passionately. Shanghai Maling Canned Goods Factory was established in the 1930s, with an interesting story behind its inception. By the late 1920s, Shanghai had already become the largest city in the Far East, with many foreign goods. During this period, canned food had already appeared in Western restaurants in Shanghai. In a shikumen house near the concession, a few Chinese individuals, drawing on their experience in Western cuisine and fueling their enthusiasm, finally developed the first bottle of tomato sauce in China through repeated experiments (Figs. 18 and 19).

Zhao Zhifang (The former Director of Shanghai Maling Canned Goods Factory): It was like the emperor's daughter never had to worry about finding a husband, the entire market was in

Fig. 17 Maling Canned Goods

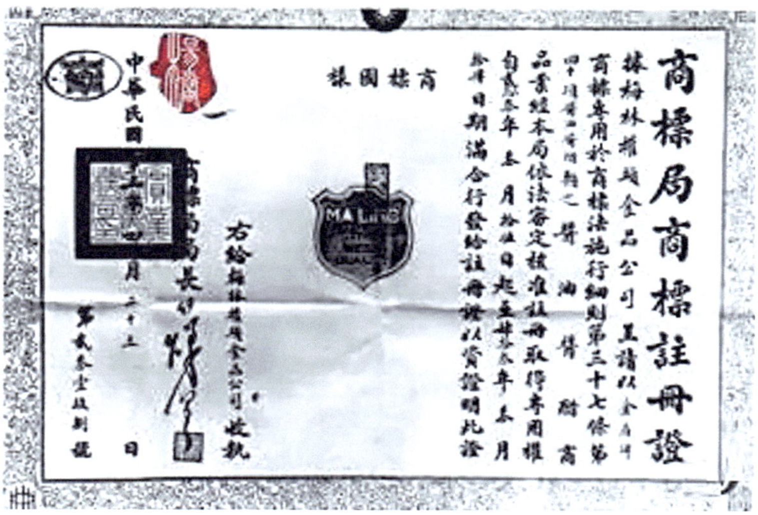

Fig. 18 Trademark registration certificate of Maling

high demand. Internationally, everyone knew that there was a Maling brand in Shanghai. At our peak, the work badge from Maling Canned Goods Factory, which featured the Maling shield, was highly valuable in Southeast Asia because people would recognize you as a part of Maling. Many people have made significant contributions to Maling. The employees in Maling have deep emotions for Maling since we all understand that quality is extremely important and hard-won.

Zhao Zhifang (The former Director of Shanghai Maling Canned Goods Factory): At that time, there were no such canned goods in China. In the Western restaurants in Shanghai, French canned peas and American tomato sauce were sold at very high prices. These items seemed to be cheaply available in our country, which meant they were just making money

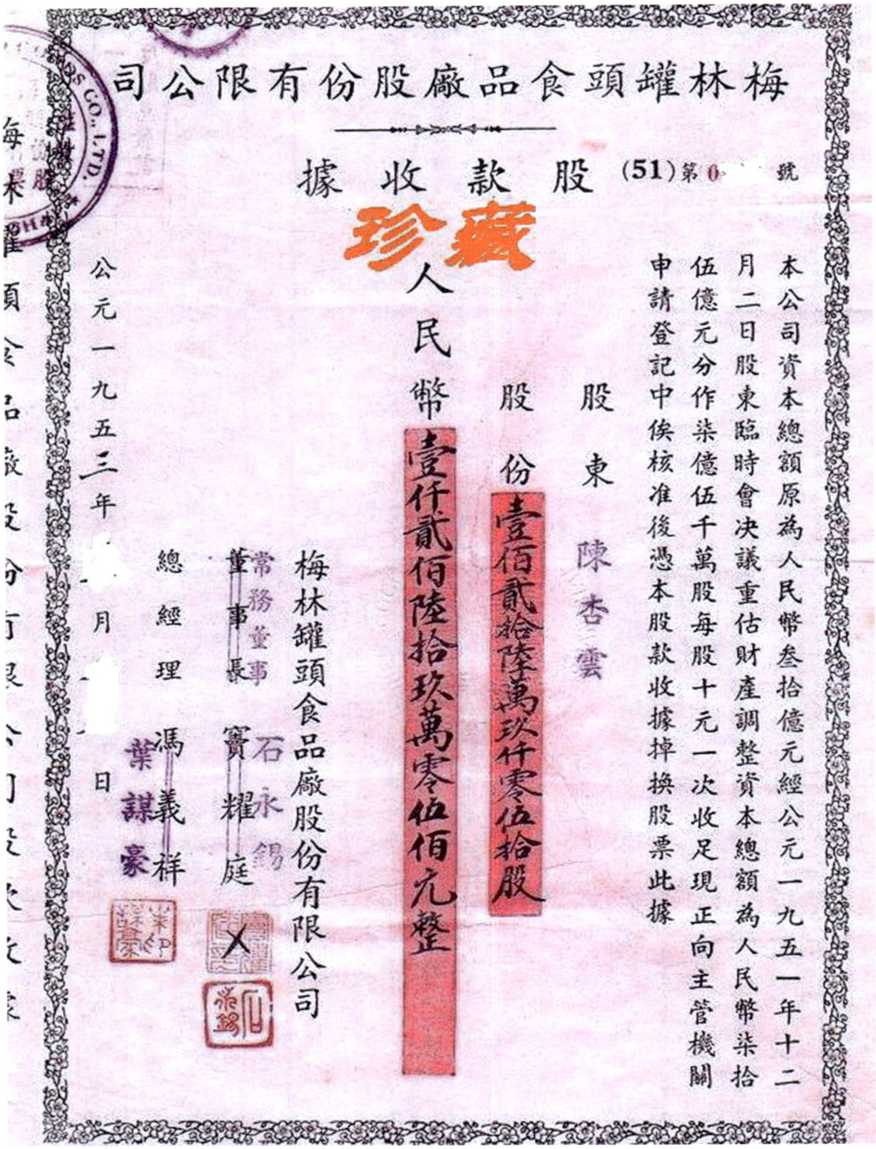

梅林罐頭食品廠股份有限公司

股款收據 (51)第0 號

珍藏

本公司資本總額原為人民幣叁拾億元經公元一九五一年十二月二日股東臨時會決議重估財產調整資本總額為人民幣柒拾伍億元分作柒億伍千萬股每股十元一次收足現正向主管機關申請登記中俟核准後憑本股款收據掉換股票此據

股東 陳杏雲

股份 壹佰貳拾陸萬玖仟零伍拾股

人民幣 壹仟貳佰陸拾玖萬零伍佰元整

梅林罐頭食品廠股份有限公司

董事長 竇耀庭

常務董事 石永錫

總經理 馮義祥

葉謀豪

公元一九五三年 月 日

Fig. 19 Precious Maling stock in 1953-Collector's edition

off us, with a huge price difference. So, many chefs in Western restaurants and a few people held in the vegetable business figured out this situation and realized that there was a huge price difference, which held profitable opportunities. We all knew how much peas cost and what price they were sold. They felt that we should resist imported goods and promote our domestic products. With this mindset, they wanted to make canned food.

In October 1930, Shanghai Maling Canned Goods Factory was established and later converted into Shanghai Maling Food Co., Ltd. The term "Maling" was derived from the poem "The fragrance of plum blossoms comes from the bitter cold," symbolizing the factory's resilience and perseverance in the face of adversity, just like plum blossoms blooming in the harsh winter. The abundance of plum blossoms would symbolize prosperity and beauty. In August 1933, Maling applied to register the "Golden Shield" trademark, thus pioneering the canned food industry in China. The factory evolved from small-workshop production to large-scale manufacturing. Maling's slogan was "Production Saves the Nation." The company advocated for domestic products and aimed to produce well-known local canned goods to resist imported goods and earn foreign exchange. By 1938, Maling's exported canned products had reached 126 varieties.

Zhao Zhifang (The former Director of Shanghai Maling Canned Goods Factory): At that time, establishing a brand was essential for export. Therefore, in 1933, we registered the "Maling Shield" brand and began exporting in 1937. Our factory initially targeted Western restaurants in Shanghai and later expanded to Guangzhou, Wuhan, and Nanjing. Considering the goal of the export market, the "Golden Shield" trademark was registered in 1933, enabling exports.

During the War of Resistance Against Japan, canned food became a sought-after item given its ease of storage, leading to unprecedented growth for Maling Canned Food. Despite the tight blockade by the Japanese, Maling took risks to establish a supply channel to the United States. According to records, from 1940 to May 1941, a total of 15,637 cases of Maling canned food were distributed to the United States. On April 25, 1940, 600 cases of fresh bamboo shoots were delivered to Chicago.

Zhao Zhifang (The former Director of Shanghai Maling Canned Goods Factory): In 1949, several national capitalists transferred the funds of Maling, amounting to over $200,000 or HK$200,000, to the branch in Taiwan, leading to a suspension of production. Afterward, our country organized the Workers' Committee and later implemented the public–private partnership. The real development of Maling took place after the founding of the People's Republic of China.

After the liberation of Shanghai, Maling first underwent the process of public–private partnership and later merged with Shanghai Yimin No.2 Food Factory, greatly enhancing its strength. The factory was also relocated to its current address at No. 224 Jungong Road (Figs. 20 and 21).

Zhao Zhifang (The former Director of Shanghai Maling Canned Goods Factory): The new location of Maling is the original site of Shanghai Yimin No.2 Food Factory, which was a military factory of the Japanese Puppet Government and the Kuomintang and produced canned food for their troops. After the Japanese surrendered and before the establishment of the People's Republic of China, the Kuomintang took over and turned it into a state-owned military supply factory, enhancing the equipment and technical capabilities. After the

Fig. 20 Chinese and foreign managers posing at the entrance of Maling

Fig. 21 Ribbon-cutting ceremony for Maling Food Co., Ltd.

establishment of the People's Republic of China, it became a military factory of the People's Liberation Army of China. During the War to Resist US Aggression and Aid Korea, braised beef and pork produced here were sent to the Korean battlefield.

In 1957, Maling Food Co., Ltd. hired Czech experts to guide production, leading to the development of a specially crafted Western-style luncheon meat canned food, which was exported to Europe. In 1959, Western-style high-temperature ham and Chinese-style eight-treasure rice canned food were developed, which were well received in overseas markets (Fig. 22).

Zhang Qingfeng (General Manager of Shanghai Maling Aquarius Co., Ltd. and Maling Food Co., Ltd.): Our first can of luncheon meat was developed in 1957, which was guided by a Czech expert in our factory on Jungong Road. At that time, due to the outdated equipment and simple production process, most of the work was done manually.

Zhao Zhifang (The former Director of Shanghai Maling Canned Goods Factory): I remember when I joined the factory in 1962, the production of luncheon meat canned food was pushed one by one using the stomach, which was unimaginable. There was no decent production line. The production of steamed port had to go through an exhaust box in the hot summer, which was passed one by one. Later, to meet the requirements of square canned luncheon meat production, Maling Canned Goods Factory imported a machine from Italy.

In order to meet the production needs of Fangting luncheon meat, Meilin Food Factory specially imported a machine from Italy (Fig. 23).

Zhao Zhifang (The former Director of Shanghai Maling Canned Goods Factory): Luncheon meat canned food was initially packaged in round cans domestically, while it needed to be in square cans internationally. Hence, the factory purchased the imported machine. With

Fig. 22 Exterior view of Shanghai Maling Aquarius Co., Ltd.

Fig. 23 The Czech experts (middle) guided the production of canned luncheon meat for Maling in 1957

> this machine, the production process was carried out in stages, where you just had to put the ingredients in, and they would instantly take shape. Then, they would be sealed in the sealing workshop. In this way, the number of empty cans increased, and only with enough empty cans could the canning production proceed. This imported machine has been in use since 1964 and has been used since the arrival of the electric square can machine.

During the planned economy era, the export of canned goods was centrally managed and arranged by the state. Canned goods exported to the Soviet Union and Eastern European countries used the Great Wall brand trademark unifiedly, while those exported to the Western countries and other regions were operated by port companies in Shanghai, Tianjin, Guangzhou, etc., each having one or two dedicated trademarks. The Maling brand was the dedicated trademark for Shanghai. At that time, canned goods from six provinces and one city were unifiedly exported with the Maling brand (Fig. 24).

Fig. 24 Workers processing chicken at Shanghai Maling Canned Goods Factory in the 1950s

Zhao Zhifang (The former Director of Shanghai Maling Canned Goods Factory): Many canned food factories contributed to the development of Maling, including Shanghai Food Import and Export Company, COFCO, and six other provincial food import and export corporations. Otherwise, it seems impossible that we could produce over 10,000 tons for export in 1978 during the planned economy era. The presence of such a vast sales network and factories in six provinces working together made it possible to export over 10,000 tons to more than 70 countries across five continents. Therefore, the great international influence of the Maling brand should be attributed to our country's policies.

From the 1950s to the 1970s, Maling canned goods were exported to Eastern European socialist countries such as the Soviet Union and the Czech Republic, as well as countries and regions such as Singapore and Malaysia, and eventually inflowed to markets of Africa and the Middle East. Maling products such as Eight Treasure Rice Canned, Tomato Sauce, and Ham Canned became popular worldwide. Among them, canned luncheon meat was particularly sought after, leading to a popular dish "Maling Luncheon Meat with Rice" in the Philippines. In Hong Kong, Maling canned luncheon meat is also the preferred choice for many restaurants and hotels.

Zhang Qingfeng (General Manager of Shanghai Maling Aquarius Co., Ltd. and Maling Food Co., Ltd.): After the reform and opening up, Shanghai Maling Canned Goods Factory and Shanghai Food Import and Export Company formed a joint venture. Then, Maling's factory on Jungong Road obtained the right to export independently. Currently, our main export products are canned luncheon meat, which is sold in Southeast Asia and has an annual export value of 50 million US dollars.

As a "time-honored" brand with nearly a century of history, Maling Canned Goods remains active in the global market. To win the favor of young people, Maling has also launched a new "Cute Pig" luncheon meat and adopted the popular live-streaming marketing model. This represents the combination of a century-old Maling brand with the Internet, as well as the new departure of traditional Chinese products in the new era.

5.2 *Shanghai Friendship Store: Witness of the New China's Diplomatic History*

The Shanghai Friendship Store was once a place that many people in Shanghai yearned for. In the years of scarce commodity supply, it served as a window to showcase friendship to foreign countries and symbolized status and privilege internally. The history of the Shanghai Friendship Store reflects the unique circumstances of China during a special period.

Since the mid-1950s, interactions between China and Eastern European countries became increasingly frequent. To meet the growing shopping demands of foreign guests, the Shanghai Friendship Store was opened at No. 345 East Nanjing Road, Donghai Building, and trial operation began on February 26, 1958. This comprehensive store served foreign guests, overseas Chinese, Hong Kong, Macao, and Taiwan compatriots, as well as senior officials. It mainly supplies Chinese specialties, scarce food, and daily necessities in the market, as well as imported goods (Figs. 25 and 26).

In 1970, amid the rallying cries of "The East Wind Blows, the War Drum Beats," the Shanghai Friendship Store relocated to the former British Consulate site at No. 33 Zhongshan East 1st Road on the Bund. Due to the barriers of fences and greenery, the Shanghai Friendship Store became somewhat "In inner chambers bred, to the world was unknown", with only the prominent slogan "Our friends are all over the world" being particularly eye-catching.

In 1985, the Shanghai Friendship Store settled at No. 40 Beijing East Road, marking the beginning point at which many Shanghai residents' impression of the Shanghai Friendship Store (Fig. 27).

The Shanghai Friendship Store used to be the epitome of "imported" goods in the minds of Shanghai residents. In addition to selling top-notch Chinese products such as high-end Hangzhou silk tapestries and Suzhou double-sided embroidery, it also offered a plethora of unheard-of foreign goods for the Chinese people, such as whiskey, Marlboro cigarettes, and Hershey's chocolate (Figs. 28 and 29).

> Ge Tao (Researcher at the Institute of History, Shanghai Academy of Social Sciences): At that time, the Shanghai Friendship Store was perceived as a high-end store with a wide range of handicrafts, such as silk, fine wines, premium teas, and fabrics that couldn't be available elsewhere. The shopping environment inside was also excellent, even better than that of the Shanghai No.1 Department Store at that time.

Fig. 25 The Shanghai Friendship Store on East Nanjing Road

Fig. 26 The Shanghai Friendship Store at No. 33 Zhongshan East 1st Road

Fig. 27 Shanghai Friendship Store at No. 40 Beijing East Road

Fig. 28 Items supplied by the Shanghai Friendship Store were all highly sought-after commodities

Fig. 29 Athletes participating in the Afro-Asian Ping Pong Friendship Invitation Tournament selecting paddles on the ground floor of the Shanghai Friendship Store

> Chao Gangling (Professor at Shanghai University of Finance and Economics): To buy items at the Shanghai Friendship Store, one had to use foreign currency. That was the situation back then because it mainly catered to foreign tourists. Many locals were curious and liked to sneak a peek inside, not knowing what it was really like.

The customers of the Shanghai Friendship Store were primarily government delegations visiting China and foreigners traveling to Shanghai. The store's visitor records vividly illustrated the trajectory of China's diplomacy. In the 1950s, Soviet guests dominated, accounting for 90%. In the 1960s, guests from the socialist camp still took the lead. From the normalization of Sino-US relations and Sino-Japanese relations in the 1970s, guests truly spread all over the world. Prince Norodom Sihanouk, Henry Kissinger, Kakuei Tanaka, and Antonio Samaranch have all visited. Among them, Prince Norodom Sihanouk had a special fondness for the Shanghai Friendship Store and visited annually from 1971 to 1974.

In 1972, it was a significant year for the People's Republic of China. On February 21, 1972, US President Nixon led a delegation to Beijing, establishing diplomatic relations between China and the US. A week later, the delegation visited the Shanghai Friendship Store, marking the first time the store received U.S. officials. In September of the same year, with the normalization of Sino-Japanese relations, Tanaka Kakuei led a delegation of 246 people to visit the Shanghai Friendship Store (Figs. 30, 31 and 32).

Ge Tao (Researcher at the Institute of History, Shanghai Academy of Social Sciences): It is hard to imagine that in an era of scarce resources, the everyday items we now take for granted were considered luxury goods. If you had a foreign exchange certificate, you could

Fig. 30 Former Olympic President Samaranch left messages at the Shanghai Friendship Store

Fig. 31 Japanese guests returning with full loads

Fig. 32 Guests from the Princess Cruise visited the Shanghai Friendship Store

go in and have a look. Otherwise, it was likely beyond your reach. You couldn't even see them, let alone touch or taste them.

Chao Gangling (Professor at Shanghai University of Finance and Economics): I have also been to the Shanghai Friendship Store. I have some relatives overseas and some foreign exchange certificates, but I didn't buy anything. I just went in to take a look.

Due to the initial purpose of the Shanghai Friendship Store being to serve foreigners with foreign exchange certificates, security guards would prohibit customers who didn't look like foreigners from entering. Back then, Shanghai residents would often peek outside the store, curious about the items being sold, creating a unique scene of that era in Shanghai.

Ge Tao (Researcher at the Institute of History, Shanghai Academy of Social Sciences): The history of the Shanghai Friendship Store, from its establishment to its decline, illustrates how Chinese people yearned for openness and integration into the world. The process was not simple. To absorb some foreign exchange and showcase our culture globally to give Chinese people a sense of pride, we gathered the best products and displayed them at the most appropriate prices. This was not just a display of goods. It was a cultural exhibition.

6 Opening a New Chapter in Foreign Trade Reform

6.1 Reform of the Foreign Economic and Trade System

The Third Plenary Session of the 11th Central Committee of the Communist Party of China held in December 1978 established the fundamental policy of invigorating the domestic economy and opening up to the outside world. This marked a historical turning point in the development of Shanghai's foreign economy and trade. From 1978 to 1990, Shanghai creatively carried out a series of innovative reforms and

Fig. 33 Establishment of Shanghai Foreign Trade Corporation

explorations aligned with the central government's direction for foreign trade system reform, tailored to local conditions.

6.1.1 Hierarchical Management and Joint Leadership

Following the central government's directive to " Implement graded management of import and export, expand the scope of local business commodities" the Shanghai Foreign Trade Corporation was established in December 1979, which was the first local foreign trade corporation (Fig. 33).

The Shanghai Foreign Trade Corporation operates under the Shanghai Foreign Trade Bureau as "one leadership team, two signs," functioning as a government-enterprise combined unit. It focused on managing the import and export business of Shanghai. It jointly leads and manages 15 branch companies and related foreign trade enterprises and institutions in Shanghai with professional export–import companies under the Ministry of Foreign Trade. This reform has had a certain impact on the centralized and unified foreign trade system nationwide, showing signs of loosening.

6.1.2 Streamlining Administration and Delegating Powers, Separating Government and Enterprise

In August 1979, the Shanghai Foreign Trade Bureau began piloting the streamlining administration and delegating power. Making full use of the powers delegated by the central government, it vigorously developed local foreign trade enterprises and

Fig. 34 Shanghai Toy Import and Export Company-Embroidery

reversed the monopoly of specialized foreign trade companies and the separation of industry and trade. Export–import companies combining industry and trade operations were successively established, including those in toys, instrumentation, and electronics. Additionally, several comprehensive local foreign trade companies such as Shenxin, Huajian, Aijian, and Yongfeng were formed. In January 1980, Shanghai's first industrial and trade import–export company, Shanghai Toy Import and Export Company, was established after the reform and opening up (Fig. 34).

In 1981, the Shanghai Foreign Trade Corporation was separated from the Shanghai Foreign Trade Bureau and became an independent economic entity. At the end of 1983, the Shanghai Municipal Government integrated the Municipal Import and Export Office, Municipal Foreign Trade Bureau, and Municipal Foreign Economic Bureau into the Shanghai Foreign Economic and Trade Commission to reduce the administrative levels and facilitate centralized management. In 1984, the Shanghai Foreign Trade Corporation was changed into a local comprehensive foreign trade enterprise, with the manager responsibility system, operating independently, self-accounting, and self-bearing profits and losses.

6.1.3 Integrating Industry and Trade, Liberalizing Business Operations

In the planned economy era, conflicts between industry and trade were inevitable due to the insufficient understanding of the international market enterprises and their lack of enthusiasm for exporting products. To this end, Shanghai implemented the "Four Alliances, Two Public" system, which involved uniting in "office operations, external negotiations, production arrangements, and dispatch of personnel abroad for inspections”. Additionally, the commodity sales prices of foreign trade enterprises and the production costs of manufacturers were made public. This system was used to strengthen the cooperation between industry and trade, fully mobilizing the enthusiasm of both parties.

In 1988, the Shanghai foreign trade-related government departments and various production departments jointly established 550 joint ventures, of which 262 were in Shanghai. By the end of 1990, there were 115 enterprises (including subordinate enterprises) with import and export rights in Shanghai, which can be roughly divided into seven types: specialized foreign trade companies, industry-focused industry-trade integrated companies, departmental foreign trade companies, comprehensive local trade companies, technology-oriented planning-trade integrated companies, industry-trade integrated foreign trade companies, and production enterprises independently operating export businesses.

6.1.4 Enterprises Contract, Self-Bearing All Profits and Losses

Since 1986, Shanghai has actively promoted the reform of the management mechanism of foreign trade enterprises, fully implemented the Manager Responsibility System and Contracting System in 18 specialized foreign trade branches, and promoted the Contracted Managerial Responsibility System nationwide in the foreign trade system in 1988. Compared with the previous situation where enterprises “focused solely on exports, ignoring profits and losses”, this marked a significant advancement. Afterward, the central government delegated power to local governments, allowing specialized foreign trade branches to be under local jurisdiction, and severing ties with the Beijing headquarters. This measure greatly mobilized the local enthusiasm for developing foreign trade.

The implementation of the contracting system has enhanced enterprises’ focus on efficiency and stimulated market competitiveness, which has been conducive to the rapid development of foreign trade. However, in the early stages of reform, due to a lack of experience and hasty steps, issues such as regional blockades and restrictions, enterprises focusing only on immediate benefits, and neglecting long-term development have also emerged.

6.1.5 Multiple Ways, Export Agency

Since 1985, Shanghai has piloted the Export Agency System in industrial enterprises such as the Jiafeng Cotton Textile Factory, Shanghai Fourth Cotton Textile Factory, Micro-bearing Factory, Yuejin Electric Motor Factory, and the Third Wool Spinning Factory. Based on this experience, Shanghai fully implemented the Export Agency System in the textile industry in 1989.

Due to the different foundations of various textile production enterprises, Shanghai's Export Agency System mainly features three ways: implementing internationally accepted export agency forms in a few well-managed industrial enterprises, taking a leap forward; implementing complete export agency in most enterprises, adopting the "Five Agencies, Five Public"; implementing primary export agency in a few industries such as clothing, maintaining the original procurement system in terms of trade relations. Shanghai's Export Agency System has achieved remarkable results. Taking Jiafeng Cotton Textile Factory as an example, after the trial implementation of the export agency system in 1985, it earned 4 million US dollars in foreign exchange that year, with a profit of 5.08 million RMB. In 1988, it earned 14 million US dollars in foreign exchange, with a profit of 25 million RMB. In just a few years, both foreign exchange earnings and profits increased by 2.5 times and 3.9 times, respectively, compared to 1985.

6.2 *Exploration of Foreign Economic and Trade Business*

The reform and opening up have invigorated the vitality of Shanghai's foreign economic and trade activities but also posed severe challenges. Due to the nationwide implementation of reforms in the foreign trade planning system and adjustments in the allocation of export sources to Shanghai, the number of imported goods from other provinces and cities gradually decreased. In 1979, the amount of imported goods from other provinces reached 4.3 billion yuan, but by 1981, it had plummeted to only 1.7 billion yuan. The significant reduction in export sources directly led to a decline in Shanghai's export volume. In response to the new problems faced during the reform and opening up, Shanghai adopted a series of measures.

6.2.1 Utilizing International Resources to Address Raw Material Shortages

To tackle the issue of insufficient raw materials, Shanghai primarily relied on expanding processing with supplied materials and developing the "Three-plus-one" trading mix. In 1989, Shanghai's foreign exchange used for processing supplied materials reached $1.1 billion, with a trade volume of $2 billion, accounting for nearly 40% of Shanghai's exports. This measure has proven effective. According to statistics, in 1989, Shanghai's trade volume for the "Three-plus-one" trading mix reached $269 million, accounting for 5.3% of Shanghai's total exports. Due to cumbersome customs procedures and slow progress, this type of business only developed rapidly in certain companies, such as Shanghai Silk Import and Export Company, which deals in kimono and silk fashion, saw over 70% of its exports coming from processing with supplied materials.

6.2.2 Adopting Various Forms to Promote Export Production

In response to the gradual decrease in the supply of goods from other provinces, Shanghai, based on the principle of "prioritizing domestic resources and seeking external support as a supplement", has readjusted its relationship with inland provinces and cities. The focus was on strengthening horizontal economic ties and establishing export production bases in various regions. Shanghai explored 10 forms of economic cooperation in practice, including allocation, outright repo, product compensation, export agency, two-way transportation, joint operation, cooperative production, joint venture, and group establishment. At the same time, to promote local export production, various effective measures have been taken. Firstly, secure funds from multiple sources to support export production. Secondly, implement incentive measures to stimulate production enthusiasm. Thirdly, engage in foreign trade and industry to develop joint ventures. These measures have yielded remarkable results. In 1990, the value of goods purchased from other provinces reached 5.981 billion yuan, setting a new historical record. Shanghai Foreign Trade Bureau established 373 joint ventures with other provinces, with 343 of them providing products for export. The acquisition of export sources reached 19.3 billion yuan, accounting for 70% of Shanghai's total export value.

6.2.3 Implementing Sales Strategies to Expand Export Markets

Since the reform and opening up, foreign trade enterprises have sprung up across various regions, but due to limited operational capabilities, they often flocked to markets such as Hong Kong and Macau. In response to this trend, Shanghai promptly carried out strategic adjustments, leveraging its geographical location, urban functions, and advantages in foreign trade to implement a global sales strategy, expand export markets, and focus on developing transoceanic markets in Europe and the United States. This approach proved effective, leading to a continuous expansion of sales markets. By 1990, Shanghai had established partnerships with 171 countries and regions. Among them, Hong Kong ranked first with an export value of 1.029 billion US dollars; Japan ranked second with an export value of 759 million US dollars; the United States ranked third with an export value of 745 million US dollars; followed closely by Germany, Singapore, the Soviet Union, Italy, the United Kingdom, and Australia.

6.2.4 Transforming Business Style and Expanding Trade Methods

To address the intensified internal competition after the opening of foreign trade, Shanghai adopted three effective measures to transform its business management style. First, it prioritized product upgrading and modernization. Multiple economic measures were used to encourage the development of marketable, innovative, and high-end products, supporting the advancement of deep processing, precision

processing, and electromechanical instrument products. Second, Shanghai shifted away from the traditional business styles. Transform the original management practices and operating mechanism, actively seeking out business opportunities. Not only carry out overseas promotion but also establish enterprises abroad. By 1990, Shanghai had established 150 economic and trade institutions across five continents. Third, a flexible trading approach was adopted. On the one hand, expand visibility through promotion methods such as advertising and exhibitions. On the other hand, improve the level of internal and external competition by accepting OEM production, expanding Shanghai's export trade through Chinese and foreign enterprises jointly creating well-known brands.

6.2.5 Enhancing Internal Conditions for an Export-Oriented Economy

In addition to a suitable institutional framework, the development of foreign trade also requires other soft and hard conditions. To this end, Shanghai has proposed a series of measures to improve the internal environment and create favorable conditions for the development of an export-oriented economy.

1. Establishing a sound administrative institution. To improve work efficiency and attract foreign investment, Shanghai established the Shanghai Foreign Investment Working Committee in 1988, providing "one-stop" services for foreign investors, which was well received. In addition, the Shanghai Foreign Economic and Trade Commission has also set up other administrative institutions, including the Technology Import and Export Office, Foreign Exchange Adjustment Center, Material Services Company, and China Import and Export Consumer Goods Quality Inspection Center.
2. Refining economic regulations. Firstly, following the development plan of Shanghai, preferential tax reductions and exemptions were utilized to guide the direction of foreign investment, such as the "Several Provisions on Encouraging Foreign Investment in Shanghai". Secondly, new solutions were proposed for foreign investment, such as the "Measures for the Paid Transfer of Land Use Rights in Shanghai". Thirdly, efforts were made to improve internal and external relations of enterprises, such as the "Regulations on Complaints and Handling Measures of Foreign-Invested Enterprises in Shanghai". Fourthly, approval procedures were simplified, exemplified by the "Interim Measures for the Application and Approval Procedures of Foreign Investment Projects in Shanghai".
3. Cultivating specialized foreign trade talent and organizations. In 1983, the Shanghai municipal government broke away from the unified employment and allocation model, pioneering recruitment through examinations. In June 1983, the first Foreign Trade Fair was held in Shanghai, with 929 companies from 38 countries and regions attending. In June 1985, the Shanghai World Trade Center

Association was established. In 1987, the first local foreign trade industry association in China, the Shanghai Foreign Trade Association, was established, with over a hundred group members.

4. Improving transportation, communication, and other conditions. Passenger routes to destinations such as Hong Kong, Japan, and other locations were opened, forming a global transportation network. Modern communication networks such as international direct dialing, video telephony, and fax were established. In 1987, the Minhang, Hongqiao, and Caohejing development zones were established, and a consulate area was opened in the Hongqiao Development Zone. A comprehensive export-oriented economic pattern took shape with the goal of full opening.

6.3 *Restarting Foreign Economic and Trade Activities*

Since the reform and opening up, the country's focus gradually shifted to economic development, and Shanghai's economic vitality has begun to burst forth, bringing new opportunities for foreign trade. In 1990, Shanghai's import and export trade expanded to 171 countries and regions, with a total import and export value of 7.427 billion US dollars, an increase of 1.46 times compared to 3.025 billion US dollars in 1978. Among them, exports increased from 2.893 billion US dollars to 5.317 billion US dollars, and imports increased from 133 million US dollars to 2.110 billion US dollars. From 1979 to 1990, the total import and export trade increased at an average annual rate of 8.5%, and the surge in imports was a notable change in foreign trade after the reform and opening up. In addition, the ranking of Shanghai's export market and the structure of import and export commodities have also changed.

6.3.1 Rankings of Export Markets

Hong Kong had always been an important trading partner for Shanghai's exports, accounting for 18.87% of Shanghai's total exports in 1978. From 1979 to 1990, this proportion remained stable and maintained the top position, accounting for 19.36% of Shanghai's total exports in 1990. The United States maintained a stable share of 14% of Shanghai's total exports from 1985 to 1990, ranking second after surpassing Japan in export volume to the United States in 1981. In 1990, Shanghai's actual exports to the United States totaled 1.063 billion US dollars, approximately 20% of Shanghai's total exports. Japan's share of Shanghai's total exports saw a slight increase, rising from 9.31% in 1978 to 14.28% in 1990. From 1985 to 1987, Japan ranked third in Shanghai's foreign trade volume, and from 1988 to 1989, it moved up to the second position. Besides Hong Kong, Japan, and the United States, Federal Germany, Singapore, and others were also important trading partners for Shanghai at that time.

In 1990, the rankings of Shanghai's export markets were as follows: Hong Kong, Japan, the United States, the Federal Germany, Singapore, the Soviet Union, Italy, the United Kingdom, Australia, and Canada. The structure of the export trade market also exhibited notable characteristics. First, exports to the United States and the Hong Kong region continue to grow. Second, exports to the Soviet Union and Eastern Europe decreased. Third, exports to the Taiwan region have increased significantly.

6.3.2 Imported and Exported Commodities Structure

In terms of exported commodities structure, the proportion of light textile products increased steadily from the early days of the founding of the People's Republic of China to the 1990s. In 1978, it accounted for 56.56%, and by 1990, it increased to 63.7%. The share of electromechanical instruments increased from 12.26% in 1978 to 23.85% in 1990. Light textile products and electromechanical instruments maintained a dominant position in exports for many years. Conversely, the proportion of agricultural and sideline products in exports continued to decrease, dropping from 31.18% in 1978 to only 12.45% in 1990.

Regarding the imported commodities structure, the import of production materials accounted for over 70% from 1978 to 1990, with the import of machinery and equipment continuously increasing. In 1990, various fibers, artificial cotton, wool, etc. accounted for 20% of the total imports. Steel and non-ferrous metals accounted for 12.2% of imports. From 1985 to 1990, the proportion of imported technical equipment was not high, with transaction amounts being modest, around 100–200 million US dollars.

Overall, from 1978 to 1990, Shanghai's foreign trade developed rapidly, and the initial effects of institutional reforms became evident. On the one hand, major trading partners such as Hong Kong, the United States, Japan, Federal Germany, and the United Kingdom established their positions in Shanghai's import and export trade. On the other hand, the structure of imported and exported commodities underwent changes, with light industrial products and textiles accounting for over 60% of exports. Light industrial raw materials and machinery and equipment became the main imported commodities, and technology imports also began to take shape.

6.4 Customs System Reform: Restoration of Customs Duties

Since 1978, under the unified direction of the central government, Shanghai took the lead in a series of reforms and actively explored the establishment of a market-oriented modern foreign trade system. Among them, there was a strong call for the restoration of customs duties and the customs system reform. In the archives of the Shanghai Customs Building, there is a letter from 43 years ago. This letter was written by 9 young customs officers in Shanghai, appealing for the restoration of customs duties and the customs system reform. The letter was dated "January 5, 1978," and

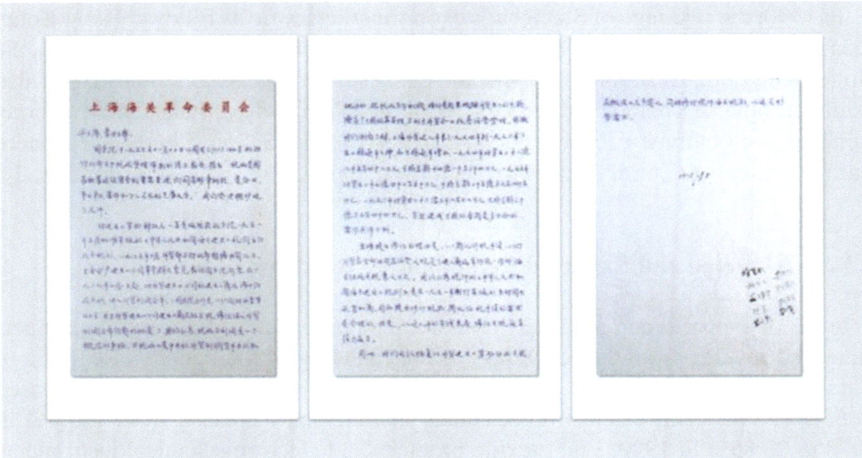
上海海关革命委员会

Fig. 35 The handwritten letter of the 9 young customs officers in 1978

the urgency of the customs system reform was evident in the letter. At the end of the letter, there were the joint signatures of the 9 young customs officers (Fig. 35).

> Gu Zhenxing (former Deputy Director of Shanghai Customs): This letter was sent on January 5, 1978, and there were 9 names in the lower right corner of the letter. Five of them were colleagues from the cargo management team at that time, and four were from our office. Together, they made up 9 people, and my name was included among them.

For a long period after the founding of the People's Republic of China, foreign trade was centrally managed by the state, and the customs belonged to the Ministry of Foreign Trade. Various specialized import and export companies under the Ministry of Foreign Trade were responsible for operating the national import and export business. After the 1950s, the Soviet Union and Eastern European countries became the focus of our foreign trade. The country implemented a centralized tax collection system, and import and export companies replaced the customs in collecting tariffs and taxes. As a result, tariff collection became a redundant process.

> Gu Zhenxing (former Deputy Director of Shanghai Customs): One reason was the combination of tax revenue with profits. Sometimes, when foreign trade suffered losses, these losses were offset by tax payments. Why did foreign trade suffer losses? It became difficult to discern the actual losses, which obscured the reality of the situation and hindered foreign trade companies from improving their management practices. Another reason was that for the country and the Ministry of Finance, tariffs were supposed to be collected immediately and directly deposited into the national treasury. However, foreign trade profits were settled once a year, so the Ministry of Finance could not receive the tax payments promptly, which posed challenges for government spending when funds were needed.

Starting from July 1967, import tariffs were suspended, and the tax payments were included in the unified profit deposit by foreign trade companies. However, with China's reform and opening up, the drawbacks of tariff exemption gradually became apparent treasury was depleted, which hindered the construction of essential infrastructure such as railways, highways, and power facilities. Statistics show that from 1950 to 1977, during a period of rebuilding and limited openness, while trade through Shanghai did develop, the pace was relatively slow, with an average annual growth rate of only 13.7%.

Gu Zhenxing and his colleagues considered whether they could use a letter to the people to directly report the current situation of customs.

> Gu Zhenxing (former Deputy Director of Shanghai Customs): Later, we drafted a letter appealing to the central leadership to restore taxation. This letter addressed the issue of restoring taxation, discussing existing tax payments, competition with foreign trade companies, merging them with foreign trade profits, and also reflecting on some existing problems. We wrote this letter to the central leadership.

At that time, the functions of the customs were weakened to only include goods supervision and the collection of personal import postal taxes. The role of tariffs in national finance and economic leverage almost vanished. Gu Zhenxing remembered that shortly after sending the letter, they received a letter from the Ministry of Finance's petition office, stating that they were in contact with the Ministry of Foreign Trade to handle the matter. To draw attention from the central government, they subsequently sent two more letters to the central leadership within the next six months, strongly urging the restoration of customs taxation and customs statistics, reforming the customs system, and advocating "hoping to separate tax and profit, restore the customs' direct collection of import and export goods taxes (payments)" and "also hoping to resolve the customs system as soon as possible, to adapt to the needs of national economic adjustment, development, and external activities."

> Gu Zhenxing (former Deputy Director of Shanghai Customs): On August 17, 1979, I remember that around this time, the documents submitted by the Ministry of Finance, the National Commission for Discipline Inspection, and the Ministry of Foreign Trade were approved by State Council, which aimed to improve the "Customs Taxation Measures" and "Customs Management System." The State Council issued a notice regarding this. Later, several ministries, including the Ministry of Foreign Trade, formally announced the restoration of customs duties starting January 1, 1980.

From January 1, 1980, customs officially resumed the separate collection of tariffs on foreign trade imports and exports. In February of the same year, the State Council decided to reform the customs system and established the General Administration of Customs, directly under the State Council. As China's customs business entered a new stage of development, China's foreign trade also began to accelerate its growth.

On April 18, 1990, the Communist Party Central Committee and the State Council officially announced the development and opening up of Pudong. In June 1990, the State Council approved the establishment of the Waigaoqiao Free Trade Zone in Shanghai Pudong. In July 1990, the Waigaoqiao Free Trade Zone Development Company was established, injecting new strong momentum into Shanghai's foreign trade for a new round of development, and thus Shanghai embarked on a new chapter in history.

Chapter 4
Standing on the Tide (1991–2024)

1 Introduction

Backed by the Yangtze River, facing the Pacific Ocean, Shanghai, which has long been the leader of China's openness, is in full bloom.

Over the past one hundred years, the winds on both sides of the Yangtze River have stirred and given rise to great changes. The city of Shanghai, with the determination of "success need not be mine, but may well depend on me", has been steadfastly pursuing development and become an important window of communication and trade between China and the world. In the new era and new pattern, Shanghai is gradually moving towards the center of the global economic and trade arena, writing a new chapter of development that shines with splendor.

2 Shanghai Trade: Born from Reform and Prospering from Openness

In December 1978, the Third Plenary Session of the Eleventh Central Committee of the Party pointed out that China began to implement the policy of internal reform and opening up to the outside world, and opened a new chapter in its history with the courage to conduct unprecedented exploration.

Shanghai, as a witness, has participated in this magnificent process.

© Fudan University Press Co., Ltd. 2025

W. Shengqiao, *Century of Shanghai Trade*,
https://doi.org/10.1007/978-981-96-8701-5_4

2.1 The New Game Just Began: China's Reform Chess Game Settles in Pudong

If you looked down on Shanghai from above before 1990, you would see that the west side of Yangtze River, the area known as Puxi, was densely lit up, while the other side, Pudong, was dimly lit. This river-crossing city was like a lame giant.

For a long time before 1990, one-sixth of the central government's finance was contributed by Shanghai. Since 1960, Shanghai had been at the top of the GDP list of all provinces, autonomous regions and cities for 20 years. Reform flood waves surged, the supply and marketing mechanism under the planned economy, planned deployment of various resources had gradually been moving towards market allocation. However, when the whole country was striding forward, Shanghai as a representative of the planned economy, had to find its way under heavy burden, and watched her brother regions to catch up. During 1980–1990, Shanghai continues to decline in the GDP list, until it fell out of the top ten.

Life in Shanghai used to be so cramped that not a single household in Pudong had piped gas before 1987. The city's transportation was congested and infrastructure outdated, and it ran a fiscal deficit for quite a few years. Traffic was congested, infrastructure was outdated, and there were fiscal deficits for several years. In the 1980s, on the front page of *Jiefang Daily* 'Shanghai's ten firsts and five lasts' had been counted, seeking for a direction for the city's development (Figs. 1 and 2).

The transition from 'striker' to 'defender' was not easy to bear. With the five special economic zones along the coast of South China taking the lead, and the Pearl River Economic Belt rising to prominence, the spring breeze of reform had blown throughout the country. As Shanghai being left behind, the development in the Yangtze River Delta and even the region along the Yangtze River had stagnated. In China's pattern of coastal opening from the south to the north, how could Shanghai resign itself to the breaking point of linked development? (Fig. 3).

> Prof. Xiong Yuezhi (Distinguished Professor of Fudan University): In 1980s, as the center of the country's openness first allocated in Guangdong, Shenzhen and so on, tentative experiments were carried out little by little in these places. Because they accounted for a relatively small plate in the whole country's economic volume, it was more secure to do the test there. Were there any problems, small boats turn around faster, and the problems would not become too big. Shanghai at that time was still the country's largest economic center, problems were not allowed to arise here, so in 1980s Shanghai was in its era of the rear-guard during the reform and opening up

In 1990, Deng Xiaoping, who spent the Spring Festival in Shanghai, looked from Puxi to Pudong, thinking about the game of Chinese reform and how to eliminate the heavy concerns about reform and opening up. His mind was made up, 'Opportunities should be seized, decisions should be made in time ...... Shanghai is our trump card, getting Shanghai up is a shortcut'; 'Grasp the development of Pudong, do not waver, until the completion'.

On April 18, 1990, the Party Central Committee and the State Council announced the development and opening of Pudong. Half a month later, in Pudong Avenue, No.

Fig. 1 The streets of Shanghai in the early days of reform and opening up

Fig. 2 Citizens riding bicycles to work (near Zhapu Road Bridge in Hongkou District in the 1980s)

解放日报

JIEFANG RIBAO

19

上海市市政工程管理局

关于换发车辆购置附加费凭证的通告

中外经济技术合作的丰硕成果

上海大众汽车公司庆祝成立五周年

李鹏总理出席大会并作重要讲话

李鹏总理在上海宣布

中央同意加快开发浦东

将实行经济技术开发区和某些经济特区的政策

为发展中国的轿车工业而努力奋斗

李鹏

在上海大众汽车公司成立五周年庆祝大会上

李鹏总理的讲话

李鹏总理在沪会见科林巴总统

朱镕基市长设宴欢迎中非贵宾

李鹏看望好八连

勉励官兵保持和发扬光荣传统

李鹏总理会见哈恩董事长

Fig. 3 News on "Development of Pudong" published in Jiefang Daily in 1990

141, 'Shanghai Municipal People's Government Pudong Development and Opening Office' was established. The working conditions were poor due to scarcity of materials, a desk had to be shared by several people, one drawer for each, but everyone was full of energy.

Coinciding with economic globalization and worldwide industrial restructuring, the development and opening up of Pudong offered tremendous chances for the multinational enterprises seeking for capital investment. 'Standing beside the globe, planning for Pudong', we decided to benchmark the best, to the world's financial center such as London and New York, a seemingly late start had the advantage of latecomers because of the high starting point (Fig. 4).

From conquering difficulties in the initial reform of the socialist market economy system, to combating the 1997 Asian financial crisis, to joining the World Trade Organization in 2001 and converging with international standards, as well as assuming a new round of reform and opening-up pilots in the midst of the unprecedented changes of the century, Pudong had lived up to its mission to develop and open up at a high level, laying the foundation for the strategic upgrade of China's reform and opening-up (Figs. 5 and 6).

Fig. 4 Pudong Development Office of Shanghai Municipal People's Government and Pudong Development Planning Research and Design Institute were established

Fig. 5 Lujiazui Financial District, Pudong, early 1990s

Fig. 6 At the beginning of the twenty-first century, Shanghai Lujiazui had become one of the most influential financial centers in China

2.2 The Situation Became Lively: Establishment of the Lujiazui Financial and Trade Zone

In April 1990, the Party Central Committee and the State Council announced the development and opening up of Pudong, Shanghai, and put Lujiazui to the forefront of reform and opening up. As the only state-level development zone named after finance and trade, Lujiazui Finance and Trade Zone is a symbol of Shanghai's reform and opening up (Fig. 7).

Forty-two years ago, it was still a patchwork of farmland with waving reeds.

In June 1995, Yindu Building was completed and the Shanghai Branch of the People's Bank of China was officially settled in Lujiazui, becoming the leader of the financial industry in Lujiazui. Subsequently, the Shanghai Stock Exchange and the headquarter of the Bank of Communications also moved in one after another.

In the following few years, many Chinese and foreign banks and other financial institutions had been stationed in Pudong, leading to the emergence of a financial center, which witnessed the birth of a number of 'China's first': in 1992, the first foreign-funded insurance company, American International Assurance Company opened; In 1995, the first foreign-funded bank, the Shanghai branch of Japan's Fuji Bank, opened. Since then, the first foreign-funded bank, the first Sino-foreign joint venture fund, and the first Sino-foreign joint venture exhibition center have come and gone. Thus Lujiazui had become a shining business card of Pudong to the world (Figs. 8 and 9).

Fig. 7 View of Pudong from Puxi in the 1980s

Fig. 8 The People's Bank of China moved into Lujiazui Financial District in 1995

Fig. 9 Lujiazui Financial District at the end of the twentieth century

Back then, there was a trail in Lujiazui called 'Lannidu Road', which means muddy ferry road. Designers from five countries including China, Italy, Japan, France and the UK had put forward five different instruction plans. The Shanghai Joint Working Group considered the advanced concepts and layout features of all these plans, listened to the opinions of experts repeatedly, and finally came up with a plan for the Lujiazui Finance and Trade Zone that fully embodied the international concepts (Fig. 10).

This was the first time in China's history that an international consultation was conducted for a regional plan, giving birth to the first planning program that brought together international wisdom.

Fig. 10 Pudong Lujiazui has evolved from a suburb in the 1990s to the thriving scene it is today (Top photo taken in 2017, bottom photo taken in 1990)

Fig. 11 Century Avenue in Pudong starts with the Oriental Pearl Tower and ends with a giant sundial sculpture

The northern part of the former "Lannidu Road" has now been incorporated into the newly constructed Yincheng Middle Road, while the southern part has been renamed as Puming Road. Nowadays, this 'muddy ferry road' can no longer be found on the map of Pudong, replaced by a string of many financial buildings on Yincheng Road. When the Oriental Pearl Tower, Jin Mao Tower, Shanghai World Financial Center, Shanghai Center and other famous landmarks had been completed, Lannidu Road and the residential area of humble old houses had disappeared, replaced by a world-impressed Lujiazui Financial (Fig. 11).

In the core area of Lujiazui Finance and Trade Zone which covers only 1.7 km^2, there are numerous multinational headquarters, and headquarters of central enterprises, private enterprises and financial institutions densely packed in high-rise buildings, which makes this place like a "headquarter brain" gathering area, and there are countless commands sent to the whole country, and even to the whole of Asia every day from here.

In addition to the core zone, the entire Lujiazui Finance and Trade Zone, which covers an area of 31.78 km^2, the headquarters economy is still extending into the hinterland and gradually highlighting its role.

From the center of Lujiazui along the Century Avenue all the way to the east to the Huamu Administrative and Cultural District, this area is gradually forming a 'Golden Corridor of finance and headquarters'. This golden corridor concentrates most of the financial institutions and headquarters organizations in Lujiazui, and has become an important economic artery in the Lujiazui Finance and Trade Zone.

2.3 The Rapidly Changing City Skyline

Along with the tide of development and opening up of Pudong, the heights of Shanghai have been constantly refreshed.

At one time, the 24-m-high Dongchang Road Fire Watch Tower was the "first height" in Pudong (Figs. 12 and 13).

Breaking this height was the completion of the 463-m Oriental Pearl Radio and Television Tower, which was officially put into use in 1995 and was once hailed as "the symbol of the rise of the new Shanghai.

In 1997, the 420.5-m Shanghai Jin Mao Tower was topped out.

In 2008, the 492-m Shanghai World Financial Center was completed (Figs. 14 and 15).

In 2016, the 632-m Shanghai Center Tower was completed. This "vertical city" can accommodate 20,000 to 30,000 people, which is almost equivalent to the population of a small to medium-sized city in Europe, and has a full range of services such as restaurants, accommodations, and stores. The Duoyun Bookstore on the 52nd floor of the building is a cultural complex in the sky that combines bookstores, exhibitions, and recreation, and the Guanfu Museum on the 37th floor displays artifacts and art treasures from the collection of collector Ma Weidu through the ages, which gives Lujiazui Financial City not only height, but also breadth, depth, and warmth, and enhances the quality of the city with culture (Fig. 16).

Fig. 12 Dongchang Road Fire Watch Tower, once the tallest building in Pudong

Fig. 13 The construction of the Oriental Pearl TV Tower began in July 1991 and was completed in October 1994

Shanghai Center Tower, as the highest point of Shanghai, is the first world-class super high-rise building in China, led by a Chinese team, supported by Chinese technology and Chinese manufacturing, which has promoted the rise of a large number of Chinese manufacturers and Chinese brands, which have been standing at the global first-line level of the industry.

In 2020, the GDP of Pudong New Area has reached 1273.4 billion yuan, which is 211 times more than that of 6.024 billion yuan in 1990; the per capita GDP has reached 238,000 yuan, or 36,800 US dollars, and has entered the level of middle to upper-developed countries. With 1/8000 of the country's land area, Pudong has created 1/80 of GDP and 1/15 of total import and export of goods, and has become one of the important "high points" of Shanghai and even China's economic growth.

Fig. 14 The continuously growing Lujiazui Finance and Trade Zone in Pudong (photographed in April 2008)

Fig. 15 The Duo Yun bookstore Flagship Shop

Fig. 16 The completion of Shanghai Center once again refreshed the city skyline of Shanghai

2.4 Aiming for the Future, Creating a World-Class Core Business Landmark

As the development of Lujiazui, after entering the "first track" of global financial cities, the enhancement of resource allocation capacity during the "14th Five-Year Plan" period becomes even more crucial.

The newly issued "*Opinions of the Central Committee of the Communist Party of China and the State Council on Supporting Pudong New Area to Carry out High-level Reform and Opening up and Build a Leading Area for Socialist Modernization Construction*" clearly stated that Pudong should enhance its ability to allocate global resources and serve the construction of a new development pattern. Improving the financial market system, product system, institutional system and infrastructure system is the basis for strengthening functions. Lujiazui had proposed a roadmap for this in Shanghai's "14th Five-Year Plan": accelerate the construction of a world-class top-level asset management center, a national financial leasing industry center, and an international insurance and reinsurance center, strive to build a high-energy licensed institution gathering highland and the core area of Shanghai's financial technology center, and guide finance to better serve key industries and the real economy.

According to the Global Financial Centers Index (GFCI) rankings, Shanghai has firmly remained in sixth place globally since 2022 (the top five are the old financial centers such as New York, London, Singapore, Hong Kong, and San Francisco). It has performed outstandingly in five core areas including talent, business environment, market development degree, infrastructure, and overall competitiveness, demonstrating the strong competitiveness and attractiveness of a world-class financial center (Fig. 17).

Fig. 17 Thirty years after the development and opening up of Pudong, both sides of the Yangtze River are prosperous

Quan Heng (Party secretary of the Shanghai Federation of Social Sciences Circles): Pudong is inherently endowed with an open gene and a mission of taking the lead in trying out new things. Although located in Shanghai, it was initially positioned as the "leader" and highland of the national regional development strategy, and undertakes the strategic mission of "developing Pudong, revitalizing Shanghai, serving the whole country and facing the world".

The practice of Pudong's development and opening up for thirty years was carried out in the historical process of China's realization of its first hundred-year goal, and the development of the next thirty years coincides with the historical process of China's realization of its second hundred-year goal (Fig. 18).

Chen Gaohong (Vice President of China Institute of Urban Governance, Shanghai Jiaotong University): Looking back at the 30 years of development and opening up of Pudong, the reason why we have kept moving forward is that the most fundamental guarantee and the most profound experience is that we have always been loyal to the overall situation of the Party and the country's development, we have always dared to bravely take up the mission when the Party and the country are faced with the risks and challenges, and we have always been adept at realizing the national strategy by scientifically grasping the international and domestic situation.

In the new era, Pudong, which is in its prime, stands even taller at the forefront. It aims to become a model for the governance of mega-cities in China, an important window to show the building of a powerful socialist modern country, a functional highland to deeply integrate into the global economic pattern, and an open banner for China to promote and lead economic globalization.

Fig. 18 Pudong Rises from Reform and Opening-up

3 From Bonded Area to Free Trade Zone

In Pudong, just like Lujiazui, a series of new areas are also lit up one by one by the "magic wand" of opening up. Zhangjiang, Jinqiao, Waigaoqiao and other three bonded areas, Lingang New Area, Expo Park and Disneyland International Tourist Resort, etc.

Pudong has had its confusions. When the policy dividends, resource dividends and labor dividends are gradually released, where is the staying power? As the wind of opening up blows strongly, many shortcomings that are not in line with and cannot be connected with international prevailing rules are exposed. What should we do?

The thinking of Pudong New Area is that, Pudong's taking the lead in trying out new things is not like "running a red light", but rather creating a "new traffic light system", and paying more attention to "local breakthroughs" and "pioneering spirit".

When the problems arising from development became increasingly acute and complicated, China once again came to a crucial moment of reform. After the national comprehensive pilot reform, the central government first entrusted the burden of the pilot free trade zone to Shanghai and Pudong. Pudong should adhere to taking institutional innovation as the core and taking the construction of the pilot free trade zone as a breakthrough to fully deepen the crucial reform.

3.1 Pioneering Exploration: Establishment of Bonded Areas

On April 18, 1990, Premier Li Peng announced at the fifth anniversary conference of the establishment of Shanghai Volkswagen Automotive Co., Ltd. the major decision of the CPC Central Committee and the State Council on developing and opening up Pudong, Shanghai: Agree that Shanghai will accelerate the development of Pudong area and implement the policies of economic and technological development zones and some special economic zones in Pudong.

Lujiazui, Jinqiao and Waigaoqiao are undoubtedly the first three areas in Shanghai to "eat crabs", kicking off the development of Shanghai's financial district, bonded area and free trade zone.

> Chen Zilei (professor of Shanghai University of International Business and Economics): With the establishment of Pudong New Area in the early 1990s, Shanghai has obtained greater policy space for development. While implementing national policies, it promotes local economic development and in turn nourishes the development of the national economy with local economy.

While Lujiazui was under construction, the first export processing zone (Jinqiao Export Processing Zone) and the first bonded area (Waigaoqiao Bonded Area) jointly established the foundation for Pudong's export-oriented economy. When introducing foreign capital, Pudong has been highly selective from the very beginning and set a "high threshold". The enterprises carefully chosen to enter have ample technological content and strong driving capacity, giving rise to numerous industrial chains. For example, Roche Pharmaceuticals set up its Shanghai company in Pudong in 1994 and became the first Sino-foreign joint venture to settle in Zhangjiang. It took the lead in constructing a complete pharmaceutical value industrial chain including research and development, production, and marketing. At present, its business spreads throughout the country (Fig. 19).

Five months later, the Jinqiao Export Processing Zone Development Company, the Waigaoqiao Bonded Area Development Company, and the Lujiazui Financial and Trade Zone Development Company were established concurrently. Pudong New Area has drawn lessons from Shanghai's past urban development pattern of "spreading like a pancake". It divides regions according to urban functions. Finance and trade are located in the Lujiazui area on the east side of the Huangpu River, just across the river from the former financial street, the Bund. The only development zone in China mainly centered on "export processing" is placed in Jinqiao. Port handling and logistics warehouses are situated in the Waigaoqiao area at the estuary of the Huangpu River (Fig. 20).

The Jinqiao Export Processing Zone covers a total area of 20.48 km^2. Within the zone, industrial plants and R&D office buildings with a total area of approximately 1 million square meters have been constructed. Currently, thousands of enterprises have settled here, including Fortune 500 companies such as Huawei, General Motors, Cadillac, and Castrol, along with a large number of their supporting factories.

The Waigaoqiao Bonded Area is the first bonded area in the country after reform and opening up and also a testing ground for reform. The reformers have incorporated their ambition and far-sightedness into the English name of the Waigaoqiao Bonded Area: Free Trade Zone, which literally translates to "free trade zone" (Fig. 21).

Fig. 19 Jinqiao Export Processing Zone established in 1990 with approval

> Chen Zilei, a professor of Shanghai University of International Business and Economics, said: For the earliest Waigaoqiao Bonded Area, Premier Zhu Rongji named it "FTZ", which stands for Free Trade Zone in English. So Premier Zhu Rongji's idea at that time was to take the construction of a free trade zone as the ultimate policy goal. Therefore, in the bonded area, we do not levy tariffs on incoming and outgoing goods. Goods can be stored here. They can be transported in from overseas and out from the area. Goods can flow freely without tariff levying.

At that time, people were still very unfamiliar with the concept of bonded areas. The so-called "bonded area" refers to a special area under the supervision of the customs, operating in a way of "domestic territory but outside customs territory". Goods entering the bonded area can enjoy policies of "exemption from certificates, exemption from taxes, and bonded status", and can carry out import and export processing, international trade, bonded warehousing, commodity display, etc. This was one of the economic areas with the highest degree of opening up, the most convenient operating mechanism, and the most favorable policies in China at that time (Fig. 22).

> Zhou Hanmin (Dean of Shanghai Socialist Institute): A total of 15 bonded zones have been established in China, with Waigaoqiao being the largest, covering an area of 10 km^2. At the time of planning and research, we all believed this was the highest goal, representing the greatest level of openness. We called it a bonded zone, aiming for the skies, a remarkable achievement.

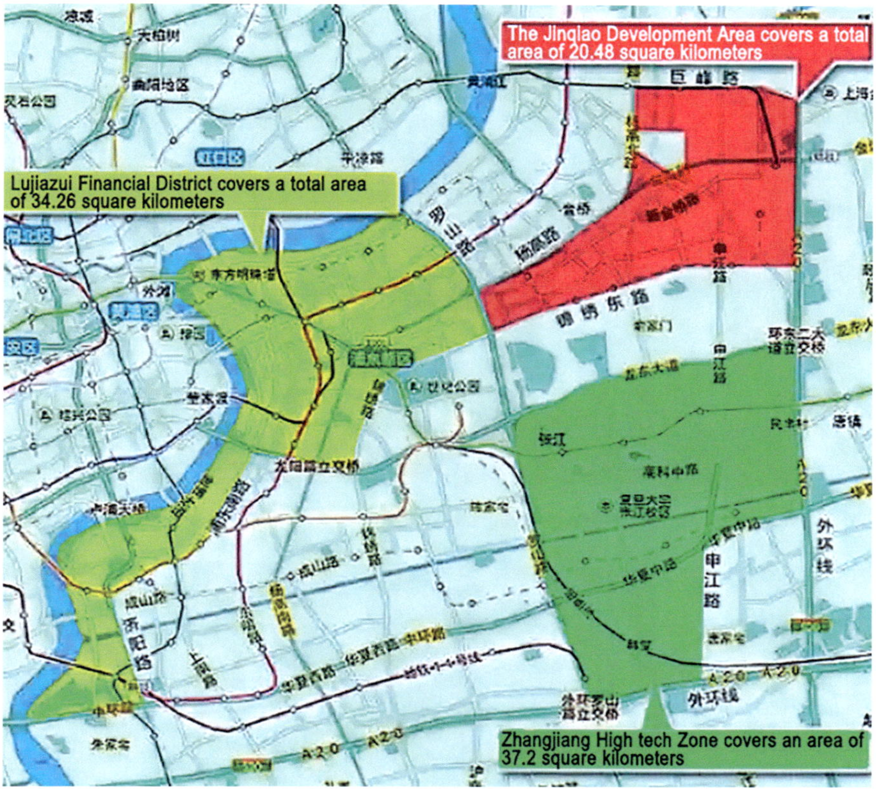

Fig. 20 Schematic diagram of the planned area of Jinqiao Development Area, Lujiazui Financial Area and Zhangjiang High-tech Area

3.1.1 Transformative Development—Construction of the Bonded Zone

Reflecting on the early 1990s, the northeastern part of Pudong, where Waigaoqiao is located, was still covered by vast rice fields, and the area leading to the Yangtze River estuary was a large reed marsh. In August 1991, construction began on the first four square kilometers of Waigaoqiao Bonded Zone. The bonded zone's isolation facilities and checkpoints became the first foundational engineering project designed by Shanghai Customs for the bonded area. At that time, there were few bus routes in Pudong; people had to bike more than 20 km to reach Waigaoqiao. There were no canteens in the area, so workers would bring food from home or dry rations for lunch and request hot water from nearby farmers.

Building the bonded zone's perimeter wall was unprecedented in China. The design had to be aesthetically pleasing, cost-effective, and functional. After reviewing a large amount of materials and referencing international standards, a construction standard was designed specifically for the bonded zone, outlining the "necessary

Fig. 21 Waigaoqiao Bonded Area of Shanghai, 1990

Fig. 22 The Waigaoqiao Bonded Area received strong support from national policies at that time

Fig. 23 Waigaoqiao Bonded Zone Perimeter Wall Construction

conditions for Waigaoqiao Bonded Zone acceptance," which was then provided to the construction company—Shanghai Waigaoqiao Free Trade Zone Development Company.

The perimeter wall of the initial 0.453 km^2 spanned a total length of 3.35 km, with a height of 3 m. The bottom section was a 50 cm concrete brick wall, followed by a 215 cm metal mesh, separated by a 5 cm gap, and topped with three rows of barbed wire spaced 10 cm apart. At the intersection of Latitude D and Yanggao Road, a customs checkpoint was constructed, including a 21-square-meter inspection room and a 900-square-meter cargo inspection area. Latitude D was designed as an entry and exit passage with separate lanes for pedestrians and vehicles, with widths of 4 and 12 m, respectively (Fig. 23).

From March 7 to 9, 1992, a national customs acceptance team led by then-Deputy Director of the National Customs General Administration, Liu Wenjie, inspected the isolation facilities of the initial phase of the Waigaoqiao Bonded Zone. During the acceptance review meeting, the team questioned, "Why has the wall height been shortened by a few centimeters?" It was later discovered that since the project was built on rice paddies, the wall had sunk slightly after early completion. Upon learning of this, the construction unit immediately made adjustments. On March 9, the first phase, covering 0.453 km^2, passed the inspection and officially began operations.

With experience from the first phase inspection, subsequent inspection processes went more smoothly. By March 1993, the new round of isolation facilities, built by the Waigaoqiao Joint Development Company, had largely been completed, spanning 9.36 km and covering approximately 2 km^2.

By the end of 1994, an additional 3.5 km^2 was completed, raising the Waigaoqiao Bonded Zone's total operational area to 5.5 km^2. By this point, the Waigaoqiao

Fig. 24 Official Operations of the First Phase of the Waigaoqiao Bonded Zone

Bonded Zone had transformed from a prototype to a mature zone, with numerous modern manufacturing plants, commercial buildings, and warehouses springing up, making it the fastest-developing bonded area in the country (Fig. 24).

> Wang Zhan (Chairman of the Shanghai Social Science Association): Since the 1980s, we have been utilizing foreign investment, but the profits were largely made outside of China. In simple terms, it was "high in and low out"—imported components entered at high prices, while finished products, processed domestically, had their prices depressed for export, with profits primarily generated outside of China, resulting in most foreign-invested enterprises showing losses within China during the 1980s.
>
> We discussed why a bonded or free trade zone was needed: our hope was that Waigaoqiao would allow for the bonded display of various foreign components, giving us insight into real prices and avoiding total control over supply and demand by foreign entities.

3.1.2 An Open Door—Itochu Corporation's Entry

At the beginning of the Waigaoqiao Bonded Zone, although the door was open, there were still many regulatory restrictions on establishing trade companies in China. The approval authority for foreign trade companies was centralized under the Ministry of Foreign Trade and Economic Cooperation, with no authorization given to the Shanghai Municipal Government. It wasn't until 1992 that Itochu Corporation established Shanghai Itochu Trading Co., Ltd., marking the breakthrough of foreign investment in China and witnessing the development and opening up of Pudong (Fig. 25).

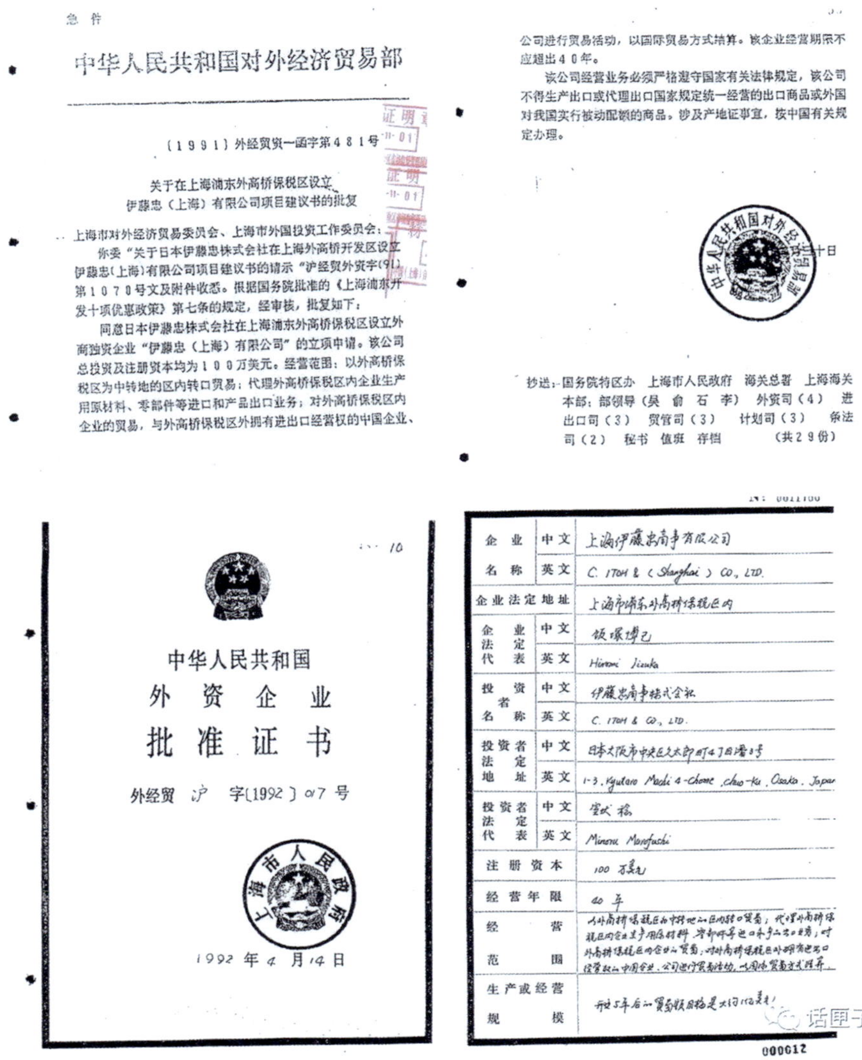

急件

中华人民共和国对外经济贸易部

〔1991〕外经贸资一函字第481号

关于在上海浦东外高桥保税区设立伊藤忠（上海）有限公司项目建议书的批复

上海市对外经济贸易委员会、上海市外国投资工作委员会：

你委"关于日本伊藤忠株式会社在上海外高桥开发区设立伊藤忠（上海）有限公司项目建议书的请示"沪经贸外资字(91)第1070号文及附件收悉。根据国务院批准的《上海浦东开发十项优惠政策》第七条的规定，经审核，批复如下：

同意日本伊藤忠株式会社在上海浦东外高桥保税区设立外商独资企业"伊藤忠（上海）有限公司"的立项申请。该公司总投资及注册资本均为100万美元。经营范围：以外高桥保税区为中转地的区内转口贸易；代理外高桥保税区内企业生产用原材料、零部件等进口和产品出口业务；对外高桥保税区内企业的贸易，与外高桥保税区外拥有进出口经营权的中国企业、公司进行贸易活动，以国际贸易方式结算。该企业经营期限不应超出40年。

该公司经营业务必须严格遵守国家有关法律规定，该公司不得生产出口或代理出口国家规定统一经营的出口商品或外国对我国实行被动配额的商品。涉及产地证事宜，按中国有关规定办理。

十日

抄送：国务院特区办 上海市人民政府 海关总署 上海海关
本部：部领导（吴 俞 石 李） 外资司（4） 进出口司（3） 贸管司（3） 计划司（3） 条法司（2） 秘书 值班 存档 （共29份）

10

中华人民共和国
外资企业
批准证书

外经贸 沪 字〔1992〕017 号

1992 年 4 月 14 日

企业名称	中文	上海伊藤忠商事有限公司
	英文	C. ITOH & (Shanghai) CO., LTD.
企业法定地址		上海市浦东外高桥保税区内
企业法定代表	中文	饭塚博己
	英文	Hiromi Iizuka
投资者名称	中文	伊藤忠商事株式会社
	英文	C. ITOH & CO., LTD.
投资者法定地址	中文	日本大阪市中央区久太郎町4丁目1番3号
	英文	1-3, Kyutaro Machi 4-Chome, Chuo-Ku, Osaka, Japan
投资者法定代表	中文	室伏稔
	英文	Minoru Murofushi
注册资本		100万美元
经营年限		40年
经营范围		以外高桥保税区为中转地的区内转口贸易；代理外高桥保税区内企业生产用原材料、零部件等进口和产品出口业务；对外高桥保税区内企业的贸易；对外高桥保税区外拥有进出口经营权的中国企业、公司进行贸易活动，以国际贸易方式结算。
生产或经营规模		开业5年后的贸易额目标是大约1亿美元！

000012

Fig. 25 Approval Letter for Establishing Itochu (Shanghai) Co., Ltd. in Waigaoqiao, Pudong

Chao Gangling (Professor at Shanghai University of Finance and Economics): In trade, we maintained strict regulations. We allowed foreign capital to invest initially only in manufacturing and production enterprises, enabling us to benefit from their investment and technology. At the time, there was a policy of "exchanging markets for technology," meaning the first step in opening up focused on production, with trade remaining restricted and strictly regulated. Even joint ventures in commerce were not permitted.

Itochu Corporation, founded in 1858, was recognized by the State Council as a friendly trading company in 1972 and was the first of Japan's top five trading companies allowed to reopen Sino-Japanese trade.

A fresh breeze from the east heralded new opportunities. In this regulatory environment that restricted foreign trade companies, Itochu's breakthrough in Shanghai's Pudong opened new horizons. Three months later, the central government transferred approval rights for foreign trade companies with registered capital under $500,000 to Shanghai, making Pudong a haven for foreign investment.

Itochu's business in China grew alongside the country's economic reform and development. In the 1990s, Itochu mainly imported large equipment for sale to Chinese companies. After 2000, with rising Chinese purchasing power and consumer upgrades, Itochu began introducing high-end, safe raw materials and food products into the Chinese market. After 2010, it ventured into industrial investments, establishing joint ventures with promising companies to explore new markets.

> Chen Zilei (Professor at Shanghai University of International Business and Economics): The Itochu model transformed China's traditional trade system, challenging it significantly. Once policy barriers were removed, investment naturally followed. Shanghai's geographic location, its economic position nationally, and its global economic connections made it an ideal location for these companies, exemplifying the original mission of the bonded zone: to promote trade liberalization.

> Mizutani Hidefumi (General Manager of Itochu (Shanghai) Co., Ltd.): Itochu has been operating in China for 46 years, and our most important market is China, not Europe or the U.S. Starting from the first trading company, Itochu now has 17 branches and over 750 employees in China, with businesses in six sectors: fibers, machinery, energy and chemicals, food, metals, and living materials. Beyond trade, we also engage in finance, such as banking and investments. With further market openings due to China's reform and opening up, I am confident that Itochu's business in China will continue to expand.

Reform is the continuous improvement of systems. The central government's decision to transfer trade approval rights to local governments in 1992 officially launched China's trade liberalization. However, Waigaoqiao Bonded Zone's ambitions extended beyond this.

Bonded display and trade have always been core functions of the bonded zone. In the 1990s, foreign companies were still only partially open in trade, limited to foreign trade and unable to engage in domestic trade, which made Waigaoqiao Bonded Zone an isolated island separated from the Chinese market. Recognizing the strong demand within the zone for domestic trade, Waigaoqiao Bonded Zone established a platform for international and domestic trade, creating a bonded goods market. It also launched specialized trading platforms for key import–export goods such as wine, cosmetics, pharmaceuticals, and high-end machinery.

Thanks to its advantageous location, flexible policies, and vast market, Pudong quickly became the first choice for foreign companies entering China. By the end of 2020, Pudong had attracted over $100 billion in actual foreign investment, with 36,300 foreign enterprises registered, including 245 foreign R&D centers and 359 regional headquarters of multinational companies. From Itochu's pioneering entry 28 years ago to today's thriving and competitive landscape, Pudong has seen a remarkable transformation.

3.2 Progressive Opening: The Comprehensive Bonded Zone

The abundance of imported goods and attractive duty-free prices in bonded zones provided an "overseas" shopping experience without leaving China. However, after China's entry into the WTO and subsequent tariff reductions, the original advantages of bonded zones gradually diminished.

In comparison, comprehensive bonded zones could be established in inland areas, offering policies like import duty rebates and unlimited storage for bonded goods, functioning as customs special supervision areas with bonded port capabilities. These zones save significant time and operational costs for companies (Fig. 26).

Ma Lingyuan [Business and Sales Operations Director at Maserati (China) Automobile Trading Co., Ltd.]: With bonded warehousing, companies can pay relevant taxes only after receiving orders, allowing for faster cash flow and scaling operations more effectively.

On November 18, 2009, the Shanghai Comprehensive Bonded Zone was officially inaugurated, marking the beginning of a coordinated operation between the Port of Yangshan, Waigaoqiao Port, Pudong Airport, and three bonded areas: Yangshan Bonded Port Area, Waigaoqiao Bonded Area, and Pudong Airport Comprehensive Bonded Area. This transformation from isolated operations to integrated collaboration allowed each bonded area to clarify its unique role and fully leverage its strengths.

In essence, the comprehensive bonded zone represents the highest level of openness in China, offering the most favorable policies and the most complete functions and simplified procedures, except for free trade zones.

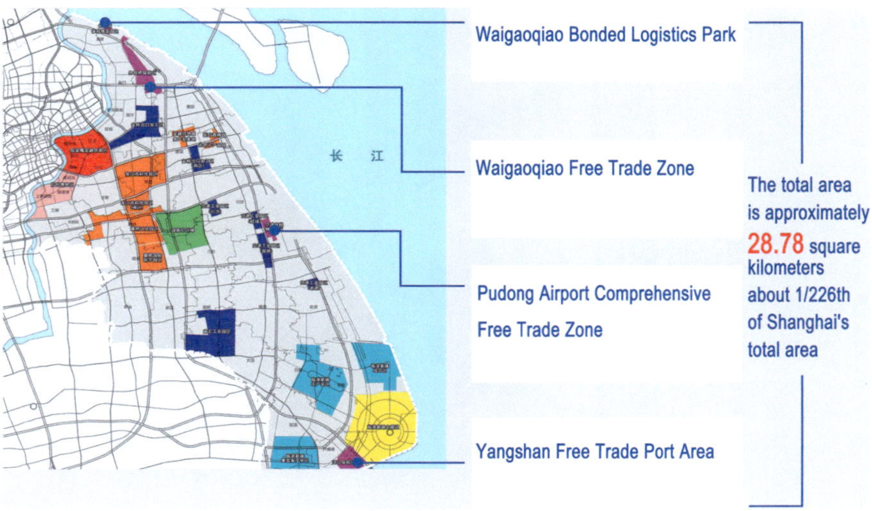

Fig. 26 "Three Ports, Three Zones" Linkage in the Shanghai Comprehensive Bonded Zone

3.2.1 Functional Roles of Shanghai's Major Bonded Areas

1. **Yangshan Bonded Port Area**

The Yangshan Bonded Port Area focuses on building a comprehensive experimental zone for international shipping development and vigorously develops multi-level businesses such as international transshipment, modern logistics, commodity exhibition, bonded warehousing, and bonded delivery of futures (Fig. 27).

International purchasers can implement unified allocation and management of goods in the Yangshan Bonded Port Area, effectively integrating the logistics chain and the trade chain. Meanwhile, enterprises can take advantage of the policy benefit of "tax refund upon entry into the area" in the Yangshan Bonded Port Area and the feature of the concentration of routes to Europe and the United States, which facilitates the development of container export consolidation business and the opening of offshore accounts, providing convenience for financing their overseas businesses. By utilizing the tax-free environment of the Yangshan Bonded Port Area, goods under the bonded status are incorporated into the delivery system, enabling enterprises in the area to take into account both the domestic and international markets simultaneously.

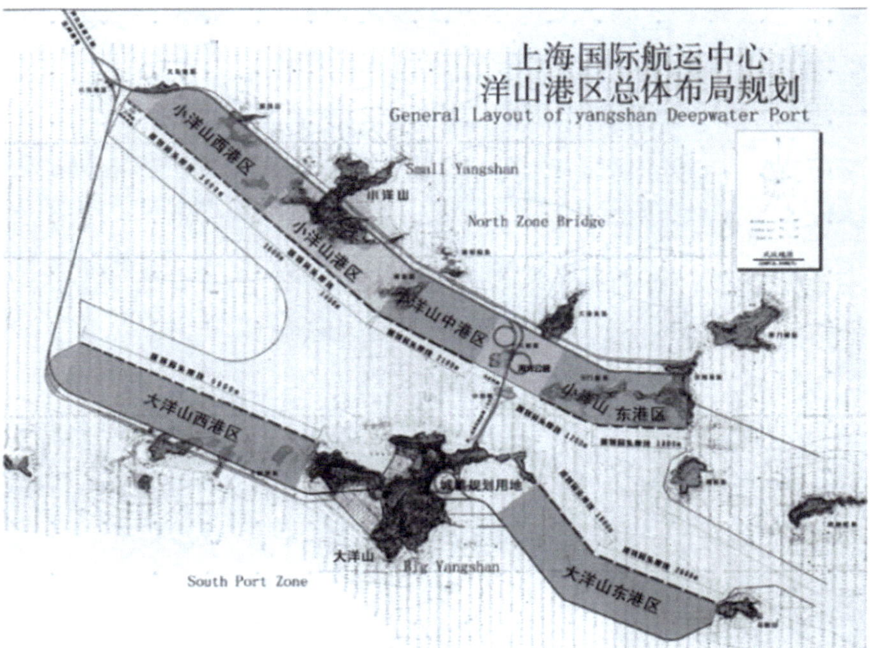

Fig. 27 Master Layout of the Yangshan Port International Shipping Center

Fig. 28 Customs Oversight of Imported Vehicles in Waigaoqiao Bonded Area

2. **The Waigaoqiao Bonded Area (including the Waigaoqiao Bonded Logistics Park)**

Focuses on becoming a demonstration zone for international trade, promoting import–export trade, transit trade, bonded display, warehousing, and distribution services. It enables customs-regulated storage, processing, and sales of bonded goods, allowing efficient distribution to both domestic and international markets (Fig. 28).

Additionally, Waigaoqiao piloted centralized fund management for multinational companies, exploring foreign exchange settlement under the combined transit trade model and enhancing offshore trade operations, ultimately strengthening trade capabilities.

3. **Pudong Airport Comprehensive Bonded Zone**

Relying on its role as an aviation hub at Pudong International Airport, this zone focuses on express air freight, distribution, third-party logistics, air-cargo bonded storage, and value-added logistics services like inspection and repair. It also hosts SPVs (Special Purpose Vehicles) for aircraft leasing, providing leasing services of aircraft and engines to domestic and international airlines (Fig. 29).

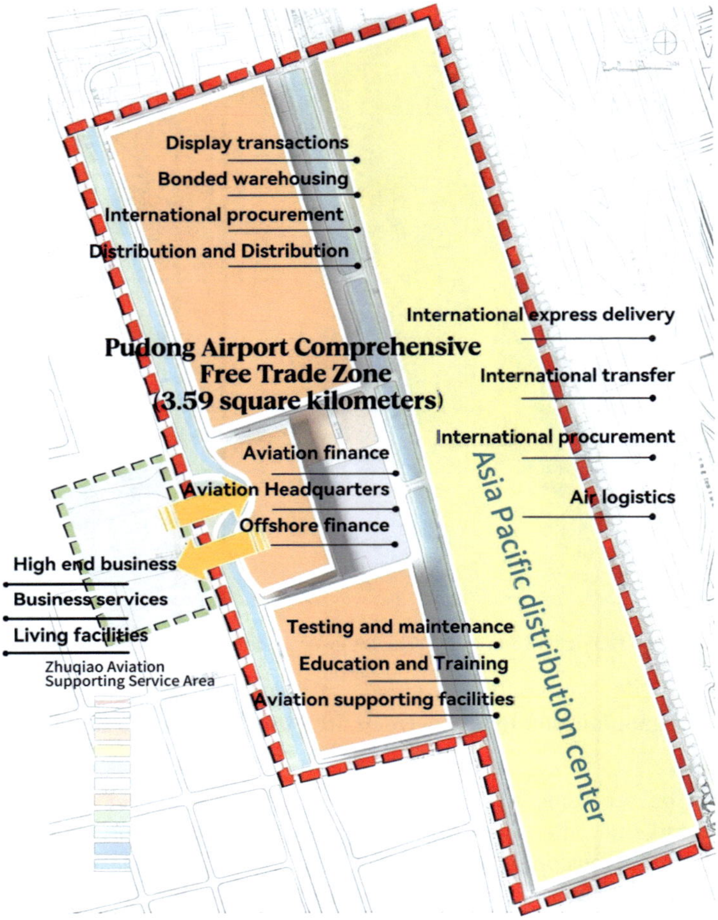

Fig. 29 Layout of Pudong Airport Comprehensive Bonded Zone

3.2.2 Policy Advantages of the Shanghai Comprehensive Bonded Zone

The Shanghai Comprehensive Bonded Zone combines policies of bonded zones, bonded port areas, comprehensive bonded zones, bonded logistics parks, and export processing zones, achieving a level of regulatory, customs, foreign exchange, and inspection convenience unmatched nationwide. Advantages include duty-free and deferred taxation, export rebates, bonded processing, efficient customs declarations, flexible foreign exchange policies, and more.

Moreover, the zone embraces a spirit of "pilot-testing and innovation," consistently advancing institutional innovation and guiding industrial transformation to position Shanghai as a leader in China's high-quality economic development.

Since 2019, Shanghai has received national approval and completed acceptance inspections for five comprehensive bonded zones in Caohejing, Fengxian, Songjiang, Qingpu, and Jinqiao, all transformed from export processing zones, and they are becoming new heights for Shanghai's open economy. For example, in the Caohejing Comprehensive Bonded Zone, customs successfully handled the country's first bonded storage vehicle for domestic sale, paving new pathways for inbound storage, certification, and taxed domestic sales of special vehicles. The Qingpu zone processes 400,000 semiconductor wafers annually, contributing to Shanghai's integrated circuit industry cluster; and a new energy vehicle company in the Songjiang zone expects to produce 100,000 vehicles per year in its initial phase, creating over 2000 jobs.

3.3 Cultivating a "Testing Ground": China (Shanghai) Pilot Free Trade Zone

On September 29, 2013, the China (Shanghai) Pilot Free Trade Zone was officially established. Many were unaware that this 28.78-square-kilometer area in Pudong was China's strategic move for deepening reform, aimed at driving reform through opening-up and regulatory innovation, with Pudong transforming once again and "institutional innovation" becoming its defining hallmark (Fig. 30).

Fig. 30 The China (Shanghai) Pilot Free Trade Zone Officially Launched in 2013

Fig. 31 The FTZ, a National "Testing Ground," Is Charged with Developing Replicable and Scalable Experiences

As one U.S. financial site noted, "Just as Deng Xiaoping's establishment of Special Economic Zones was a policy reform signal, the Shanghai FTZ's experiment will provide direction for future reforms.

Initially, the Shanghai FTZ included the Waigaoqiao Bonded Zone, Waigaoqiao Bonded Logistics Park, Pudong Airport Comprehensive Bonded Zone, and Yangshan Bonded Port Area. Within just over a year, it expanded to include the Jinqiao Export Processing Zone, Zhangjiang High-Tech Park, and Lujiazui Financial and Trade Zone, increasing in size from the original 28.78 km^2 to 120.72 km^2 (Fig. 31).

Sun Yuanxin (Professor at Shanghai University of Finance and Economics): Institutional innovation, or systemic reform, was necessary to expand foreign investment access, enhance trade facilitation, transform government functions, and open financial markets. If such reforms were implemented nationwide, they could pose risks, so a pilot area was chosen for experimentation. The Shanghai Comprehensive Bonded Zone, with Waigaoqiao at its core, was selected due to its primary role in import–export trade, giving it the title "Free Trade Zone."

Since its establishment, the Shanghai FTZ has adhered to a "pilot-first, innovation-driven" approach, fostering a business environment grounded in legal standards and global practices. Utilizing just one-fiftieth of Shanghai's land, it has contributed a quarter of the city's GDP and tax revenue, producing over 120 institutional innovations, many of which have been replicated nationwide.

The establishment of the Shanghai FTZ has driven significant growth in both the secondary and tertiary sectors, particularly through favorable policies that benefit the steel, automotive, financial, logistics, commercial, trade, cultural, and social services sectors. The FTZ's access to China's most prosperous city and province, along with its proximity to ports and international airports, advantageous policies, and excellent infrastructure, has accelerated the development of Shanghai's service sector.

If China's economy is likened to an ocean, free trade zones are like big fish one after another. Since the Shanghai FTZ's founding eight years ago, China has established 21 free trade zones nationwide, including in Guangdong, Tianjin, Fujian, Liaoning, Zhejiang, Henan, Hubei, Chongqing, Sichuan, Shaanxi, and Hainan, creating a pilot layout that spans east, west, south, and north.

3.4 New Mission in a Changing Landscape: Lingang New Area

With economic globalization and digital trade advancing, deeper "Belt and Road" cooperation, and escalating U.S.-China trade tensions, the domestic and international market environment has grown increasingly complex. To meet the need for further openness, the central government decided to establish the Lingang New Area within the existing Shanghai FTZ, entrusting it with a higher historical mission to promote the liberalization of goods, services, investment, finance, and data under trade security and risk control conditions.

In August 2019, the State Council issued the "Overall Plan for the Lingang New Area of the China (Shanghai) Pilot Free Trade Zone" along with official approval for its establishment. The initial Lingang New Area covers 119.5 km^2, including three main sections: the southern area of Lingang (76.5 km^2), Xiaoyangshan Island (18.3 km^2), and the southern section of Pudong Airport (24.7 km^2).

The Plan clearly puts forward that on the basis of applying various open and innovative measures of the free trade pilot zones, the new area should be supported to focus on freedoms in investment, trade, capital, transportation and employment of personnel, etc., and promote the liberalization and facilitation of investment and trade. The Lingang New Area places greater emphasis on the free flow of various economic factors. It not only needs to improve the facilitation level through innovation in the government supervision mode, but also achieve a higher level of openness.

On August 20, 2019, the Lingang New Area was officially inaugurated by Dishui Lake, marking the second expansion of the FTZ since its initial establishment in September 2013. Thirteen companies received the first business licenses that same day, with investments spanning fields such as integrated circuits, biopharmaceuticals, and artificial intelligence, totaling over 30 billion yuan (Figs. 32 and 33).

Following fifteen years of development and construction, the Lingang area has evolved into an advanced manufacturing industrial base, attracting a cluster of leading enterprises with high-tech content from both domestic and international markets.

Fig. 32 The Lingang New Area of the China (Shanghai) Pilot Free Trade Zone

Fig. 33 Establishment of the Lingang New Area in the China (Shanghai) Pilot Free Trade Zone

Fig. 34 Tesla's Shanghai Gigafactory, Phase One, has a production capacity of 250,000 vehicles annually, with exports to Europe and the Asia–Pacific region

Moreover, the Lingang area is advantaged by its excellent transportation infrastructure. Leveraging the international freight hub capabilities of the Yangshan Deepwater Port and Pudong Airport, it serves as a crucial underpinning for the growth of industrial and trade functions.

The introduction of the Lingang New Area is not simply a matter of expanding space or relocating policies; it is about establishing a new system, new functions, new industries, and a new economy that drives outward openness, positioning itself as a new hub in the global economic network. The Lingang New Area aims to develop four core sectors—cutting-edge technology, cross-border finance, international trade, and high- level shipping services—to form world-class industry clusters, foster new economic drivers, and boost China's global competitiveness (Fig. 34).

Owing to the "6 + 2" open policies and systems of the new area, along with the recently introduced "50-item" supporting policies in Shanghai, the Lingang New Area has a significant attraction for enterprises. The "6" specifically implies convenient investment and operation, free in-and-out movement of goods, smooth capital flow, highly open transportation, unrestricted professional practice of personnel, and rapid information interconnection. The "2" stands for an internationally competitive tax system and a comprehensive risk management system. This array of incentive policies guarantees that the Lingang New Area can enjoy advantages that are unparalleled by other regions.

> Chen Yin (Executive Vice Mayor of Shanghai and Director of the Lingang New Area Administration): Our aim is for the Lingang New Area to be the city's most attractive region for policy resources, drawing in talent and projects on a large scale.

On August 12, 2021, the Shanghai Municipal Government released the "14th Five-Year Plan for the Development of the Lingang New Area of the China (Shanghai)

Free Trade Pilot Zone", which defined the development goals of the new area: By 2025, the regional GDP will quadruple on the basis of 2018, with an average annual growth rate reaching 25%. Three 100-billion-level industrial clusters of intelligent new energy vehicles, integrated circuits, and high-end equipment manufacturing will be cultivated and formed, and advanced manufacturing industrial clusters such as biomedicine, artificial intelligence, and civil aviation will be expanded and strengthened. Industries such as cross-border financial services, new forms of international trade, modern shipping services, digital information services, and scientific and technological innovation services will be vigorously developed, and a number of influential functional platforms will be formed.

General Secretary Xi Jinping once highly praised the Shanghai Pilot Free Trade Zone, "Living up to the great trust and high expectations, working in close cooperation, overcoming difficulties, focusing on the core of institutional innovation, actively serving the national strategy, making significant progress in many aspects, replicating and popularizing a batch of important achievements across the country, and generally fulfilling the original intention…".

The evolution from bonded zones, comprehensive bonded zones to free trade pilot zones is a preemptive move in a new round of national reform. It is also an important experimental field where opening-up drives reform and institutional innovation spurs the comprehensive deepening of reform. A batch of pilot experiences such as the negative list management model and the reform of the commercial registration system have been replicated across the country. As the "leading goose" in the "formation of geese" of China's free trade pilot zones, the Shanghai Free Trade Pilot Zone will continue to strive to become a central node in the domestic circulation and a strategic link in the domestic and international dual circulations. It will play a better leading and radiating role in the integrated development of the Yangtze River Delta.

4 The Fruit of Global Trade: China's Indigenous Commercial Aircraft, the C919

Manufacturing and trade are twin pillars of a country's economy. Over the past four decades of reform and opening up, China has steadily integrated into the global trade system, transitioning from a manufacturing powerhouse to a global manufacturing leader across various industries, from toothbrushes and batteries to cars, ships, and even large aircraft. The birth of China's domestically developed large aircraft, the C919, in Shanghai symbolizes the rise of China's high-end manufacturing sector as a new emblem.

4.1 From Dream to Reality: The Journey to Chinese-Made Commercial Aircraft

The development level of civil aviation manufacturing reflects national strength, contributing to economic and technological advancement. As one of the world's most complex and technologically intensive products, large commercial aircraft represent the pinnacle of a country's industrial capability and achievements. China's path to developing large aircraft has been challenging and arduous.

In 1903, the Wright brothers ushered in the modern aviation era. Few know that, during the early twentieth century, China was the only Asian country comparable to Western aviation development. In 1909, Feng Ru, known as the "father of Chinese aviation," created China's first domestically manufactured aircraft, predating even Russia and Germany. In 1913, Pan Shizhong, an aviator from Shanghai, designed and built a dual-wing military aircraft, with both power and body parts independently developed.

Back in those days, only a few countries around the globe were capable of independently designing and manufacturing aircraft. China's aviation industry got off to an early start. At that time, numerous patriotic and ambitious individuals regarded contributing to the nation via aviation as a shortcut to overtake the powerful foreign countries and realize national rejuvenation. Nevertheless, under the circumstances of warlord separatist strife and chaos, each faction pursued its own development, with no unified consensus, not to mention a long-term blueprint. It was all but a fleeting illusion. By the eve of the breakout of the War of Resistance against Japanese Aggression, China's initial edge in the aviation industry had vanished without a trace (Fig. 35).

In 1949, during the grand founding ceremony of the People's Republic of China, a formation consisting of 17 aircrafts from the newly established People's Liberation Army Air Force soared majestically over Tiananmen Square. These planes were all acquired from the Kuomintang. Subsequently, under the aegis of Soviet assistance, China embarked on an endeavor to replicate the Soviet Union's aircraft design benchmarks, regulations, models, and manufacturing processes. Alas, under the duress of the international geopolitical climate, China was compelled to channel all its energies into the arduous pursuit of the atomic bomb, hydrogen bomb, and artificial satellite. Consequently, the aircraft research and development program was indefinitely postponed. By the twilight of the 1960s, with the meteoric rise of the international civil aviation sector, the era of jetliners supplanting propeller-driven airliners had irrevocably dawned (Fig. 36).

Wu Xingshi (Member of the National Large Aircraft Project Expert Committee, and Member of COMAC's Science and Technology Committee): The People's Republic of China made four major decisions to develop large commercial aircraft, initially beginning in 1970.

In August 1970, with Premier Zhou Enlai's approval, China agreed to Shanghai's proposal to trial the production of a transport aircraft, marking the official launch of "Project 708" to develop the country's first large commercial aircraft, the Y-10, manufactured by the Shanghai Aircraft Manufacturing Factory.

Fig. 35 Feng Ru, the "Father of Modern Chinese Aviation," designed China's first domestic aircraft

Fig. 36 Pan Shizhong, a Shanghai-born aviator, and the self-designed "No.1" aircraft

Yang Zuoli (former deputy director of the Shanghai Aircraft Design and Research Institute): More than 100 of us came to this place in the first batch. There was neither an office nor a place to sleep. We worked in the large canteen and even designed airplanes in the cabin of small aircraft. We could sleep in basements and warehouses. At that time, we said that as long as we could put a desk, we would work, and as long as we could put a bed, we would sleep.

Shanghai Aircraft Manufacturing Factory (now COMAC's Assembly and Manufacturing Center) undertook 12 major campaigns to accelerate production, achieving record productivity increases, with the entire factory contributing 22 million unpaid man-hours.

Support for the Y-10 project poured in from all over China. More than 300 factories, research institutes, and universities across the country participated in the Y-10's development, making it an unprecedented endeavor in terms of scope, scale, and technical demands in the history of the People's Republic (Fig. 37).

Cheng Bushi (Deputy Chief Designer of the Y-10): The intelligence and diligence of the Chinese people are fully reflected in this project. Despite the hardships, we successfully completed the aircraft. It demonstrated our nation's capability – China can build this kind of plane.

After ten challenging years, on September 26, 1980, the Y-10 successfully completed its maiden flight at Dachang Airport in Shanghai. However, due to an outdated military-centric manufacturing model, the Y-10 faced barriers to commercialization. To this day, a Y-10 prototype still stands on the lawns of COMAC's base in Pudong. Its worn-out interior and aged seats remind visitors of the pioneering

Fig. 37 The original Y-10 prototype at Dachang Base, now relocated to the Zhujiao Base

Fig. 38 Shanghai Aviation Industrial Corporation's partnership with McDonnell Douglas in the 1980s to assemble the MD-82 aircraft (a partnership that ended in 1996 when McDonnell Douglas was acquired by Boeing)

spirit of early Chinese aviation, serving as a historic testament to China's initial steps toward its "aircraft dream" (Fig. 38).

> Wu Yue (Director of COMAC's Science and Technology Committee and General Manager of the C919 Project): The civil aviation industry reflects the overall industrial capability of a nation, and its development requires a comprehensive and advanced industrial system. Without a high level of industry, it is impossible to succeed.

In the late 1980s and 1990s, China launched further international cooperative projects to develop commercial aircraft. Although these efforts encountered various setbacks, China's aviation industry steadily built up its industrial chain, enhanced through collaborations and subcontracting. By the end of the century, China had become a significant player in global aviation manufacturing.

With China's rapid economic growth and the expansion of its civil aviation industry, the potential for large-scale aviation presented new opportunities. Developing a commercial aircraft with independent intellectual property rights once again became a priority, following the "three-step" strategy for civil aviation: regional jets, single-aisle jets, and wide-body jets.

In 2002, the State Council approved the ARJ21-700 regional jet project, and after over a decade of effort, it received type certification from the Civil Aviation Administration of China in late 2014, marking the completion of the development, certification, and delivery of China's first independently developed regional jet. This achievement laid the groundwork for the development of the C919 narrow-body jet (Fig. 39).

The ARJ21, China's first domestically developed, fully proprietary regional jet, seats 78–90 passengers and has a range of 2225 km, ideal for regional routes between

Fig. 39 China's domestically developed ARJ21-700 regional jet, which officially entered service in 2016

central and smaller cities. Expanding regional aviation is an efficient and economical way to connect dispersed populations and foster economic growth in China's remote western regions.

The ARJ21 has accumulated more than 460 orders, with nearly 60 aircraft delivered, operating on 107 routes and holding a 1% market share. With over 100,000 safe flight hours, it has achieved a breakthrough for Chinese commercial jets on domestic routes and significantly advanced China's civil aviation capabilities.

Yet, as the twenty-first century began, embarking on the C919 project was a bold decision. Developing a large commercial aircraft requires high technical skills, significant funding, considerable risk management, and a lengthy development cycle of approximately eight years. Only a few countries, such as the U.S., Canada, and European nations, can independently design and manufacture large commercial aircraft, with Boeing and Airbus forming a global duopoly.

In April 2001, a group of over 20 senior scientists, led by Wang Daheng, a renowned scientist who contributed to China's nuclear programs, petitioned the central government to restart the development of large commercial aircraft. In 2003, Wang made another appeal to then-Premier Wen Jiabao, reiterating the need for China to develop its large aircraft (Fig. 40).

> Wu Xingshi (Member of the National Large Aircraft Project Expert Committee and ARJ21 Chief Designer): The late Wang Daheng, one of China's most esteemed scientists, left us with eight words to inspire the next generation: "Preserve the old, explore the new, seek the best, and forge ahead."

Fig. 40 Wang Daheng (1915–2011), a distinguished scientist and pioneer in China's aviation industry

In June 2003, the national planning group for China's medium-to-long-term technology development launched the Large Aircraft Project, conducting rigorous feasibility studies. By February 2007, the State Council approved the large commercial aircraft project, formally establishing the Commercial Aircraft Corporation of China (COMAC) in May 2008, headquartered at the same site where the Y-10 was once built. In November of that year, the C919 project officially began. The "C" in C919 represents both COMAC and China, symbolizing China's ambition to join Boeing and Airbus as a leading player in commercial aviation. The C919 single-aisle jet (comparable to the Boeing 737 or Airbus A320) is expected to become the workhorse model in the Chinese market. According to COMAC, there will be a need for around 26,000 single-aisle jets over the next 20 years, with nearly a trillion dollars in market value within China alone.

More significantly, large commercial aircraft have extensive supply chains and high downstream impacts. Components like avionics, onboard maintenance systems, and display systems, along with countless subsystems, have driven the growth of both China's aviation and related industries.

4.2 *Building a Complete Industrial System from the Ground Up*

On May 5, 2017, a momentous day in Chinese civil aviation, the C919 completed its maiden flight, taking off from Shanghai Pudong International Airport and landing smoothly after 79 min, witnessed by thousands of cheering spectators. Designed and developed by COMAC, this aircraft marked a major milestone in China's aviation industry. The C919, comprising 724 cables, 2328 tubes, nearly 80 km of wiring,

Fig. 41 The C919 successfully completed its test flight at Pudong Airport

and 2.5 million parts, was created through independent Chinese design, overcoming complex challenges in system integration and achieving a near 60% domestic production rate. The scene of the successful test flight of the C919 still remains fresh in the memory of Chinese people. Although the first flight time was repeatedly postponed, its smooth takeoff and landing mean that China's civil aviation industry has completed a milestone leap (Fig. 41).

The market positioning of the C919 is a narrow-body passenger aircraft with 150 seats and a range of more than 4000 km, which can meet the direct flight between any two cities in China. Judging from the range, number of seats and engine performance parameters, the C919 is benchmarked against the Boeing 737 MAX 8 and the Airbus A320neo. The latter two are respectively one of the best-selling models of Boeing and Airbus, and are also the mainstream models in the entire international civil aviation industry.

Compared with the competing models of Airbus and Boeing, the C919 reduces air resistance by 5%. "The layout of components such as wings, fuselage, empennage, engine, and landing gear, the parameters of range and seat class, as well as engine class and power supply power… The most critical part of the C919 joint conceptual design is completely independently designed by our country.

> Wu Guanghui (Academician of the Chinese Academy of Engineering and Chief Designer of the C919): The C919 sets the benchmark for the future of China's equipment manufacturing sector. It plays a critical role in enhancing our nation's capabilities in equipment manufacturing and advancing scientific and technological levels.

Fig. 42 C919 Final Assembly Line at COMAC's Shanghai Aircraft Manufacturing Facility (July 5, 2018)

The C919 follows the internationally prevalent "main manufacturer + supplier" model, with COMAC as the primary manufacturer and companies such as AVIC and CETC from China, as well as global suppliers like Safran, Honeywell, and United Technologies (Fig. 42).

> Wu Yue (Director of COMAC's Science and Technology Committee and General Manager of the C919 Project): The development of aviation systems in China, from aircraft-level to system-level integration, has reached a strong, cohesive, and systematic level with the C919. COMAC integrates the aircraft-level system, while suppliers handle subsystem integration, establishing a structured model for the entire supply chain. Our framework is taking shape, though not yet fully mature.

Over the past decade, China has largely established its civilian aircraft manufacturing industry: COMAC serves as the primary manufacturer, bringing together a supply chain involving over 200 first-tier suppliers from 15 countries, including the Aviation Industry Corporation of China (AVIC) and General Electric (GE). This collaborative approach has fostered joint ventures between foreign suppliers and Chinese companies, further enhancing China's capabilities in aviation structure, avionics, materials, and component standards. In the C919 project, over 200 enterprises from 22 provinces and cities across the country and over 200,000 people participated in the research and development. The creators of C919 can be regarded as the pioneers in domestic large aircraft manufacturing (Fig. 43).

Fig. 43 Two workers assemble the C919 at the COMAC Shanghai Assembly Facility

4.3 A Product of Global Collaboration in the Aviation Industry

International cooperation has been essential to the success of the C919 project. When the project was initiated, former Premier Li Keqiang emphasized a guiding principle for China's commercial aircraft: "independent design, systems integration, global procurement, and progressive localization." Building a high-quality commercial aircraft required both innovation and access to global resources.

Our independent innovation can be carried out completely under the condition of opening up. We can integrate advanced technologies and mature products at home and abroad to make global scientific and technological resources available for our use. Yuan Wenfeng, director of the C919 project office, said that the C919 has always adhered to the technical route of "independent research and development, international cooperation, and international standards", and has conquered more than 100 core technologies and key technologies including the integrated design of aircraft engines and the control laws of fly-by-wire flight control systems (Fig. 44).

> Wu Yue (COMAC Science and Technology Committee Director, C919 Project General Manager): Civil aviation is a global industry where innovative resources flow freely, enabling worldwide collaboration and resource utilization. Our strategy is to set standards and incorporate the most suitable resources into our platform to deliver customer-satisfying products.

Through global bidding, the C919 attracted top companies from China and abroad, strengthening the entire industrial ecosystem. More than 200 enterprises across 22 provinces and nearly 200,000 individuals participated in the C919 project, significantly boosting innovation in China's civil aviation industry. As the project progressed, research institutions conducted over 700 technology research projects, such as strength testing on tail sections, composite material repairs, brake

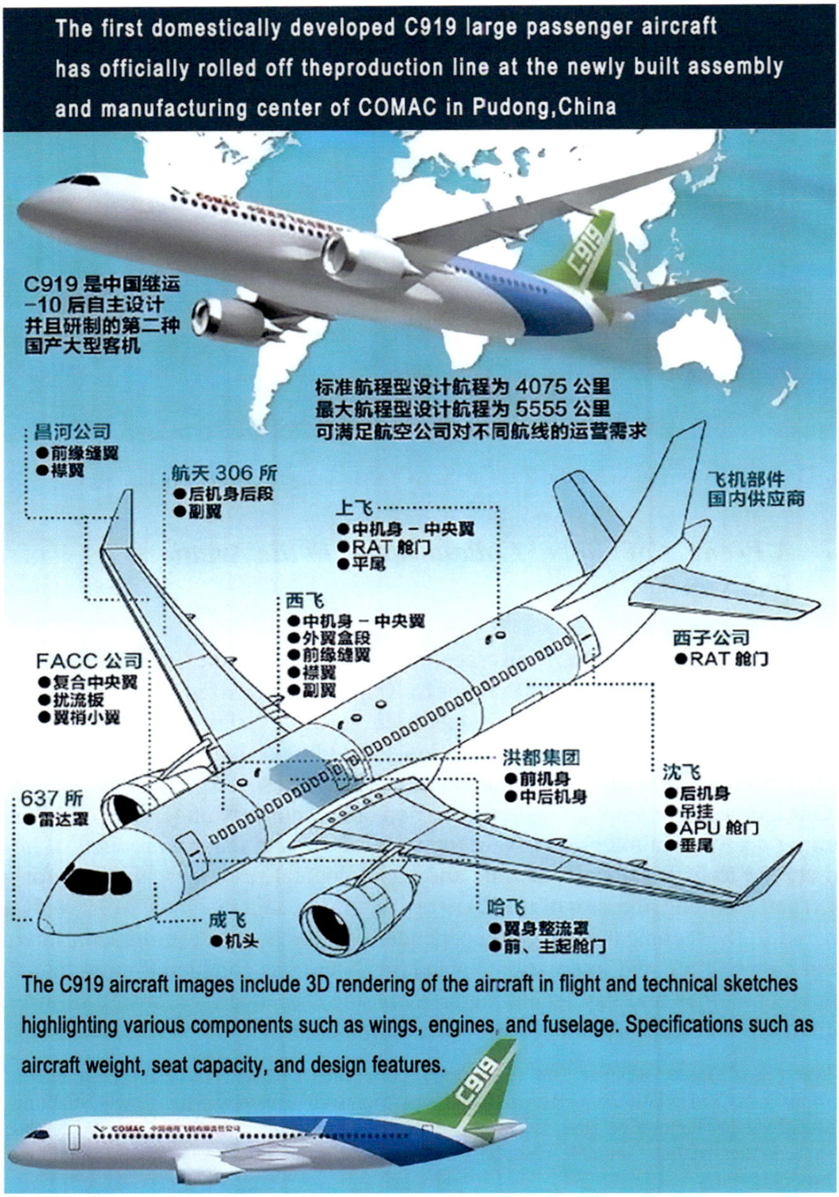

Fig. 44 The domestically produced large aircraft C919 has promoted the formation of a technological innovation system in the domestic civil aircraft industry

Fig. 45 The first LEAP-1C engine for the C919 is delivered

system innovations, electrical system data processing, and aerodynamic designs for ultra-critical wings (Fig. 45).

However, key components like the engine remain challenging for China's aviation industry to produce independently in the short term. The C919 currently uses the LEAP-X engine, developed by CFM International. While around 20 companies globally can build airplanes, only a handful can manufacture jet engines. Since 2010, China has designated jet engine development as a major national initiative, investing billions of yuan annually to gain mastery over this critical "crown jewel" of modern industry.

For the C919 to truly compete globally, it must achieve a fully independent supply chain for essential components, such as the engine and avionics, and navigate international certification barriers. The two most authoritative airworthiness certificates worldwide are issued by the U.S. Federal Aviation Administration (FAA) and the European Union Aviation Safety Agency (EASA). To gain international market entry, the C919 must meet at least one of these standards, allowing it to compete with products from Boeing and Airbus in the commercial aviation market.

4.4 Flying Higher: China's Path in Advanced Manufacturing

Driving along the Yingbin Expressway past Pudong Airport's Terminal 2, a series of impressive buildings comes into view upon turning onto Shangfei Road 919. This is COMAC's Pudong base, where China's first domestically made large commercial jet, the C919, was assembled and rolled out for its first test flight.

Fig. 46 COMAC Chairman He Dongfeng unveils the "Never Give Up" sculpture at COMAC's Pudong Base

In the plaza at COMAC's Pudong Base, near the Y-10 prototype, stands a silver, torch-shaped sculpture inscribed with the words "Never Give Up," commemorating the perseverance of the Y-10 team and the generations of aviation experts who dedicated their careers to the Chinese aviation industry. "Never Give Up" embodies the indomitable spirit of Chinese aviation: a determination to conquer technical and managerial challenges, to see Chinese-made jets fly worldwide, and to fulfill the long-standing dream of producing a domestic aircraft (Fig. 46).

> Dang Tiehong (Deputy Director of COMAC's Market Department): In the past, China was often said to have to export billions of shirts just to import a single aircraft. Every year, our country spends a significant amount of foreign currency to purchase airplanes. With C919, we are laying the groundwork for a future where we dominate the civil aviation market, strengthening both domestic and international trade.

Over the past nine years, COMAC's Shanghai base has seen the rollout of ten C919 test aircraft and successfully delivered them to domestic airlines such as China Eastern Airlines, Air China, and China Southern Airlines. Production efficiency has improved with five advanced assembly lines for final assembly, central wings, mid-fuselage, horizontal tails, and overall aircraft integration. A streamlined, tact-based production mode has enhanced both production efficiency and precision management. Additionally, the introduction of "dark factory" automated production lines has significantly boosted the automation level in aircraft manufacturing. Moving forward, Pudong New Area's "One Valley, One Park" strategy aims to establish a dedicated industrial cluster for the aviation sector, anchoring China's ambitions in large aircraft manufacturing.

5 Build an International Shipping Center: The Construction of Yangshan Deep-Water Port

5.1 Ranking Third Globally: Shanghai Entered the Leading Camp of International Shipping Center

On July 11, 2021, the 2021 Xinhua Baltic International Shipping Center Development Index Report was released, making Shanghai rank among the top three international shipping centers for the first time, second only to Singapore and London. The report, released by the China Economic Information Service and the Baltic Exchange, measures the development level of international shipping center cities from three dimensions: port conditions, shipping services and comprehensive environment (Table 1).

"By 2020, Shanghai will basically build itself into an international shipping center with a high concentration of shipping resources, sound shipping service functions, excellent shipping market environment, efficient modern logistics services, and the ability to allocate global shipping resources." That was the goal of the State Department that was set out in 2009. In 2021, Shanghai broke the six-year three strong situation of Singapore, London and Hong Kong, China, and became one of the most developed shipping centers in the world. The change in the list ranking has witnessed the rise of Shanghais international shipping industry.

Then comes a more intense competition. On "2020 China navigation day BBS", vice mayor of Shanghai Shang Zhiping said, will promote the construction of a new round of international shipping center, "attract and cultivate more international, national shipping organization and functional institutions in Shanghai, actively participate in international maritime technology rules, promote Shanghai to participate in international shipping affairs, the ability of global service".

He pointed out that Shanghai needs to play a leading role in promoting the formation of a world-class port group in the Yangtze River Delta with reasonable division of labor, mutual cooperation and strong strengths, and promote the Yangtze River Delta region to become an important node of the international logistics network.

5.2 Yangshan Deep-Water Port: To Build a New Global Model of Modern Port Construction

After the reform and opening up, the Huangpu River in Shanghai has been unable to carry the new generation of container ships, and the heavy responsibility of shipping

Table 1 TOP10th ranking of Xinhua Baltic Sea International Shipping Center Development Index

Ranking	The year 2020	The year 2019	The year 2018	The year 2017	The year 2016	The year 2015	The year 2014
1	Singapore	Singapore	Singapore	Singapore	Singapore	Singapore	Singapore
2	London	Hong Kong	Hong Kong	Hong Kong	London	London	London
3	Shanghai	London	London	Hong Kong	Hong Kong	Hong Kong	Hong Kong
4	Hong Kong	Shanghai	Shanghai	Hamburg	Hamburg	Rotterdam	Rotterdam
5	Dubai	Dubai	Dubai	Shanghai	Rotterdam	Hamburg	Hamburg
6	Rotterdam	Rotterdam	Rotterdam	Dubai	Shanghai	Shanghai	Dubai
7	Hamburg	Hamburg	Hamburg	New York—New Jersey	New York—New Jersey	Dubai	Shanghai
8	Athens	New York—New Jersey	New York—New Jersey	Rotterdam	Dubai	New York—New Jersey	Tokyo
9	New York—New Jersey	Houston	Tokyo	Tokyo	Tokyo	Busan	New York—New Jersey
10	Tokyo	Athens	Busan	Athens	Athens	Athens	Busan

must be handed over to the sea. At the beginning of Pudongs development and opening up, in order to ease the urgent need of international freight transportation, the Shanghai municipal government decided to carry out the Yangtze Estuary waterway control project and build a container terminal in Waigaoqiao.

Wang Zhan (former Secretary and Director of the Party Leadership Group and Director of the Development Research Center of Shanghai Municipal Peoples Government): If the containers enter the Huangpu River, its draft is obviously not enough, so there is the channel management of the Yangtze River estuary. We plan to divide it into three phases, and then from the district to the city. In this process, our container terminal is actually constantly transferring outward, transferring from Zhang Huabang to Waigaoqiao, but in fact, the iteration of the container is very fast. At that time, when we were doing this research, it should be in 1995 that the international containers would move from the third generation to the fourth, the fifth and the sixth generation, which could not meet the draft requirements even the Yangtze Estuary waterway.

In 1990, after the CPC Central Committee and the State Council announced the development and opening of Pudong, the development of Shanghai Port was faced with a series of challenges. First, the continuous expansion of foreign trade scale and the rapid growth of cargo transportation volume led to the chronic shortage of cargo handling capacity at the terminal. In the project evaluation of Waigaoqiao Phase II, the core issue of the controversy is the expectation of the future box volume growth. At that time, it was proposed that after the completion of Waigaoqiao Phase II, the volume of boxes could be increased from about 600,000 boxes in the first phase to 1.5 million to 2 million boxes. But some people doubt that reaching a few million boxes is a big deal. In fact, later developments have far exceeded expectations. Secondly, the trend of large-scale container ships has begun. At that time, container ships have reached 2000–3000 boxes, and then there were 4000–5000 boxes of fourth generation ships and fifth generation ships, about 40,000–50,000 tons, and 50,000 tons of ships to reduce load outside the Yangtze River Estuary. At the same time, Shanghai is also facing fierce competition with Taiwan, China Kaohsiung, Busan, South Korea, and Kobe, Osaka, Japan. In 1994, the container volume of Shanghai was only 1 million boxes, which is still an order of magnitude gap compared with these ports, and Shanghai is under great pressure.

From the perspective of historical development, "Port is for the city," is an important rule of the urban development; from the geographical location, Shanghai is located at the mouth of the Yangtze River in the middle of the eastern coast of Chinese mainland; From the perspective of port conditions, unlike the international transit port of Singapore, Shanghai is a hinterland port backed by the most economically developed Yangtze River Delta region in China. These factors determine that Shanghai must have a deep-water port, which is both to Shanghai and the Yangtze River Delta region. It means a lot for the whole of China. The construction of the Yangshan deep-water port is on the horizon.

5.2.1 The Construction of Yangshan Deep-Water Port Has Been Kicked off

From the 1990s to the beginning of the 20 00 s, the trend of economic globalization accelerated, and the scale of international trade continued to expand, which promoted the major changes in the pattern of the world shipping industry. The development and change of the international container transportation market gradually show the characteristics and trend of "large-scale ships, management alliance and trunk routes".

However, at that time, the annual international container throughput of Shanghai Port was only about 500,000 boxes, while in the same period, Hong Kong, China and Singapore have entered the ranks of tens of millions of containers. Kaohsiung Port in Taiwan has also reached the annual throughput of more than 5 million boxes, ranking among the top five container ports in the world. In addition to the gap in the number of berths, there is no deep-water port for super large container ships to dock, which becomes the most prominent and fatal "short board" for Shanghai port to become an international hub port (Fig. 47).

Fang Huaijin (Vice President of Shanghai International Port Group Co., LTD.): The early modern industries of Shanghai, from grain processing and cotton textile industry, were all spread out along the Suzhou River. At the beginning of the twentieth century, the Huangpu River gradually became the main water channel of Shanghai port, but whether Suzhou River and Huangpu River, it was an inland river, and the water depth conditions and the width of its channel were very limited. Take the Huangpu River as an example, the natural water depth of the Huangpu River is about 6 m, the sunken bed is only 8 m, and the Suzhou River is more shallow. So Shanghai is not actually a harbor, to be precise, it is just a river port, and it is an inland river port.

In this context, Shanghai began to actively look for deep-water ports that can meet the future shipping development. In the mid-1990s, the main leaders of the Shanghai

Fig. 47 Reclamation and sand blowing at Yangshan Port

Municipal Party Committee and the municipal government innovatively put forward the bold idea of "jumping out of Shanghai to see Shanghai" and building deep water alleys outside the sea. After a series of exploration and preliminary analysis, it is considered that Yangshan sea area is the alternative port site of Shanghai deep water port. It has obvious comprehensive advantages. Located in Shengsi County, Zhoushan City, Zhejiang Province, the Yangshan Islands is 27.5 km away from Shanghai Nanhui Luchao Port, only 104 km away from the international route, and has a water depth of 15 m. If a sea bridge is built between the island and the mainland, it could be the nearest deep-water port to Shanghai.

Shanghai in 1995 formally proposed the construction of a deep-water port, and in March 2002, The State Council approved the approval of the Yangshan Port construction project. Since then, the Shanghai Deep Water Port Construction Headquarters has been responsible for the construction of the project. In December 2005, the first phase of the project (including the Donghai Bridge) was completed and put into operation, taking about ten years, which can be called "a port in ten years". However, the Yangshan Port is located in the outer sea, which is about 30 km away from the Luchao Port in the Nanhui district of Shanghai. Only through the construction of a cross-sea bridge can the port area be easily connected with the transportation network of Shanghai. Therefore, the Donghai Bridge is the cross-sea bridge project officially opened, it is the cross-sea channel connecting Shanghai Nanhui New Town and Yangshan Town, Shengsi County, Zhoushan City, Zhejiang Province, is a part of the southern end of Shanghai Expressway, is also one of the key supporting projects of Yangshan deep water port. The Donghai Bridge leads the Shanghai port to the outer sea, providing a strong transportation guarantee for improving the carrying capacity of the port (Fig. 48).

> Dai Angang (professor of fudan university): can be said to be the source of Shanghai port, first port, trade, city, financial, industrial, so the port is one of the most important economic driving force in Shanghai, and Shanghai port has been advancing with The Times, for example from qinglong port to shop 16, from sixteen to waigaoqiao, from waigaoqiao to yangshan deepwater port, its trajectory is to follow the navigation of the world. So now some people describe the port of Shanghai is from Shanghai to the sea, which is very image.

In April 2002, Chinas "tenth Five-year Plan" major construction project, the Shanghai international shipping center, was officially launched. In the first phase, the magnificent building is the cross-sea bridge. Design as a two-way eight-lane bridge, it not only connects land and island, but also spans Zhejiang and Shanghai, marking the beginning of a new round of regional economic cooperation between Zhejiang and Shanghai in the new century. Yangshan Container deep-water Port is an important basic project for the construction of Shanghais aviation hub port, information port and seaport, and an important platform for building Shanghai into a modern international metropolis—international shipping center.

Fig. 48 The Donghai Bridge

5.2.2 Construction of Yangshan Port Phase I to Phase IV

On June 26, 2002, the first pile was laid on the 32.5-km cross-sea bridge. Thus, the construction of the Yangshan deep-water port wharf began.

In the first to fourth phases of Yangshan Port, the builders spent countless sleepless nights on this island in the ocean. In December 2005, the first phase of the Yangshan deep-water Port project was completed and opened, with a total investment of about 13 billion yuan. The construction of the first phase of the project has three main parts. The first part is to build a berth with 1600 m long coastline, five fifth and sixth generation container ships and 8000 teUS ships on Xiaoyangshan Island. Annual design throughput capacity of 2.2 million TEU. The second part is the construction of a 32.2-km long bridge from Luchao Port to Yangshan Island, of which the bridge is 27.5 km long. The third part is the construction of highway, substations, water transmission pipelines and other supporting infrastructure.

The completion of the first phase of Yangshan Deep-water Port is an important milestone in the construction of Shanghai as an international shipping center. It marks that Shanghai Port has changed from an inland port to a port with deep water berths, laying an important hardware foundation for the construction of Shanghai as an international shipping center.

The second phase of the Yangshan deep-water Port area has been extended westward along the first phase of the project, with the wharf coastline of 1400 m long, and four special berths for 70,000–100,000-ton containers being built, with a total land area of about 888,300 m^2 and a designed annual container throughput of 2.1

Fig. 49 Construction of Yangshan Port Phase I Project

million TEUS. The construction contents of the second phase mainly include 4 million cubic meters of sand throwing (blowing) and filling, 861,000 m^2 of road yard, 15 single houses with a total construction area of 15,187.7 m^2, 60 sets of large loading and unloading process equipment, and port production management system, etc. The successful completion of the second phase of the project will further play the scale effect of Yangshan deep-water port area, and further improve the comprehensive competitiveness of Shanghai port to participate in the international container transportation (Fig. 49).

At the end of 2006, the second phase of the project was completed and opened in the port. At that time, Yangshan deep-water port area had become the main port area of Shanghai international shipping center. According to the overall plan of Yangshan deep-water port area, the north port area was planned to have a coastline of more than 10 km, 30 container berths, and a handling capacity of about 15 million TEUS.

In 2008, the third phase of Yangshan Deep water Port Area (phase I) built four special berths for 70,000–150,000-ton containers, with an approved annual handling capacity of 2.8 million teUS. It was completed and officially put into trial operation in June 2008. With the operation of the third phase of the project (phase 1), 13 large container deep water berths have been built in the Yangshan deep water port area, which has effectively alleviated the shortage of deep water berths in Shanghai Port (Figs. 50 and 51).

Fang Huaijin (Vice President of Shanghai International Port Group Co., LTD.): In Waigaoqiao, we have built 6 docks and 6 port areas, from Waigaoqiao Phase I to Waigaoqiao Phase VI. But that does not meet the requirements. After entering the twenty-first century, the trend of large-scale ships and operation alliance in the international shipping industry is becoming more and more significant. At present, the container ships on the main international trunk lines are 14,000 boxes, 18,000 boxes and 20,000 boxes. The latest one has 23,000 boxes, 60 or 70 m longer than the worlds largest aircraft carrier. The load is 1.5 times that of the

Fig. 50 Construction of Yangshan Port Phase II Project

Fig. 51 Construction of Yangshan Port Phase III Project

current aircraft carrier, which is equivalent to the size of our Liaoning. Obviously, Shanghais ports and docks along the Yangtze River estuary are not adapted to this general trend.

The total land area of the fourth phase project covers an area of about 2.23 million square meters, with a coastline of 2350 m, with two 70,000 ton berths and five 50,000 ton berths. The designed handling capacity will reach 4 million teUS a year at the beginning, and will reach 6.3 million teUS a year in the future, which can meet the requirements of many large container ships berthing at the same time.

Compared with the traditional wharf, the fourth phase of Yangshan Port project adopts automatic equipment and control system for the first time, controlling the bridge crane to load and unload containers, and using the unmanned automatic transport vehicle to transport containers. Compared with the first, second and third phases of Yangshan Port, the wharf in the fourth phase has the shortest coastline and the least land area, and its handling capacity is more than twice the total number of the previous three periods. Currently, the super port has only nine people, but the operating efficiency can be increased by 30 percent (Fig. 52).

Guimo (former Party Secretary and Chairman of Shanghai Yangshan Tongsheng Port Construction Co., LTD.): The first phase of the project should reach 3 million teTUS. The second phase of the project is 3 million teUS.... its development is, more than 2 million, 5 million later, a gathering effect. All the routes, all the containers will converge, more and more to you. This is a characteristic of the international hub port.

From Phase I to Phase IV, now Yangshan Deep Water Port is not only the largest container port in China, but also the container port with the highest degree of full automation in the world. In the past, a bridge crane required dozens of workers; now one worker can serve several bridge cranes (Fig. 53).

Fig. 52 Construction of Yangshan Port Phase IV Project

Fig. 53 Opening of Yangshan Phase IV Automatic Wharf

> Fang Huaijin (Vice President of Shanghai International Port Group Co., LTD.): In 1978, the container throughput of Shanghai was only 7,951 boxes, but in 2019, the container throughput of Shanghai port was 43.31 million boxes, an amazing increase of 5,000 times. In 1978, Chinas total import and export volume was 35.5 billion yuan. By 2019, Chinas total import and export volume reached 3.154 trillion yuan, an increase of more than 880 times. The connection between ports and trade can be seen clearly in terms of quantity and scale. Port is used for the city and the city prospers the port, which has been repeatedly proved by the development of history.

At the beginning of the planning, the fourth phase of Yangshan Port took smart port, green port, science and technology port and efficiency port as the standards and norms for construction, and boldly adopted the fully automated container construction scheme to realize the terminal operation from traditional labor-intensive to automatic and intelligent modern new terminal. Among the more than 40 automated terminals that have been built and are under construction in the world, the diversified yard operation interaction mode is pioneered. The application of innovative technologies such as electric drive technology of container transport vehicles, second-generation port-based power supply and solar auxiliary heating have laid a solid foundation for the construction of zero-emission "green terminal" at Yangshan Port.

Since 2014, the fourth phase of Yangshan Port project has been built into a world-class fully automated terminal in three years. The design capacity of this intelligent terminal is 4 million teUS in the beginning and 6.3 million teUS in the future. The container throughput of Yangshan Port accounts for more than 40% of Shanghai port, which is an important support point for Shanghai to become an international shipping center. The opening of the automated terminal of Yangshan Port will boost the annual container throughput of Shanghai Port to exceed 40 million TEUS, equivalent to the sum of the throughput of all ports in the United States, and the United States with a volume of 1 / 10 of the annual throughput of the current global ports.

The Yangshan Port automatic terminal will eventually be equipped with 26 bridge cranes, 120 sets of rail cranes and 130 sets of automatic guidance transport vehicles. Such a large automated terminal has been built and put into operation at one time.

5.2.3 The Completion of the Yangshan Deep-Water Port is an Important Achievement in the Construction of Global Modern Ports

From 2002 to 2017, four phase of construction, yangshan deep water port by the first phase of construction five container deep water berths, wharf coastline 1600 m to the second phase of engineering construction four container deep water berths, wharf coastline of 1400 m, to the third phase of engineering construction, construction of seven container deep water berth, wharf coastline of 2600 m, to the fourth phase of project construction, the construction of seven container deep water berth, wharf coastline of 2350 m, after years of unremitting construction has now created the glory of yangshan deep water port.

Yangshan deep-water port has achieved good economic and social benefits, and has improved the container handling capacity of Shanghai port. The deep-water port has a coastline of 30 km and can build more than 50 super Panamanian container berths with an annual throughput of more than 20 million teUS. 16 container deep-water berths, one LNG ship berth and five refined oil berths have been built. In addition, supporting facilities such as working ship wharf and Xiaoyangshan Passenger Transport Center have been built along the route, providing supporting services such as ports, logistics, processing zones and comprehensive service areas.

On January 5, 2021, the National Development and Reform Commission held a special press conference, pointing out that the fourth Phase of Shanghai Yangshan Port has been built into the worlds largest and most highly automated container terminal. Yangshan deep water port has become an important achievement and typical symbol of modern port construction in China and even the world (Fig. 54).

The construction of Yangshan Port will have an important impact on the trade development of Shanghai at two levels: one is the overall impact on Shanghai city; the second is the direct influence on the rear base of the port area.

First, the construction of deep-water container port will greatly enhance Shanghais competitive position in the international port, thus greatly enhancing Shanghais agglomeration and radiation capacity. With the sustained and rapid development of Chinas economy and the rapid growth of Chinas foreign trade, Shanghai has grown into the worlds top three major ports and shipping center. This status inevitably requires the corresponding finance, trade, talent, management, air and land transport and other aspects of high-level, high-quality services. Different from the first and second generation international shipping centers which mainly focus on the distribution of tangible commodities, the third generation international shipping centers also participate in the international distribution and allocation of production factors.

Fig. 54 Construction of automatic wharf of Yangshan Port

Such international shipping center cities inevitably require the strengthening of corresponding economic center, financial center and trade center. The construction of the Shanghai international shipping center will promote the formation of the other three major centers.

Second, the construction of Yangshan Port will directly drive the development of urban economy. The huge project construction of Yangshan Port construction not only drives the port construction, bridge construction and rear port supporting construction, but also directly drives the urban construction. The port industry and its induced trade, logistics and a large number of services will bring considerable industrial development and peoples livelihood employment opportunities for the economic development.

Yangshan Bonded Port Area has become the core carrier of the construction of Shanghai international shipping center. It is further improving various functions, promoting the prosperity of the shipping market, serving the economic development of the Yangtze River Delta and the Yangtze River basin, and promoting the development of Chinas foreign trade.

5.3 *Enhancing Soft Power: Improve the Business Environment and Promote the Development of Global Trade*

To build Shanghai as an international shipping center, we should focus on infrastructure construction and improve the soft power of service, and adhere to both hands.

First, optimize the modern shipping collection and distribution system. The basic framework of Shanghai shipping collection and distribution system has been basically formed, but it needs further improvement, including the integration of port resources in the Yangtze River Delta, forming the port pattern of cooperation, complementary advantages and orderly competition; promote the linkage development with inland river shipping, make full use of the golden waterway of the Yangtze River, and accelerate the direct connection in Yangshan deep water port area, we should vigorously develop the transfer of water to water, mainly to solve the impact of container land transport on the city. Once this problem is solved, the development of ports can be more smooth.

Secondly, to develop a modern shipping service system. Shanghai international shipping center of hardware facilities from the current basic is complete, but service soft environment needs to further improve, Shanghai give full play to the international main route location advantage, and industrial base, human resources, business environment, develop ship trading, ship management, shipping brokerage, shipping consulting, shipping technology and other kinds of shipping services, expand shipping service industry chain, extend the development of modern logistics and other related industries, constantly improve the shipping service function.

5.3.1 Enhance the Port Competitiveness and Improve the Business Environment of the Ports

In 2020, the container throughput of Shanghai Yangshan Port was 20.22 million TEUs. In January 2021, the container throughput of Yangshan Port broke the historical record with 1.965 million teUS, with a year-on-year growth of 17.8% and another record high. Both ships and personnel entering and leaving (port) from Yangshan Port have reached a new high. According to the statistics of Yangshan Border Inspection Station, in 2020, the gate, prevented the situation, helped the resumption of work, and inspected more than 8400 inbound (port) ships, and released more than 196,000 inbound (port) personnel (Fig. 55).

The new high data of Yangshan Port is behind the steady growth of port competitiveness. Yangshan Port is backed by the Yangtze River Delta and radiates to the whole of China. It has a very superior geographical position and has more than 70 stable air routes, covering six continents and three oceans. In 2019, a number of new routes to the United States and Europe were added. At the end of 2019, the "Cherry Express" with direct Chile to China moved to Yangshan Port. The dense ocean routes

Fig. 55 Yangshan Port Container Terminal

narrowed the distance between China and the world. In addition to increasing the routes, in order to meet the needs of the market and the situation, major shipping companies have increased their capacity. From 2019 to 2020, more than 50 new container ships over 20,000 teEU have been put into operation (Fig. 56).

Yangshan Port is less than 24 h, which is one of the most efficient ports in China. There is the worlds leading loading and unloading operation speed here. On the basis

Fig. 56 Yangshan Port Wharf

of the first, second and third phases of Yangshan Port, the designed throughput of Yangshan Port, the monthly throughput reaches 348,000 TEUS. During the second CIIE, the Yangshan Port intelligent heavy truck demonstration operation project was put into trial operation. Relying on the 5G system, driverless containers were put on the road, further improving the capacity of the Donghai Bridge and the transit speed of containers. The big customs clearance mode here is in the forefront of the country.

Behind the new high data of Yangshan Port is the continuous improvement of the business environment at the port. Efficiency is competitiveness, and the business environment is even more competitiveness. Yangshan Border Inspection Station has thoroughly implemented the reform spirit of "delegating power, administration and service" of the National Immigration Administration. Since 2019, it has successively launched work measures such as "immediate, online, appointment, front, relay, coordinated, time-limited and one-time". Measures for the port to win the efficiency, for the enterprise to win the benefits, to achieve "data more errands, the masses run less". In terms of the protection of seafarers rights and interests, Yangshan Border Inspection Station and Yangshan Customs established a mutual recognition mechanism for the baggage inspection and supervision of Chinese seafarers. The two sides designed and activated the baggage inspection and seal, avoiding the repeated inspection of luggage and articles, benefiting hundreds of Chinese nationals who left the ship boatman.

Yangshan border Inspection, together with customs and maritime departments, jointly carried out joint boarding, ranking first among open ports in China. It takes less than half an hour for the joint boarding inspection to complete all the entry inspection procedures, which greatly shortens the non-production berthing time of ships, improves the operation efficiency of ports and shipping companies, and reduces the operating costs. After the establishment of Lingang New Area of the Free Trade Zone, the inspection units of Yangshan ports took customs clearance as an important measure to build the frontier window of reform and opening up and serve the CIIE, and ensured the rapid entry of exhibits from Turkey, France, Italy and other countries through joint boarding.

5.3.2 Establish the Shanghai Shipping Exchange to Promote the Development of the Shipping Service Industry

In order to develop the shipping service industry and enhance Chinas voice in the international shipping field, Shanghai innovatively explored the establishment of the Shanghai Shipping Exchange. On November 28, 1996, approved by the State Council, by the ministry of communications and the Shanghai municipal peoples government jointly formed the Shanghai shipping exchange officially opened, this is Chinas first shipping market, regulate the behavior, the shipping trade price, adjust the function of shipping trading information communication, for the development and development of the national shipping market demonstration guiding role (Fig. 57).

Fig. 57 Shanghai shipping exchange

5.3.3 Prepare the International Shipping Index to Enhance the Voice of International Shipping

On April 13, 1998, the "China Export Container Freight Index" presided over by the Ministry of Communications and compiled by Shanghai HNA Exchange was released for the first time, which had a wide international influence. Now, the "China Export Container Freight Index" has been known as the worlds two largest shipping freight index, together with the worlds "Baltic dry bulk freight index", which has become a reliable data cited in the United Nations document.

So far, the Shanghai shipping exchange compiled index including China export container freight index, Shanghai export container freight index, Chinas coastal (bulk) freight index, Chinas coastal coal freight index, China imported dry bulk freight index, China imported crude oil freight index, Chinas import container freight index and the Taiwan strait, container freight index, etc. Greatly enhanced Chinas international shipping voice.

5.3.4 Develop the Cruise Industry and Build Wusongkou International Cruise Port

Wusongkou is close to the main channel of the Yangtze River Estuary, and the construction of cruise port can make up for the lack of large cruise terminal in Shanghai Port, realize complementary functions and dislocation development with the North Bund International Passenger Transport Center, and jointly form the largest and most complete international cruise home port and cruise industry center in China.

In July 2009, Shanghai Wusongkou International Cruise Terminal water project officially started construction, and officially opened on October 15, 2011. For the implementation of the national "Belt and Road" construction and the deployment of the Yangtze river economic belt development strategy and Shanghai "innovation driven development, economic transformation and upgrading of" work requirements, construction began on June 18, 2015, Shanghai wusong mouth international cruise terminal follow-up project, new two large cruise berths, makes wusong mouth international cruise port with four ships by ability. On July 13, 2018, the follow-up project of the wharf was officially put into trial operation. On the same day, three Shengshi Princess, Nuoweizhen Joy and Mediterranean Brilliant cruise ships over 130,000 tons docked at the same time, officially opening the new era of cruise operation of "three ships living together" at Wusongkou International Cruise Port.

Now, Shanghai has become the busiest international cruise home port in the Asia–Pacific region, and the passenger delivery volume of the cruise home port remains the fourth in the world and the first in Asia (Fig. 58).

Fig. 58 Mediterranean Glory cruise ship

5.3.5 Implement the Tax Rebate Policy and Institutional Innovation of the Port of Departure

In accordance with relevant regulations, Shanghai has implemented the tax rebate policy at the port of departure, provided international transit and pooling service, reduced the cost of international container transit, and encouraged Chinas foreign trade containers to be transferred in the Shanghai International Shipping Center. As the worlds largest container port, Shanghai Port is located at the intersection of the coastline and the center of the golden waterway of the Yangtze River. With the advantages of many policies such as the pilot free trade zone, it has a good ability to complete the international transit and pooling service. In October 2014, Shanghai Port completed the first international transit collection, which can reduce the cost of international shipping logistics. At present, the international container transit volume of Shanghai Port is increasing year by year. In 2020, Shanghai Port International transit exceeded 5.3 million teUS, with a year-on-year growth of more than 14%, and the water transfer ratio reached 51.6%, up 3% year on year.

The construction of Shanghai international shipping center is also faced with some institutional and mechanism problems, such as the registration of "convenience flag". At present, Chinas fleet has a large scale and large volume, but the five-star red flag is limited, From the construction of Shanghai international shipping center, ship registration is very important, ship registration here, related maritime services will be handled here, otherwise shipping insurance and other shipping services will be difficult to develop. This needs to be solved through the next step of institutional reform.

In fact, the construction of Shanghai international shipping center is a process of continuous exploration, continuous unified understanding and continuous innovation, which has created many firsts in China and even in the world. In terms of port construction, the offshore island is the first in China, the first in the world, and the first in China. In the field of system and mechanism, the cooperation in port construction is also the first in China, and the cooperation with Zhejiang in recent years is still further deepening innovation.

6 The Never-Ending China International Fair: Writing a New Maritime Legend

In November 2018, the first CIIE (hereinafter referred to as CIIE) was held in Shanghai. Shanghai, Chinas largest economic center, has once again attracted the attention of the world.

6.1 Born with the Trend

At present, the trend of openness and integration is rolling forward, and economic globalization is gradually deepening. Only by actively participating in leading the process of economic globalization and developing an open economy at a higher level can we open up broad space for Chinas development and make greater contribution to building an open world economy. In the severe environment of anti-globalization, protectionism and unilateralism, slow economic growth, populism and trade protectionism, and the new round of scientific and technological revolution such as e-commerce and artificial intelligence, China holds up the banner of comprehensive opening to the outside world and injects more "Chinese power" to building an open world economy and promoting the construction of a community with a human destiny, demonstrating the responsibility and responsibility of a great country.

Since the reform and opening up, after 40 years of sustained development, China has become the world's second largest economy and an important supporting force for global economic growth. However, the development of the country needs to continue to deepen the reform and opening up, the industrial structure needs to be adjusted, the system and mechanism reform needs to be deepened. In this context, the Expo was born with the trend.It is a platform led by China, creating opportunities for trade cooperation and exchanges among many enterprises and entities, embodying free and fair trade, and thus triggering a "green storm". It has not only built an economic bridge between China and the rest of the world, but has also grown into a major platform for international procurement, investment promotion, people-to-people exchanges and open cooperation. As an open platform for trading goods and services, the Expo will better promote trade balance.

The year 2021 is the first year of the 14th Five-Year Plan. At the new historical node, the 14th Five-Year Business Development Plan clearly emphasizes the promotion of trade platforms, giving full play to the role of important exhibition platforms such as the CIIE, and becoming a task in the 14th Five-Year Plan for national economic and social development. The CIIE provides an effective channel for multinational enterprises eager to find trade opportunities, and truly solves the survival problem of individual enterprises. This is also the real meaning of the existence of the CIIE.

6.2 The CIIE Becomes a Window for Foreign Trade

In the golden autumn of 2018, the first CIIE with the theme of “New Era, Shared Future” opened in Shanghai.

At the opening ceremony, Chinese President Xi Jinping announced to the world that the CIIE is for China, but also for the world. As the worlds first and only national expo with import as the theme, China International Trade Expo is a great initiative in the history of international trade. The first CIIE attracted 172 countries, regions and international organizations, and more than 3600 enterprises participated.

> Yu Mingyang (Professor of Shanghai Jiao Tong University): When the Canton Fair started, China was badly blocked by foreign countries. We were in urgent need of foreign exchange. A lot of our construction needed to buy a lot of equipment, including “two bombs and one star”, which needed a lot of foreign exchange. At this time, we must open a window, so the Canton Fair opens a small window for Chinas foreign exchange acquisition and the integration of Chinese products into the international system, so the significance of the Canton Fair is very significant. Today into the expo very big reason is that the world in the globalization, China as a big bear to tell the world, we are open, open mind, so we actively to introduce a lot of good things abroad, in this way, on the one hand, show the big bear, on the other hand to promote the development of global trade system, rather than isolation.

6.2.1 The First CIIE—Weigh Anchor and Sail Away

This event is the first state-level event with the theme of “import”. It drew a blueprint for cooperation and development and injected strong “Chinese energy” into building an open world economy. Chinese President Xi Jinping attended the opening ceremony of the conference and delivered a keynote speech titled “Building an Innovative and Inclusive Open World Economy”, emphasizing the importance of open cooperation from three dimensions of history, reality and the future.

The CIIE has announced to the world that Chinas firm attitude towards further opening-up. Accelerating the pace of opening up and holding the International Import Expo is a highly targeted measure. This just creates new opportunities for countries

Fig. 59 Poster for the first CIIE

and regions that hope to maintain and develop sound commercial cooperation with China. Among them, the United Kingdom has high hopes for this expo, claiming that it will bring opportunities to the "golden era" of China-UK relations. Other participating countries and regions are also very eager to showcase themselves in this supermarket in China and try to obtain as much market share as possible. After all, business and trade relations based on fairness and openness are win–win. For the countries and regions participating in this expo, it is an opportunity to increase import and export trade for themselves (Fig. 59).

With so many countries and regions willing to carry out business activities with China, it is also a rare opportunity for China to gain strength because of the turbulent tide of anti-globalization. While products and services with comparative advantages around the world rush into China, they will bring great pressure and challenges to relevant domestic industries and enterprises, and will also inspire them to constantly change, improve and pass.

Transformation and upgrading will make our products and services more competitive in the market. In the long run, the CIIE will help accelerate the process of Chinas supply-side structural reform.

Overall, the conference was fruitful, with a year of $57.83 billion. In addition, the conference also held more than 370 supporting activities, 1178 exhibitors and 2462 buyers from 82 countries and regions conducted several rounds of one-to-one on-site negotiations, reached 601 further field visits, 657 intended transactions. The international community spoke highly of the CIIE, saying that it is an international public good to promote inclusive and mutually beneficial global development and will provide more opportunities for China (Fig. 60).

The first CIIE is just the beginning, and the expo itself is only a window, followed by a steady stream of transnational commercial activities. With the influx of a large number of imported goods and services into China, it will not only bring the Chinese

Fig. 60 Exhibition picture of central and Eastern European countries

people more and better choices in life, but also make many countries and regions willing to develop commercial cooperation with China benefit from the "China energy".

6.2.2 The Second CIIE—Remote Overweight Mountain

In November 2019, the second CIIE was held in Shanghai. Shanghai, Chinas largest economic center, has once again attracted the attention of the world. The cumulative intended turnover of the second CIIE reached 71.13 billion US dollars, an increase of 23% over the first year. The huge results amazed the world. In the six days, the global debut exhibits, the interaction between supply and marketing, and the sincere signing, the wonderful moments of the CIIE are unforgettable.

> Yu Mingyang (Professor of Shanghai Jiao Tong University): The first stage of trade is the transaction of things. In the second stage, when money is available, we begin to trade with money as the medium. In the third stage, regional trading begins to global trading. In the fourth stage, financial means begin to intervene, and then there are a lot of convenient financial means of payment. For example, can delay transaction, can accept bill, can trade mortgage, these means began to appear, the whole transaction process can be amplified through financial means, financial leverage. At the present stage, everything can be traded, that is to say, services, wisdom and many other invisible things can enter the state of trading.

At the venue of the second CIIE, there is a special exhibition area,—service trade exhibition area.

Fig. 61 Picture of the second CIIE

Although trade in services is invisible or intangible, it truly facilitates industrial innovation and upgrading, facilitates global trade communication, and contributes to a better life for all people. As the only exhibition area without physical goods in the CIIE, the appearance of the service trade exhibition area is enriching the progressAt the same time, the CIIE also builds a communication bridge for the global service trade suppliers and demanders (Fig. 61).

Service trade exhibition orientation for "the strongest brain build mini earth", cultural and tourism services, financial and consulting services, trade logistics and supply chain services, inspection and certification services, integrated services (construction, design, etc.) five plates, and international logistics services sustained authors efficiency, "Belt and Road" construction power enterprises to sea, tourism + science and technology to promote lifestyle change, digital can assign four bright spot. Leading enterprises in all industries attended the meeting to meet the needs of domestic and foreign trade services. The artificial intelligence robot "Dibao" invested and developed by Decathlon was also unveiled in the service trade exhibition area of the second CIIE, which can be applied in the scene of physical shopping malls to realize the automatic inventory of products of all categories. The 5G laboratory of SGS can provide testing services for the software and hardware of the Internet of Vehicles, and provide technical support for the landing application of 5G communication technology in the automotive industry. The Internet of Things coffee machine launched by Yuanxun, the global information technology partner of the Olympic

Fig. 62 The Cultural and Tourism Exhibition Area of the second CIIE

Games, can control the delivery and supplement of related materials through the Internet of Things technology. Dafei Group has launched customized refrigerated logistics solutions for Chinese food trade enterprises (Fig. 62).

Although the total value of Chinas foreign trade continues to grow and maintains a trade surplus, it has a high deficit in the service industry trade. As more and more Chinese people go abroad, tourism occupies an increasingly important share of the service trade. In the service trade exhibition area, the theme of "tourism + technology promotes lifestyle change" became a highlight, particularly eye-catching. In the special exhibition hall of tourism service, through big data, artificial intelligence and other forms of display, the three highlights of technology-enabled tourism, immersive interactive experience and the application of new scenes are centrally displayed (Fig. 63).

> Sun Jie (CEO of Ctrip): There is a lot of incomprehension between people that can be reduced in the process of travel contact and increase our friendship.If people around the world can come to China and have a look, I believe they will love China very much, and the voice of anti-China will be far reduced, which is also a contribution to world peace.

The development of tourism service trade is undoubtedly a booster to promote the cultural exchanges between China and foreign countries. Todays world is a world of economic globalization. In the process of economic globalization, countries in the world not only have economic cooperation, but also have cultural and ideological exchanges. If goods and services are the hardware of CIIE, then the

Fig. 63 Puszlo booth in the service trade exhibition area

exchange of culture and ideas is software. Todays world is faced with many contradictions. Economic growth is inseparable from the exchange of culture and ideas. The exchanges of culture and ideas promote economic development at a deeper level, promote the consultation and settlement of issues in all aspects of the world, and promote the building of a community with a shared future for mankind (Fig. 64).

Ctrip, located in Hongqiao Airport Business District, is also an exhibitor of service trade at the CIIE. Inside the busy office, the staff responded to questions from tourists from all over the country and around the world. With the continuous development of Chinas trade, Chinas weak service trade industry has also broken out a road from "bringing in" to "going out" (Figs. 65 and 66).

> Sun Jie (ctrip chief executive): this is the Chinese to show the world our strength, China has a population of 1.4 billion, Shanghai per capita GDP has reached $20,000, has reached such a consumption level, so the Chinese market is very big, every country as long as it wants to future growth, China is determined to win a market. Ctrip in this process to show our service strength, but also to show our purchasing ability to the world, so this is a good opportunity.

In the second CIIE, Ctrip, as the only OTA in the world, appeared in the service trade sector, showing the open door of Chinas new image of Chinese tourism to the world.

Liang Jianzhang, founder and executive chairman of Ctrip, said Ctrip is not only a name card for the country, but also should play an important role in the countrys overall economy. If we compare the contribution of inbound tourism income to GDP, we will find that the contribution of inbound tourism to GDP in general countries is 1% -3%. India, a major economy in Asia, is around 1%, while Thailand has the

Fig. 64 Exhibition picture of China Wind and Tourism Bureau

Fig. 65 Exhibition picture of Hainan tourism Culture

highest level at 12.48% and China has the lowest level at 0.3%. In this respect, Chinas inbound tourism still has a high potential for development (Fig. 67).

> Liang Jianzhang (co-founder and executive chairman of Ctrip): Open China shows sincerity to the world, and China is in urgent need of a global brand of trade in services. In the future, Ctrip Group has the ability and willingness to cooperate with the government in both the

Fig. 66 Gansu tourism Exhibition Map

Fig. 67 Ctrip appeared at the CIIE

development of electronic visa system and the marketing of friendly Chinese tourism image, so as to let the world understand China and enter China.

6.2.3 The Third CIIE—Has Thousands of Sails

On November 4, 2020, the Shanghai China National Convention and Exhibition Center blossomed again, marking the third China International Import CIIE. The special year of 2020 is that the COVID-19 epidemic spreads around the world, the world economy enters a cold autumn, and many countries have suspended or cancelled large international exhibitions. The special year, the year of the big exam, the third CIIE came as scheduled, announcing to the world Chinas firm determination to promote opening-up at a higher level and constantly promote the building of an open world economy.

As President Xi Jinping said at the opening ceremony, "Chinas hosting of this global trade event as scheduled on the premise of ensuring epidemic prevention and security demonstrates Chinas sincere desire to share market opportunities with the world and promote world economic recovery." As an important platform for opening up and cooperation, this CIIE has a larger scale, higher exhibition level, wider circle of friends—exhibition area of nearly 360,000 m^2, nearly 30,000 m^2 more than the last year, hundreds of new products, new technologies, new services "global debut, the first exhibition in China" (Fig. 68).

More than 3600 exhibitors from more than 150 countries and regions have gathered here. Sun Chenghai, deputy director of CIIE Bureau, said that although the global COVID-19 epidemic continues to spread, the cooperation intention of all parties is

Fig. 68 Some government and business people participating in the third CIIE

not reduced. On a one-year basis, the total transaction volume of the third CIIE was 72.62 billion yuan, an increase of 2.1% over the previous one. The proportion of world top 500 enterprises and industry leading enterprises continuous exhibition is nearly 80%, the level of exhibition arrangement has been further improved, the proportion of special decoration reaches 94%, a number of national ministries and commissions continue to launch tax incentives, customs clearance convenience, market access and other supporting policies, bringing more benefits to exhibitors.

The CIIE is a close link to China and the world. After three years of development, the CIIE has turned exhibits into commodities, exhibitors into investors, connecting China and the world. It has become four platforms for international procurement, investment promotion, people-to-people exchanges and open cooperation, and international public goods shared by the world.

From promoting the "Belt and Road" to actively holding the import Expo, this is another international product that China has provided to the world. Big pattern, big pen, big feelings, the Huangpu River slowly flows east, the night sky stars twinkle, the CIIE is not afraid of wind and rain, not afraid of the turbulent, guard guard for the sea of Chinese economy. China has always added a bright color to the world economic development with an open mind embracing all rivers.

Shanghai has business from all over the world, people gather, civilizations blend, diverse colors, backed by the Yangtze River, facing the Pacific Ocean, and led the opening up of China for a long time. To tell the story of Shanghai is to tell the story of China. In the past 40 years of reform and opening up, Shanghai has witnessed Chinas progress to the world and recorded the progress of the world into China.

6.2.4 The Seventh CIIE—As Scheduled, Continue to Release Opportunities

One year to anchor and sail, two years to climb mountains, three years to see thousands of sails. So far, the CIIE has been successfully held for seven times, as scheduled, which continues to release opportunities. From the number of exhibitors, intended turnover, new products, new technologies, new services and other indicators, each session is constantly creating new records. Especially in the current situation of slow global economic recovery and increasing uncertainty, it has been actively participated by more and more countries, enterprises and products, which shows the confidence of global enterprises in China's economic development and high recognition of China's market opportunities. China is also accumulating strength to promote the high-quality development of economy and trade with an open mind. It will integrate China's trade power into the sea of Global trade, and explain how China can share market opportunities with the world and promote the recovery of the world economy with practical actions (Fig. 69).

After holding seven sessions, the CIIE has gradually matured and has become an important carrier of China's "comprehensively improving the level of opening up". It has played an increasingly significant role in promoting global economic integration, trade liberalization, innovation and development. Its comprehensive benefits have

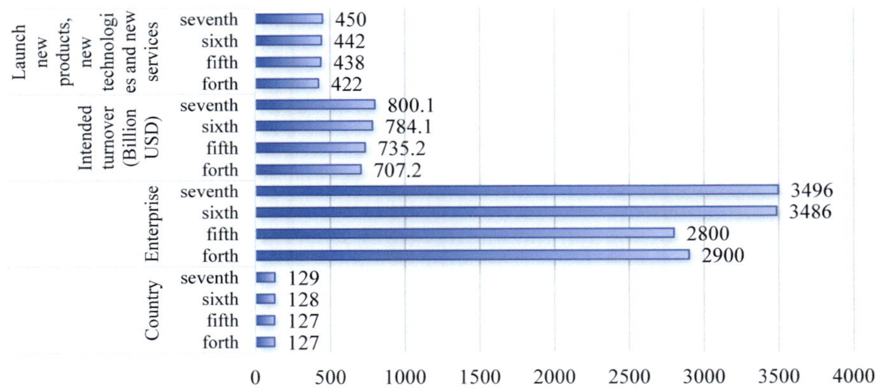

Fig. 69 Data of exhibitors, intended turnover, initial new products, new technologies and new services of the fourth to seventh CIIE

been continuously enlarged, and its communication influence is huge. It has been widely praised. In accordance with General Secretary Xi Jinping's important instruction that the fair should not only be held year after year, but also be at a high level, effective and better, each session is guaranteed as scheduled and set a new high, with the spillover effect gradually highlighted, forming a virtuous ecosystem of "exhibits become commodities, exhibitors become investors, buyers become traders", and enterprises all over the world are benefiting from it.

6.3 The CIIE Has Promoted the Improvement of Shanghais Trade Environment

As an open platform, the CIIE has not only declared to the world Chinas commitment to building an open world economy and its confidence and determination to open the Chinese market to the world, but also brought about a lot of changes in the trade management system related to imports. In addition, CIIE also plays an important role in promoting the trade environment in Shanghai, mainly reflected in the following six aspects.

First, the CIIE is a dialogue platform. While holding the CIIE, it can also hold relevant forums to promote trade exchanges between Shanghai and the outside world. For example, at the same time of holding the CIIE, the Hongqiao Economic Forum was also held, which mainly discussed some policies in the fields of trade and investment. Several forums have been held, focusing on the digital trade of e-commerce, mainly focusing on the emerging trade methods, and play a good role in promoting trade innovation.

Second, expand the effect of trade procurement, attract trade buyers to move in Shanghai "6 days + 365 days" one-stop trading service platform, integrate procurement resources, and provide convenience for import and export trade. The first two sessions of the CIIE have attracted more than 200 Fortune 500 headquarters enterprises, and also attracted more than 30,000 small and medium-sized trade buyers. The commodities of these enterprises will be promoted to the whole market through the "6 days + 365 days" one-stop trading service platform to facilitate the resource docking.

Third, to expand the effect of trade and investment, Shanghai has become a platform for investment promotion in all over the country, including some other countries and cities around the world. Through the CIIE, Shanghai has attracted some cities to hold investment promotion activities, while Shanghai itself will also hold some recommendation activities. For example, at the 2019 City Promotion Conference, Shanghai opened up some investment routes in 16 districts, inviting merchants from all over the world to visit, to explore some industrial characteristics of each place in Shanghai, and then to make investment. By the end of September 2020, Shanghai has attracted 758 regional headquarters and 458 research and development centers, and the effect of trade and investment promotion is very obvious.

Fourth, promote the adjustment of trade structure in Shanghai and gather emerging industries. As an international trade center city, Shanghai has gathered a large number of trade subjects. Through many booths, the CIIE has brought different enterprises in the fields of goods, services and digital fields to Shanghai, thus promoting the adjustment of the whole new subjects in Shanghai. For example, a large number of manufacturing industries in Shanghai will shift to the outside world and gather new service entities and digital entities again.

Fifth, promote the innovation of Shanghais trade content, and move forward to both the service field and the digital field. In the field of service, a large number of trade supervision modes in Shanghai are mainly concentrated in the field of goods. With the development of service trade, service trade needs to establish some trade supervision methods adapted to its own characteristics, such as the supervision methods of some services related to research and development and maintenance, which requires further innovative solutions. In the digital field, the development of digital trade needs a certain amount of infrastructure. In addition, there is a need to improve the connectivity of data flows globally, which requires innovative solutions in unimpeded digital trade.

Sixth, promote the expansion of Shanghais trade network outward to the Yangtze River Delta region and other cities. For the inward extension, Shanghai will further expand to the Yangtze River Delta region and the Yangtze River Basin through the extension of the industrial chain and value chain. For the outward extension, promote the trade image publicity of Shanghai to other international cities, build partnerships for more cities around the world, and play the role of Shanghai as a "bridgehead".

Epilogue

"All rivers run into sea, pursuit of excellence, enlightened and wise, atmospheric and modest" is the spirit of Shanghai. The long mainland coastline of China is like a stretched bow; The winding and twisting Yangtze River is like an arrow ready to launch; And Shanghai is at the intersection of this bow and arrow. Born and prospered by the sea, Shanghai, a century old trading metropolis, has always stood at the forefront. It is like a mirror, reflecting the vicissitudes and great changes since the reform and opening up; It is also a banner that strives towards the goals of openness, innovation, and high quality.

For a hundred years, trade has connected and changed the world.

Since the reform and opening up, Shanghai has used world standards to explore and innovate. Facing the future, Shanghai carries new historical missions, seizes new development opportunities, and writes new maritime legends.

© Fudan University Press Co., Ltd. 2025

W. Shengqiao, *Century of Shanghai Trade*, https://doi.org/10.1007/978-981-96-8701-5

Main References

1. Siwen Bao. Yangshan Port Joins the Ranks of International Shipping Center [N]. China Metallurgical News, 2005–12–10.
2. Wei Cao. Residential Buildings in Shanghai after the Opening [M]. China Architecture & Building Press, 2004.
3. Zongsheng Chai, et al. The Large Aircraft Park Takes Off with Dual Engines of Aviation Manufacturing and Services [R]. The Paper, 2020–11–19.
4. Laoli Changshu. City Memories: Human-Pulled Rickshaws and Rickshaw Pullers in Old Shanghai [EB/OL]. http://www.360doc.com/content/14/0403/09/98463_366001846.shtml. 2021–10–19.
5. Chunfang Chen. Compradors and Foreign Firms: The Beginning of Chinese Compradors [J]. Shanghai Department Store, 2017(5).
6. Chunfang Chen. Compradors and Foreign Firms: The Compradors of Foreign Firms in Shanghai Thrived in Every Situation [J]. Shanghai Department Store, 2017(6).
7. Gaohong Chen, Xiaoli Tang. 30 Years of Pudong Stories: Listen to This "800 Heroes" of Pudong Telling the Story of Development and Opening Up [N]. People's Daily Online Shanghai Channel, 2020–4–15.
8. Jiachun Chen. Shanghai Pudong New Area Bravely Shoulders New Missions, Striving to Create a Pioneer Zone for Socialist Modernization [N]. China Development Network, 2021–3–1.
9. Jing Chen. The Year of Yangshan Port: We are different this year [N]. China News Network Shanghai Channel, 2020–1–12.
10. Mingyuan Chen. Rethinking the History of Foreign Concessions in China (Part Five): The Controversial "Comprador" Class [J]. Forum of Social Sciences, 2013(10).
11. Shuang Cui. Never Give Up: The Dream of Domestic Large Aircraft Comes True [N]. Science and Technology Daily, 2018–7–23.
12. Renyi Dai. Shizhong Pan, the First Aviator in Chinese Aviation History, was from Qingpu [N]. Shanghai Observer, 2018–1–24.
13. Aibo Ding. Foreign Firms and Compradors [J]. Qilu Weekly, 2015(44).
14. Richu Ding, Renze Wang. Yu Qiaqing in the May Thirtieth Movement [J]. Memories and Archives, 1996(5).
15. Richu Ding. History of Modern Shanghai Economy (Volume 1: 1843–1894) [M]. Shanghai People's Publishing House, 1994.
16. Minsheng Fang. Deep Water Port: The Basic Conditions for Shanghai to Become an International Metropolis [J]. World Economic Papers, 1993(5).
17. Zhou Fang. Domestic Shipping Tycoon Yu Qiaqing (1867–1945) [J]. Shanghai Business, 2002(10).
18. Yuanchao Gao. The Status Quo and the Developing Tendency of the Wholesale Business in Japan and America [J]. Contemporary Finance & Economics, 2004(3).

© Fudan University Press Co., Ltd. 2025
W. Shengqiao, *Century of Shanghai Trade*, https://doi.org/10.1007/978-981-96-8701-5

19. Chengyu Guan. Urban Cultural Evolution through the Lens of Shanghai's Culinary Culture [J]. Beauty & Times, 2019(7).
20. Shuwen Hou, Chun Wang. Phoenix Nirvana: Domestic Large Aircraft Finally Embraces a Glorious Moment [N]. Science and Technology Daily, 2019–8–27.
21. Xingyang Hu. Following the Introduction of the Central Government's Important "Opinions," the Special Exchange in Shanghai, One of the Only Five in the Country, Has Ushered in a Major Development Opportunity [N]. Shanghai Observer, 2021–7–29.
22. Baisheng Huang. Yu Qiaqing's Talent for Seizing Business Opportunities [J]. Light Novel, 2009(14).
23. Weihua Ji. Functional Linkage and Dislocation Development in Shanghai Pilot Free Trade Zone, Lingang New Area, and Pudong New Area [J]. Scientific Development, 2021(7).
24. Rong Jian. Yu Qiaqing and the Shanghai Securities Exchange [J]. Memories and Archives, 1996(3).
25. Haofeng Jiang. Insights from A380 for Domestic Large Aircraft [J]. Jetliner, 2019(4).
26. Fagen Li. A Study on the Formation of the Foreign Trade Center of Modern Shanghai: From the Perspectives of War and Treaty Ports [J]. Shanghai Journal of Economics, 2016(9).
27. Hongbing Li, Weiqun Xie, Dingding He, Shaotie Shen. Legendary Pudong: The Pioneer of Opening Up [N]. People's Daily Online, 2018–9–17.
28. Ye Li. Yangshan Port Container Throughput Hits New High [N]. Liberation Daily, 2021–7–31.
29. Yongmei Li. The Development Prospects of Container Transportation in China Are Limitless [N]. China Communications News, 2005–4–15.
30. Yuyang Li, Qiyu Feng. Just Look at the Answers of These Tycoons to Understand the Significance of China International Import Expo [N]. Economic Daily, 2020–2–8.
31. Xinran Liu. Hongsheng Liu: From a Foreign Comprador to an Industrial Tycoon [J]. China Small & Medium Enterprises, 2015(5).
32. Jianhao Lu. Advocacy Coalition Framework and Industrial Policy —— The Political Economy of System Integration Strategy in the Chinese Commercial Aircraft Manufacturing Projects [D]. PhD dissertation, Peking University, 2021.
33. Jinzhang Lu. From Wusong Railway to Songhu Railway [J]. Railway Knowledge, 1994(4).
34. [U.S.] Rhoads Murphey. Shanghai, Key to Modern China [M]. Compiled by the Institute of History, Shanghai Academy of Social Sciences. Shanghai People's Publishing House, 1986.
35. Wenjie Lv. New Goals and Positioning of Shanghai Free Trade Zone Lingang New Area in the New Era [N]. People's Daily Online Shanghai Channel, 2020–1–3.
36. Xianfeng Luo. On the Role of Compradors in Early Modern Industrialization [J]. Journal of Jiaozuo Normal College, 2007(4).
37. Yujun Ma. The First Track of Songhu [J]. Shanghai Stories, 2019(6).
38. Baozhang Nie. On the Essential Characteristics of Foreign Firms Compradors-A Response to Japanese Scholar Miyata Michitaka and a Discussion with Mr. Zhongping Yan on "History of Modern Chinese Economy" [J]. Modern China, 1993(1).
39. Chenjing Nie. Xi Jinping Attended the Opening Ceremony of the First China International Import Expo and delivered a Keynote Speech [N]. Xinhua Net, 2018–22–5.
40. Chaoran Pang, et al. Research on System Integration and Innovation in Lin-gang New Area of the Shanghai Pilot Free Trade Zone [J]. Scientific Development, 2021(8).
41. Yanhua Ruan (Oral Account), Shuwei Ren (Compilation). The Barbed Wire Lowered by 30 Centimeters? Shanghai's Actions Reassures the Nation, Ensuring that Free Trade Zones Are Not Used for Smuggling [N]. Shanghai Observer, 2020–4–17.
42. Shanghai "China's Foreign Economic and Trade Series" Compilation Committee. Shanghai's Foreign Economic and Trade (1949–1990) [M]. Shanghai Scientific and Technical Literature Press, 1994.
43. Shanghai Archives Information Network. The Evolution of Shanghai Theaters [EB/OL]. https://www.archives.sh.cn/shjy/scbq/201203/t20120313_6039.html. 2021–10–19.
44. Shanghai Archives Information Network. Early Photography Studios in Shanghai [EB/OL]. https://www.archives.sh.cn/shjy/shzg/201603/t20160323_42607.html. 2021–10–19.

45. Shanghai Archives Information Network. The Earliest Modern Hotel in Shanghai: Richards Hotel [EB/OL]. https://www.archives.sh.cn/shjy/scbq/201203/t20120313_5831.html. 2021–10–19.
46. Institute of Economics, Shanghai Academy of Social Sciences, Academic Committee of Shanghai International Trade Association. Shanghai Foreign Trade (1840–1949) [M]. Shanghai Academy of Social Sciences Press, 1989.
47. Shanghai Municipal Local Chronicles Office. Shanghai Local Chronicles and Special Column for 70 Years of New China [EB/OL]. http://www.shtong.gov.cn/node2/n253144/n258132/. 2021–10–19.
48. Shanghai Municipal Local Chronicles Office. Shanghai Foreign Economic and Trade Chronicles [EB/OL]. http://www.shtong.gov.cn/Newsite/node2/node2245/node74728/index.html. 2021–10–19.
49. Shanghai Municipal Local Chronicles Office. Evolution of Shanghai Fashion [EB/OL]. http://www.shtong.gov.cn/node2/n189671/n190091/n258994/n259033/index.html. 2021–10–19.
50. Shanghai Municipal Local Chronicles Office. Shanghai Customs Chronicles [EB/OL]. http://www.shtong.gov.cn/Newsite/node2/node2245/node4466/index.html. 2021–10–19.
51. Shanghai Municipal Commission of Commerce. Shanghai's Open Economy Over 30 Years-A Review and Outlook of Shanghai's Foreign Economic and Trade Development During China's 30 Years of Reform and Opening Up [M]. Shanghai People's Publishing House, 2008.
52. Shanghai Municipal Bureau of Statistics. Historical Statistical Data on Shanghai's National Economy and Social Development: 1949–2000 (Foreign Trade and Economy Volume) [M]. China Statistics Press, 2001.
53. Wenchao Shang, Huijuan Chen. Thirty Years of Pudong: Starting anew on a new journey [N]. Guangming Daily, 2020–11–09.
54. Jialu Shen. The Past and Present of Western Cuisine in Shanghai [J]. Shanghai Wave, 2008(4).
55. Di Song. Insights from the China International Import Expo-Seeking Certainty in China [N]. Economic Observer, 2020–11–07.
56. Zhiliang Su. The Opium Trade in Modern Shanghai [N]. China Anti Drug News, 2021–06–11.
57. Zhou Su. Research on the Influence of Free Trade Zone Construction on the Upgrade of Industrial Structure-Based on the Intermediary Effect of the Opening of Shanghai Free Trade Zone [D]. Master's Thesis, Shanghai International Studies University, 2021.
58. Binggen Wang. AVIC Aircraft: Accelerating the Development of the Civil Aviation Industry [J]. Stock Market Trend Analysis Weekly, 2019(10).
59. Chuaifang Wang. The History of Foreign Businessmen-Shanghai: 1843–1956 [M]. Shanghai Academy of Social Sciences Press, 2007.
60. Juelin Wang. Hongsheng Liu and China Development Bank (Part II) [N]. China's Insurance Quote, 2021–07–02.
61. Junhao Wang. Modern Industrial Economics [M]. Zhejiang People's Publishing House, 2003.
62. Ke Wang. Research on the Development of Civil Aviation Industry in Shanghai [D]. Master's Thesis, Shanghai Jiao Tong University, 2012.
63. Tieya Wang. Compilation of Old Sino-Foreign Treaties and Agreements (Volume I) [M]. Shanghai University of Finance and Economics Press, 2019.
64. Zhiyan Wang. Shanghai: Comprehensive Bonded Zones Persist in Pioneering and Testing, with Continuous Optimization of Port Environment [N]. Liberation Daily, 2011–11–10.
65. Zitao Wang. Shanghai Yangshan Deep-Water Port Phase IV Passes Completion Acceptance [N]. China News Service, 2018–12–25.
66. Weiqun Wu. Five Cities Including Shanghai Will Take the Lead in Cultivating and Building International Consumption Centers[N]. Liberation Daily, 2021–07–20.
67. Xi Xi. Various "First Railways" in Chinese Railway History [J]. Traffic & Transportation, 2018(2).
68. Siyun Xia, Guoyi Zhang. Modern History of Shanghai's Foreign Trade [M]. Shanghai People's Publishing House, 2018.
69. Siyun Xia, et al. An Overview of Shanghai's Modern Foreign Trade History [M]. Shanghai People's Publishing House, 2015.

70. Qiaoling Xian. A Preliminary Analysis of Compradors and Early Modernization in China [J]. Journal of Beijing Union University (Humanities and Social Sciences), 2004(3).
71. Awu Xiao. The Entrepreneurial Spirit of Yu Qiaqing [J]. Memories and Archives, 2003(6).
72. Xiao Xiao. Modern Knowledge Lectures During the Isolated Island Period [N]. The United Times, 2021–7–20.
73. Hua Xin. Yangshan Port Opened, Shanghai Became the World's Largest Port [N]. China Trade News, 2005–12–15.
74. Ke Xing. Several Issues Regarding the Reconstruction Society in Shanghai During the Isolated Island Period [J]. Research on the History of Publishing in China, 2021(3).
75. Ganli Xu. Constructing Urban Lifestyles: The Modern Civilizing of Shanghai and Its Drivers [J]. Folklore Studies, 2020(5).
76. Jihua Xu. The Business Philosophy of Industrialist Yu Qiaqing [J]. Macroeconomic Management, 2012(2).
77. Yafang Xu. A Brief Discussion on the Gradual Formation of Modern Concepts Among Shanghai People After the Opening [J]. Cultural Heritage of Cities, 2013(4).
78. Ming Yan. The China International Import Expo Empowers China's Economy to Brave the Winds and Waves [N]. Tencent, 2020–11–11.
79. Zaili Yang. Theory of Late Qing Dynasty and Western Culture Influence on Chinese Women Dress-Case Analysis of Women's Dress Changes in Modern Shanghai [J]. Journal of Huaihua University, 2011(6).
80. Xianhao Yao. Materials on the History of Modern China's Foreign Trade: 1840–1895 (Volume 1) [M]. China Publishing House, 1962.
81. Jiaxin Yu. "Greater Efforts," General Secretary Proposes New Requirements for the Construction of Free Trade Pilot Zones [N]. Xinhua Net, 2021–7–11.
82. Zhu Yue. Liu Hongsheng: Founding Match Factory and Competing with "Western Matches" [J]. Youth Leadership, 2021(15).
83. Juan Zhang. How the China International Import Expo Changes Our Lives [N]. Tencent, 2020–11–14.
84. Suya Zhang, Junjun Li. Shanghai Yangshan Port Drives Regional Soaring [N]. Economic Daily, 2006–2–7.
85. Wenhua Zhang. The Evolution of Shanghai's Tram System [EB/OL]. http://www.360doc.cn/mip/820447933.html. 2021–10–19.
86. Xi Zhang. The Financial Magnate of the Republic of China Era: Zuyi Bei [J]. Zhejiang Archives, 2007(11).
87. Xiuli Zhang. The Chinese Directors of Jardine Matheson [J]. China Small & Medium Enterprises, 2013(11).
88. Jin Zhao, Hongsheng Liu. As a Chinese Industrialist, I Truly Feel Proud [N]. Study Times, 2021–8–2.
89. Chun Zhen. "Setting Up Trading Houses" and "Foreign Firms"-Early Overseas Capital and Guangdong's Import and Export Industry [J]. Chinese QiaoYuan Magazine, 1999(2).
90. Institute of Free Trade Zones, Sun Yat-sen University. 2020–2021 Annual Index of Institutional Innovation in China's Free Trade Zones Released [N]. Nanfang Metropolis Daily, 2021–7–22.
91. Xiangcai Zhong. Insights into the Evolution of Modern Chinese Society from Liu Hongsheng's Family Letters [J]. Modern China, 2021(1).
92. Yue Zhu. Domestic Large Aircraft Take Off from Pudong, Driving a Trillion-Yuan Level Industrial Chain [N]. East Day, 2020–11–12.

MIX
Papier aus verantwortungsvollen Quellen
Paper from responsible sources
FSC® C105338

If you have any concerns about our products,
you can contact us on
ProductSafety@springernature.com

In case Publisher is established outside the EU,
the EU authorized representative is:
Springer Nature Customer Service Center GmbH
Europaplatz 3, 69115 Heidelberg, Germany

Printed by Libri Plureos GmbH
in Hamburg, Germany